Th
Yo

Financial Sector Policy
for Developing Countries

Financial Sector
Policy for
Developing Countries

A READER

edited by
Gerard Caprio
Patrick Honohan
Dimitri Vittas

**A copublication of the World Bank
and Oxford University Press**

1 2 3 4 05 04 03 02

A copublication of the World Bank and Oxford University Press.

Oxford University Press
198 Madison Avenue
New York, NY 10016

The findings, interpretations, and conclusions expressed here are those of the author(s) and do not necessarily reflect the views of the Board of Executive Directors of the World Bank or the governments they represent.

The World Bank cannot guarantee the accuracy of the data included in this work. The boundaries, colors, denominations, and other information shown on any map in this work do not imply on the part of the World Bank any judgment of the legal status of any territory or the endorsement or acceptance of such boundaries.

ISBN 0-8213-5176-1

Acknowledgments

Chapter 5 is reprinted by permission of Elsevier Science from Research in Banking and Finance (Volume 2, 2002, pp. 243–263); Chapter 9 is reprinted by permission of Macmillan-Palgrave from Holger Wolf, ed., *Contemporary Economic Issues*; Volume 5: *Macroeconomic Policy and Financial Systems* (*Proceedings of the International Economic Association World Congress*, Tunis) (London: Macmillan, 1997). An earlier version of Chapter 10 appeared in *Forbes* magazine.

Library of Congress Cataloging-in-Publication Data

Financial sector policy for developing countries : a reader / edited by Gerard Caprio, Patrick Honohan, and Dimitri Vittas.
    p.cm.
    Includes bibliographical references.
    ISBN 0-8213-5176-1
    1. Finance—Developing countries. 2. Banks and banking—Developing countries. 3. International finance. I. Caprio, Gerard. II. Honohan, Patrick III. Vittas, Dimitri.

    HG195.F5365 2002
    332.1'09172'4—dc21

                                                            2002068957

43. Lester V. Chandler (1958), *Benjamin Strong,
    Central Banker* (New York: Arno Press)

This is the authorized biography of the man who was governor of
the Federal Reserve Bank of New York from 1914 until his death
in October 1928, and who played a key role in the development of
the system and in the increasing interconnections of U.S. finance
with that of Europe. President Hoover called Strong an
"appendage of Europe," but Friedman and Schwartz in their mag-
isterial *Monetary History of the United States* (see under number
24 in this list) argue that the transition, accelerated by Strong's
death in 1928, of financial decisionmaking power from New York
to Washington, where the Federal Reserve Board sat, played a crucial part in permitting the deepening of the world depression in the
United States.

44. Christopher Clay (1978), *Public Finance and Private
    Wealth: The Career of Sir Stephen Fox, 1627–1716*
    (Oxford: Clarendon Press)

This book is enormously helpful in tracing, through the life of one
man in the household of Charles II, the need for intermediaries in
lending to the crown; it also helps trace the financial revolution
from tax farming to bureaucratic tax collecting and government
expenditure. Fox, the father of Paymaster Henry Fox and grandfather of Charles Fox, a contemporary and rival of William Pitt
at the end of the 18th century, started out when the Stuarts were
in exile and lived through and helped to facilitate a series of inno-
vations and improvements in public finance and personal intermediation. He earned such trust of the monarchy that when
Charles II defaulted to the goldsmiths and other holders of his
paper (the Stop of the Exchequer of 1682), he paid Sir Stephen
regularly.

45. Count Egon Caesar Corti (1928), *The Rise of the
    House of Rothschild* (New York: Blue Ribbon Books)

There are dozens of books on the Rothschilds. Some of the best,
especially those by Jean Bouvier and Bertrand Gille, are about the
French house, based on the papers that have been made available
to scholars. Most, like this one by Corti, are journalistic rather
than scholarly. The story nonetheless is worth telling and retelling:
how the five sons spread from Frankfurt to London, Paris,

Amsterdam, Vienna, and Naples; how they worked together; and, especially in London and Paris, how they rose to the top of the ladder in banking, horse racing, and society. There may be better books than this about the Rothschilds, but as I don't know those that are not in English this one belongs on my list.

46. Joseph S. Davis (1975), *The World Between the Wars, 1919–39: An Economist's View* (Baltimore: Johns Hopkins University Press)

Davis, who was born in 1885 and retired as head of the Stanford University Food Research Institute in 1952, wrote this autobiography as he was approaching 90 years of age. He had been in the U.S. Shipping Mission in London during the First World War, served as an economist assistant on the staff of the American delegation to the Dawes Commission on German reparations in 1924, worked for the Harvard Economic Advisory Service in the 1920s, and became a member of President Eisenhower's Council of Economic Advisers after leaving academic life. The book is only partly autobiography: to a considerable extent, it is also an account of the international economy in the interwar period. Davis's comments on important figures of the times, and especially on Keynes, are of great interest.

47. Emile Moreau (1954), *Souvenirs d'un gouveneur de la Banque de France: Histoire de la stabilisation du franc, 1926–1928* (Paris: Edition Genin)

This autobiography, a favorite of mine, is I understand also recommended by Milton Friedman. It may be one of the few things on which we see eye to eye. Moreau was a canny *inspecteur des finances,* originally from Poitou, who spent 20 years at the head of the Bank of Algiers before becoming governor of the Bank of France in June 1926, in the midst of the crisis that Poincaré stabilized in July. The book is a day-by-day account of his negotiations with the French government and of his dealings with Montagu Norman of the Bank of England and Benjamin Strong of the Federal Reserve Bank of New York. Read especially how he copes with M. Aupetit, the Secretary of the Bank when he took over. Moreau left the Bank of France in 1930 to head the Banque de Paris et du Pays Bas (Paribas).

48. D. P. O'Brien, ed. (1971), *The Correspondence of Lord Overstone,* Volumes 1–3 (Cambridge: Cambridge University Press)

Samuel Jones Loyd, late Lord Overstone, was the leader of the currency school in the middle of the 19th century. The currency school would today be called monetarist. An Etonian, Cantabrigian, successful banker, and the richest man in England of his day, Overstone was also a man of strong convictions. He strikes me as the Milton Friedman of his day, powerful in debate, firm in opinion, admitting to no doubt or error. His correspondence, to a considerable extent conducted with C. W. Norman, the grandfather of Montagu Norman and member of the Court (Board of Directors) of the Bank of England, is full of views on finance and myriad other subjects. As the editor of this volume points out, Overstone delayed the adoption of the decimal system by Britain for a century. He was charitable in his private life, but not toward the ideas of others, especially those of Thomas Tooke, a merchant in the Russian trade and insurance company head. To Overstone, only gold was money, and banknotes derived their moneyness only to the extent they were redeemable in gold.

49. Fritz Stern (1977), *Gold and Iron: Bismarck, Bleichroeder, and the Building of the German Empire* (London: Allen and Unwin)

Gerson Bleichroeder, Bismarck's personal banker, was Jewish. At Hitler's accession to power, the family managed to get his papers out of Germany, and with these Fritz Stern of Columbia University has produced a financial history of Prussia and Germany from the 1830s to the 1890s. This tale details the role of finance in helping Bismarck make war on Austria and France, collect 5 billion francs in reparations in 1871 and 1872, and rescue some of the speculators and swindlers involved in the bubbles of railroad investment in 1873. There are penetrating chapters on the role of Jews in German economic and social life and on the corruption of the press by bankers. If one is looking for parallels, compare Bismarck's lack of interest in economics and finance with that of Henry Kissinger.

50. John Williamson (1971), *Karl Helfferich, 1872–1924: Economist, Financier, Politician* (Princeton, N. J.: Princeton University Press)

Helfferich is a man you love to hate. He was bright, unpleasant, and devastatingly wrong on such issues as unrestricted submarine warfare or how Germany should finance the First World War. Williamson thinks it "unfair" to call him a "financial Ludendorff" or "the most frivolous of all finance ministers": frivolous is hardly the word for a protagonist of such venom. In polemics, Helfferich's tone was so harsh that he was twice sued for slander; his personal attack on Walther Rathenau, the German finance minister, in June 1922 was said to have inspired the extremist nationalists who assassinated Rathenau.

For anyone who has found the average book in the foregoing list too lightweight, it is easy to point to heavier, although perhaps less digestible fare. I recommend, for starters:

United States:
Milton Friedman and Anna Jacobson Schwartz (1963), *A Monetary History of the United States, 1867–1960* (Princeton, N. J.: Princeton University Press)

England:
R. S. Sayers (1976), *The Bank of England, 1891–1944,* Volumes 1–3 (Cambridge: Cambridge University Press)

France:
Jean Bouvier (1976), *Un Siècle de Banque Française* (Paris: Hachette)

Germany:
Deutsche Bundesbank (1976), *Wahrung und Wirtschaft in Deutschland, 1876–1976 (Currency and the Economy in Germany, 1876–1976)* (Frankfurt: Knapp)

Contents

Foreword   *Cesare Calari*   xi

PART I   DESIGNING POLICY FOR THE FINANCIAL SYSTEM

Looking Back at the World Bank's
World Development Report 1989:
Finance and Development   3
Millard F. Long

From Good Bankers to Bad Bankers   19
Aristóbulo de Juan

Impact of Early Financial Growth Strategies
on Financial Structures and Problems in
Three Asian Crisis Countries   31
David C. Cole

Risk Management and Stable Financial
Structures for LDC, Inc.   49
Yoon Je Cho and Andrew Sheng

Eggs in Too Few Baskets: The Impact
of Loan Concentration on Bank-Sector
Systemic Risk   73
Berry K. Wilson and Gerard Caprio

PART II INTERNATIONAL AND INTERSECTORAL LINKAGES

Policy for Small Financial Systems   95
Biagio Bossone, Patrick Honohan,
and Millard F. Long

Dollarization, Private and Official:
Issues, Benefits, and Costs   129
James A. Hanson

Policies to Promote Saving for Retirement 171
Dimitri Vittas

Financial Networks and Banking Policy 205
Patrick Honohan and Dimitri Vittas

PART III TAKING THE LONGER VIEW

Retirement Reading for Sophisticated Bankers 229
Charles P. Kindleberger

This volume is dedicated to
Millard F. Long,
pioneer in the diagnosis of financial sector
policy problems in developing countries.

———

My master wades in:
Clearing driftwood, calming seas.
I can swim with him.
                              —DB

Contributors

Biagio Bossone
International Monetary Fund

Gerard Caprio
The World Bank

Cesare Calari
The World Bank

Yoon Je Cho
Sogang University, Seoul

David C. Cole
formerly Harvard Institute for International Development

Aristóbulo de Juan
A. de Juan and Associates

Patrick Honohan
The World Bank

James A. Hanson
The World Bank

Charles P. Kindleberger
Massachusetts Institute of Technology

Millard F. Long
formerly The World Bank

Andrew Sheng
Securities and Futures Commission, Hong Kong

Dimitri Vittas
The World Bank

Berry K. Wilson
Lubin School of Business, Pace University, New York

Foreword

Cesare Calari

THE DRAMATIC EVENTS OF THE LATE 1990s, which followed a wave of financial crises going back to the early 1980s, brought to center stage the issue of financial sector policy in developing countries. Many recent books have presented a chronology and interpretation of the crises, but it is little appreciated that these financial sector problems had been brewing for decades and that a small number of scholars had long been evolving an approach to understanding the structure and dynamics of these sectors.

Spearheaded by a group led by Millard Long, the World Bank began studying more than 20 years ago the problems, risks, and policy solutions surrounding private finance. This volume contains a collection of essays drawing on that accumulated experience and offering a wide perspective based on extensive real-world institutional experience. They are a useful reader on a wide range of the financial policy issues that are central in developing economies today. They reflect also the evolving approach of the Bank's financial sector team and represent the knowledge that the team has painstakingly accumulated over the years.

Today it seems natural and almost too obvious that much of the international community's policy focus should be directed to financial sector reform: to strengthening the prudential regulations and supervision of the financial system and ensuring that finance can make its most effective contribution to economic prosperity through sound, market-driven allocation of investable resources.

Despite the pioneering theoretical work of McKinnon and Shaw in the early 1970s, it was not always so. A quarter-century ago, the relationship between the international financial institutions and the financial sectors of developing countries was centered on the promotion and use of development banks as conduits for aid money, effectively serving as wholesale intermediaries for lending to the enterprise sector. This was a substantial business, but it resulted in massive misallocations of resources and ultimately foundered on a wave of mismanagement and insolvency. The incentive and information structure within which the development banks were operating was dysfunctional. Recognizing this, the World Bank began to diversify its counterparties, employing commercial banks to replace or supplement the development banks as apex institutions for these loans.

A pioneering 1983 review by Millard Long subsequently discovered that the commercial banks also were hitting problems of loan delinquency and consequential insolvency (Long 1983). Prudential supervision and regulation of banks in the recipient countries was deficient. It was this review that first identified that banking systems were not just an obstacle to the effective intermediation of World Bank loans, but also represented a wider structural development problem that was holding back economic development in numerous developing countries. From being an internal issue of World Bank practice and procedure, the need for reform of the banking sector (and, more widely, of the financial sector) to remove a key development constraint was catapulted into center stage. In parallel, pioneering work was being carried out at the International Finance Corporation (IFC)—the World Bank Group's private sector financing arm—to develop domestic capital markets and promote their access to international investors. The expression "emerging markets" was coined in this context when the IFC launched its "Emerging Markets Data Base," the first such database commercially available to institutional investors. This work, which ultimately helped put emerging markets on the map of the global investment community, was carried out by a small entrepreneurial team led by visionaries such as David Gill, Antoine van Agtmael, and Michael Barth and benefited greatly from Millard's own advice and leadership.

By 1989, the Bank's financial sector work had matured to the point where a comprehensive presentation was called for of its policy thinking to a broader audience. Millard Long's unit took the lead in the preparation of the highly acclaimed 1989 *World Development Report* (WDR), which highlighted the insolvency problems facing commercial banks in most developing countries and drew attention to the legal and regulatory foundations that were required for an efficient and robust financial system (World Bank 1989). This generated a wave of new analysis and raised awareness of the issues at stake (Long and Vittas 1992). In the first article of this volume, Long revisits these issues and considers what has changed in the intervening years. Interestingly, it was about six years after the 1989 WDR before development texts began to include a chapter on the financial system. Thanks to the efforts of Millard Long and others, the contribution of finance to development now is widely recognized.

One important new development has been the systematic compilation of databases on crises (Caprio and Klingebiel 1997) and on other aspects of the financial sector environment in developing countries (Demirgüç-Kunt and Sobaci 2000; Beck, Demirgüç-Kunt, and Levine 1999; Barth, Caprio, and Levine 2001). The findings and policy implications of a generation of econometric research, both within and outside the Bank, that followed the 1989 WDR and that is based on these and other cross-country datasets is succinctly summarized in the Bank's recent Policy Research Report, *Finance for Growth: Policy Choices in a Volatile World* (World Bank 2001). In addition to the challenge of preventing crises, *Finance for Growth* asks how the foundations of finance should best be laid, examines the role of the state as an owner of banks, and explores a world of finance without frontiers.

Bank management and the avoidance of banking crises in developing economies was and remains a central concern. Early versions of Aristobulo de Juan's famous paper, "From Good Bankers to Bad Bankers," on how good private sector bankers can slide under pressure and temptation into being bad bankers were first circulated in the late 1980s. Based on the Rumasa crisis in Spain and on a wide range of developing country experiences, the paper exemplifies the intellectual approach that evolved in the World Bank to the management and prevention of bank insolvency. This approach also drew strongly on the contrasting supervisory practice of U.S. regulators (cf. Polizatto 1990) and on management practice in leading commercial banks (Barltrop and McNaughton 1992). Observers of bank insolvency today will find that the lessons here remain painfully fresh.

In "Impact of Early Financial Growth Strategies on Financial Structures and Problems in Three Asian Crisis Countries," David Cole looks back at 30 years of financial sector policy in Indonesia, the Republic of Korea, and Thailand. The contrasting experiences of these financial systems in the crash of 1997–1998 can be directly traced to their structural differences, which evolved over decades. Cole highlights the role of personalities and institutional rivalry in creating these contrasting financial structures.

These elements inevitably came to the fore as more and more countries began to liberalize their financial sectors. Already by the early 1990s it was evident that financial liberalization must be seen as a process susceptible to temporary setbacks, and not as a one-off event (Caprio, Atiyas, and Hanson 1994). Subsequent work identified poorly prepared and poorly implemented liberalizations as being at the root of many of the late-1990s crises (Caprio, Honohan, and Stiglitz 2001). Yoon Je Cho and Andrew Sheng's 1993 paper, "Risk Management and Stable Financial Structures for LDC, Inc.," is an early and ingenious statement of the proposition that prudent financial liberalization can usefully be thought of by analogy with the task of financial management of a firm or corporation, the aims of which are good diversification and moderate leverage. If they took a rather optimistic view of the achievements of some East and Southeast Asian economies in this regard, their paper nonetheless was prophetic in its emphasis on the importance of a sound national financial structure.

Risk management emerged as the central issue for prudent bank governance. One aspect of this is the historic failure of many banks adequately to diversify their risk; a characteristic that is documented by Jerry Caprio and Berry Wilson in "Eggs in Too Few Baskets: The Impact of Loan Concentration on Bank-Sector Systemic Risk." Caprio and Wilson benchmark actual bank portfolios around the time of the crises in Chile, Malaysia, and Mexico against the risk–return frontier available in each country at that time. They find the explanation for risk concentration to lie primarily either in disaster myopia or in the deliberate attempt to seek out the highest possible return; both causes potentially are curable by ensuring that more of the banker's own funds are made subject to the same risk.

One consequence of financial liberalization and technological advances is that more and more countries seem but small components of an increasingly integrated world financial system. In "Policy for Small Financial Systems," Biagio Bossone, Patrick Honohan, and Millard Long explore the financial sector drawbacks of being small and propose some policy solutions. This increasing globalization of course has had other effects, including the important example of the spontaneous growth in dollarization. In "Dollarization, Private and Official: Issues, Benefits, and Costs," Jim Hanson looks at the complex policy issues involved in dollarization, including its implications for bank risk management and for government choice of exchange rate regime.

The 1990s saw the Bank widening its vision to more comprehensively embrace nonbank finance, building on IFC's groundbreaking work in this area. Chief among the nonbank sectors that began to be examined were contractual savings and pension reform (Vittas and Skully 1991; Vittas 1993). This examination subsequently evolved into a major Bank initiative to raise developing country awareness of the impending crisis in publicly provided pensions and of the potential for a financial sector solution through funded and privately managed pension funds (James and Vittas 1996; World Bank 1994). Pension fund development interacts with the strengthening and deepening of other aspects of nonbank finance, including securities markets and the market for annuities. These in turn require regulatory and legal underpinnings. In "Policies to Promote Savings for Retirement," Dimitri Vittas provides an up-to-date synthesis of best practice approaches to the main policy decision points facing designers of pension systems. He focuses in particular on the question of how much compulsion should be built in to the system.

This wider focus of the Bank also demanded a more comprehensive view of the role of the financial sector and the links between financial development and economic growth. With some development economists still questioning the causal role of financial sector development in generating growth, it was important to examine this issue with rigorous econometric techniques. The Bank program in this area has yielded clear and important findings (King and Levine 1993; Demirgüç-Kunt and Levine 2001). "Financial Networks and Banking Policy," by Patrick Honohan and Dimitri Vittas, describes one way of looking at the complex network of interconnections within the financial system and between finance and the real economy.

Drawing on the results both of practical experience and research work, the World Bank's policy effort in the financial sector had by the end of the millennium thus evolved to tackle issues in incentives, organization of financial regulation, financial taxation, banking crises, corporate finance, capital market development, small firm finance, insurance reform, deposit insurance, financial structure, corporate governance, collateral security, credit information, housing finance, and mortgage securitization.[1]

Finally, I particularly welcome inclusion of Charles Kindleberger's "Retirement Reading for Sophisticated Bankers." The history of finance is a long one, and it provides many lessons for the policymakers of today. Kindleberger presents his list as recommended reading for the retirement years: it thus is especially appropriate as the concluding essay in a volume dedicated to Millard Long, whose inspired leadership for many years spearheaded the World Bank's efforts in the financial sector.

xvi CESARE CALARI

As a personal note, I would like to add that I have had the privilege of working with Millard on various occasions, particularly during the early years of my career with the World Bank Group. The lessons I learned from him have stayed with me, and none is greater than the power of ideas, when supported by sound research and intellectual integrity. It gives me, then, particular pleasure to sign this foreword.

Note

1. By the mid-1990s, the International Monetary Fund was also stepping up its involvement in the field of financial sector policy, which has now been fully recognized in the work of the Monetary and Exchange Affairs Department and the newly created Capital Markets Department. Since 1999, the Fund has joined the Bank in launching a comprehensive country-by-country financial sector assessment program (FSAP), which places diagnostic work on a more systematic basis than had been possible in the past.

References

The word *processed* describes informally produced works that may not be commonly available through libraries.

Barltrop, Chris J., and Diana McNaughton. 1992. *Banking Institutions in Developing Markets*. Washington, D.C.: World Bank.

Barth, James, Gerard Caprio, and Ross Levine. 2001. "The Regulation and Supervision of Banks around the World: A New Database." World Bank Policy Research Working Paper 2588. Washington, D.C.

Beck, Thorsten, Aslı Demirgüç-Kunt, and Ross Levine. 1999. "A New Database on Financial Development and Structure." World Bank Policy Research Working Paper 2146. Washington, D.C.

Caprio, Gerard, Izak Atiyas, and James A. Hanson, eds. 1994. *Financial Reform: Theory and Experience*. Cambridge, Cambridge University Press.

Caprio, Gerard, Patrick Honohan, and Joseph E. Stiglitz, eds. 2001. *Financial Liberalization: How Far, How Fast?* Cambridge, Cambridge University Press.

Caprio, Gerard, and Daniela Klingebiel. 1997. "Bank Insolvency: Bad Luck, Bad Policy, or Bad Banking?" In Michael Bruno and Boris Pleskovic, eds., *Proceedings of the World Bank Annual Conference on Development Economics, 1996*. Washington, D.C.: World Bank.

Demirgüç-Kunt, Aslı, and Ross Levine. 2001. *Financial Structure and Economic Growth: A Cross-Country Comparison of Banks, Markets, and Development.* Cambridge, Mass.: MIT Press.

Demirgüç-Kunt, Aslı, and Tolga Sobaci. 2000. "Deposit Insurance around the World: A Database." World Bank Development Research Group, Washington, D.C. Processed.

James, Estelle, and Dimitri Vittas. 1996. "Mandatory Savings Schemes: Are They an Answer to the Old Age Security Problem?" In Zvi Bodie, Olivia S. Mitchell, and John A. Turner, eds, *Securing Employer-Based Pensions: An International Perspective.* Philadelphia: University of Pennsylvania Press.

King, Robert G., and Ross Levine. 1993. "Finance and Growth: Schumpeter Might Be Right." *Quarterly Journal of Economics* 108(3):717–37.

Long, Millard F. 1983. "Review of Financial Sector Work." World Bank Financial Development Division, Industry Department, Washington, D.C. Processed.

Long, Millard F., and Dimitri Vittas. 1992. "Changing the Rules of the Game." In Dimitri Vittas, ed., *Financial Regulation: Changing the Rules of the Game.* Washington, D.C.: World Bank.

Polizatto, Vincent P. 1990. "Prudential Regulation and Banking Supervision: Building an Institutional Framework for Banks." World Bank Policy Research Working Paper 340. Washington, D.C.

Vittas, Dimitri. 1993. "Swiss Chilanpore: The Way Forward for Pension Reform?" World Bank Policy Research Working Paper 1093. Washington, D.C. (Reprinted in Zvi Bodie and E. Philip Davis, eds. 2000. *The Foundations of Pension Finance.* Cheltenham, U.K.: Edward Elgar.)

Vittas, Dimitri, and Michael Skully. 1991. "Overview of Contractual Savings Institutions." World Bank Policy Research Working Paper 605. Washington, D.C.

World Bank. 1989. *Financial Systems and Development: The 1989 World Development Report.* New York: Oxford University Press.

———. 1994. *Averting the Old Age Crisis.* New York: Oxford University Press.

———. 2001. *Finance for Growth: Policy Choices in a Volatile World.* New York: Oxford University Press.

Part I

Designing Policy for the Financial System

Looking Back at the World Bank's *World Development Report 1989: Finance and Development*

Millard Long

Making Finance a Part of the Development Agenda

Ten years after I led the team that prepared the 1989 *World Development Report* (WDR) on finance and development, I was invited by the University of Frankfurt to review that report. Specifically I was asked to consider what was right and what was wrong with the report; to assess what the report missed, in terms of coverage; and to identify what happened in the following 10 years that would change the report. To cover all of this in a short paper is a tall order, so I shall confine my remarks to the few things I consider most important.

At about the same time that the report was published, John Williamson (1990) coined the term "Washington consensus" to describe the development ideas of the World Bank, International Monetary Fund (IMF), U.S. Treasury, and many academics. The WDR, however, was not a consensus statement on financial systems. Even as late as the end of the 1980s, improving financial systems was not part of the development agenda. I recall being told at the time by one of my bosses at the World Bank that there was no such thing as a financial sector, and that banks were merely pass-through mechanisms for channeling funds to the "real" sectors, such as industry, agriculture, and housing. Financial systems had no independent impact on the economy.

When Stanley Fischer, later first deputy managing director of the IMF, joined the World Bank in the late 1980s as chief economist, he met with all the division chiefs under his direction to find out what they thought important in their fields of responsibility. To get his attention I told him that all the financial institutions in all the developing countries were bankrupt. He knew I was exaggerating, but even an economist as well informed as Stan Fischer was unaware of the scale of the problems that many countries were facing. To back up what I had told him he had me write a note on the subject. Ten years later he gave a speech at the Bank in which he recalled our exchange. He noted that he had asked the research department in the IMF to update the information I had given him: where in the late 1980s I had listed 25 countries with financial sector problems, by the late 1990s the IMF listed more than 100 countries.

There is no lack of interest in financial systems today. The principal shareholder countries have given a mandate to the World Bank and the IMF to assess vulnerabilities in the financial sectors of member countries. A joint World Bank–IMF taskforce on finance has been established, and for the first time the two institutions have joint missions. The World Bank has a special vice presidency for finance; each of the Bank's regions maintains a department for finance; and there are a further three central (i.e. not region-specific) departments.

I would not claim that it was the 1989 WDR that put finance front and center in development work—the current level of concern is the direct result of the Mexican, Asian, and Russian crises of the late 1990s—but the report did bring more attention to financial systems. Originally controversial, the opinions expressed in the WDR have over time become the consensus both of what elements of finance we need to consider and what policies are appropriate for dealing with problems. Ten years after its publication, I contend the report remains a good statement on the importance of finance to economic development.

Brief Review of the 1989 World Development Report

The 1989 WDR consists of a prefatory chapter—the first chapter, in accordance with the practice of the time, was devoted to a review of the world economy—and eight substantive chapters on finance.

The second chapter began by outlining the modalities and testing empirically the ways in which finance affects growth. Research in the last decade has greatly strengthened this overall association made by the report, in particular through describing the mechanisms through which financial development impacts the real economy.

The third chapter presented a brief history of the development of financial systems and the fourth chapter examined the evolution of finance in developing countries after the Second World War. From the end of the colonial period, instead of building financial systems that directly addressed existing problems, most governments in developing countries used finance as a tool to develop the real sectors, directing credit at controlled interest rates to those sectors that they wanted to support. In the late 1950s and 1960s this approach worked quite well—perhaps better even than would have the alternative of developing the institutions of a financial system.

Low and often negative real interest rates failed, however, to encourage savings in financial form, credit was not allocated to investments yielding the highest returns, and failure to repay loans was not punished with bankruptcy. During the 1970s the problems inherent in this approach to domestic finance were masked by the easy availability of foreign capital, but after the Latin American crisis of 1982 and the withdrawal of foreign lenders the weaknesses in many domestic financial systems became overwhelming. The fifth chapter of the WDR dealt with the roots of the financial crises that ensued, their consequences, and the lessons to be drawn.

The sixth chapter outlined the building blocks for a healthy financial system, starting with the keystones of finance: contracts and debt recovery. Nothing is so destructive to finance as what is called in Bangladesh "the culture of default." Where business ethics are weak and fraud common, it is impossible to build a financial system, and in many developing countries debt default has become the most widespread form of white collar crime. The WDR stressed the importance of strong financial infrastructure: of a legal framework, including court system; of information flow that is based on sound accounting and auditing; and of strong and independent regulation and supervision of financial institutions.

The concluding three chapters were devoted to building financial markets in developing countries: the seventh chapter to the institutions of formal finance; the eighth to informal and semiformal finance; and the ninth to policy issues. The approach in many developing countries has been to respond to imperfections in the financial markets, such as a shortage of term finance or funding for small-scale enterprises, by either establishing a public institution to provide the missing credit or to order a private sector institution to do so. The WDR argued for an alternative approach: establish an environment and build the institutions that can mobilize savings, allocate credit efficiently, and enable market participants to hedge risk.

Developments Since 1989

When the WDR was drafted in the late 1980s, few countries had undertaken major financial policy reforms. Many countries have since implemented the policy approach that is outlined in the report. Macro policies have been stabilized, interest rates liberalized, and directed credits eliminated or greatly reduced. Competition has increased among banks and between banks and other types of financial institutions. Domestic markets have been opened to foreign funds, and some countries have permitted foreign institutions to buy domestic banks and insurance companies.

The approach in many countries is to ascertain why a particular type of finance is missing and to deal with the underlying problem, not just its symptoms. Rather than attempt to overcome problems through government fiat, these countries—notably the middle-income countries of Latin America, Central Europe, and East Asia—have sought to develop financial systems. The poorer countries of Asia and Africa are also moving in this direction. Reform, however, has often been slow and difficult, and has proved to be no panacea. Though more efficient at mobilizing funds and allocating credit, private institutions can make big mistakes, as we have seen recently in East Asia.

Much has been written on financial systems since the WDR was published, but while many of the report's themes and issues would today require elaboration I can find nothing in it that is fundamentally wrong. If I were to rewrite the report today, I would add a piece on the need to adapt financial systems to the economic structure. While all financial systems solve similar problems, they solve them in different ways, and any advice on policy or institutional development must take the unique features of the economic structure into account. I would add a section on the interrelationship between corporate finance and macroeconomic stability, which was the main source of trouble in East Asia. I would also add a section on the globalization of finance: globalization has been and is likely to continue to be a dynamic force for change in finance.

Finally, I would elaborate on what the report said about two disparate aspects of institution building: noncommercial bank finance, which became important for the first time during the 1990s, and financial supervision, which remains problematic.

Finance and Economic Structure

Transitional Economies

For the last decade I have worked primarily on the countries of Central and Eastern Europe. It is clear from the experience of these countries that the socialist model of a financial system, while wrong for a capitalist system, is not inappropriate to a planned economy. Prices and wages, output, and investment were all determined by the fiat of the plan. For both households and enterprises, cash savings were a residual between income and expenditure, not a matter of choice. Households for the most part ran a forced surplus; corporations, a forced deficit. Credit allocation was not based on the profit-risk calculus of the capitalist economy but was used to balance cash flows, with deficits in some sectors being covered by surpluses in others.

As they sought to transit from socialism to capitalism, these countries faced the need to change their financial systems, however. It was not possible to do so in one jump: in an economy undergoing a slow transition, a fully market-based financial system would have been out of sync with the real system. The International Financial Institutions (IFIs) nonetheless pushed for immediate introduction of profit-risk finance, as they wanted to use a hard budget constraint to force change at the enterprise level. The model put forward by the IFIs required the banks to operate on profit-based principles, which forced loss-making enterprises to adjust or go bankrupt. The banks were to administer work-out procedures for those enterprises that failed.

In none of the countries has this latter aspect of the model worked well. Neophyte bankers were simply in no position to administer bankruptcy and work-out procedures, and bankruptcies in any case were on a scale that would have overwhelmed even the most experienced bankers. The first part of the reform—lending based on the profit-risk calculus—also worked in few countries (Hungary, Poland, and the Baltic States are examples), and then only after an interim period of several years. For the rest (the Czech and Slovak Republics, Rumania, Bulgaria, and practically all of the former Soviet Union), the countries simply were not prepared to face at the enterprise level the discipline that this model implied. Credit continued to be used, as in the past, to cover cash-flow deficits.

The IFIs' did nothing to help design a transitional financial system that would have been in keeping with the slow pace of enterprise reform. I do not want to appear critical of the IFIs' strategy, but I would point out that the high level of nonperforming assets that we find in financial institutions is an inherent part of slow transition at the enterprise level. The lesson that I draw is that finance is not a tool that can be used on its own to drive deep economic and social reforms. Had this been recognized from the outset, the IFIs and the governments might have changed their approach and the countries would not today be burdened with so many nonperforming loans and bankrupt financial intermediaries.

Small Economies

I am convinced that we have paid too little attention to scale in financial systems. I recently did some work on Moldova, which had 21 banks but total assets of only US$300 million. This is not unusual. Fifty of the world's 150 countries have financial systems with assets of less than US$1 billion (the size of the World Bank Staff Credit Union) and 100 countries have assets of less than US$10 billion (the size of a moderate regional bank in a developed country). At this level there are issues of scale not just in the financial institutions, but also in the financial system itself. However hard one tries to tailor recommendations on competition, a system in which 21 banks divide US$300 million in assets is not likely to be efficient.

There are other questions also to resolve. For example, what rules on portfolio diversification and large exposure limits make sense for very small systems? A recent report on Macedonia recommended establishment of a credit rating agency, but no estimate was made of the cost of such an agency relative to the level of loans in the system. How much superstructure, in terms of central bank, supervisory agency, and financial infrastructure, can a small system support? When do costs exceed benefits?

For real goods, we recognize that countries must trade, but the model for thinking about the development of financial systems is surprisingly closed, with little thought given to how openness can be used to overcome the disadvantages of small size. We clearly need to pay more attention to size when thinking about and advising on financial structure (see also Bossone, Honohan, and Long, "Policy for Small Financial Systems," in this volume).

Corporate Finance and Macro Stability

The Asian financial crisis had different roots in each of the countries afflicted. In the Republic of Korea, critical to the crisis was the link between corporate finance, economic structure, and macro stability.[1] Early in its development, the Korean government decided it wanted country growth to be led by several large corporations. Building these corporations required capital that was beyond the means of any individual or business group, but as the government historically ran no deficit it was able to avail itself of bank-deposited household savings (which at 35 percent of gross domestic product (GDP) were among the highest in the world) for lending to the corporate sector. Little equity and a high level of debt equate to high leverage and a high level of credit risk, however. Excess leverage has been recognized as a potential problem at the enterprise level, but not at the macro level. What follows is far from a complete analysis of the macro consequences of corporate leverage, but it may give some insight into the problem.

Figure 1 shows how leverage affects net profits. Vertical line "A" represents the situation of a firm financed primarily with equity; line "B," a highly leveraged firm. The diagonal represents the situation where earnings before interest and taxes (EBIT) are equal to interest expenses for a given rate of interest. Higher levels of EBIT will lead to profits; lower levels to losses. Clearly, firm A is profitable at lower EBIT than firm B. If one thinks of the space in probability terms, the probability of earnings exceeding interest is higher in any period for firm A than for firm B. The impact of a higher rate of interest can be shown by pivoting upward the diagonal line. In the crisis year, interest rates rose sharply and exchange rates fell—both of which are factors that affect a firm's ability to service its debts. Furthermore, much of the corporate debt was short-term; it was the refusal of foreign creditors to roll over the maturing debt that produced the liquidity crisis.

An unleveraged firm does not easily get into debt trouble, but should it do so it is likely to realize a very poor rate of return on invested capital. A highly leveraged firm, in contrast, may realize a reasonable return on invested capital despite showing a loss—a small improvement in pre-interest earnings, a fall in interest rates, or an improvement in the exchange rate can in fact make a leveraged firm quite profitable in terms of return on equity. It is this characteristic that has enabled the Republic of Korea's rapid return from crisis in 1997 to recovery, albeit a fragile recovery.

Economic structure also is intimately connected to finance
(see Figure 2). High corporate leverage implies high risk for
lenders. To compensate for the risk, lenders ask for guarantees;
these in Korea were provided explicitly by other members of the
family of firms and implicitly by government. The *chaebol* structure and the close links between the government, corporations,
and financial institutions were related to leverage; high debt mul-
tiplied by high interest rates led to high interest expense; and this
in turn meant low earnings after interest and taxes, little potential
for finance through retained earnings, and further dependence on
external funding.

Korea's economic and financial organization, which was very
different from the capitalism of the West, thus was characterized by
highly leveraged firms, the *chaebol* structure, passive financial
intermediaries, an interventionist government, and high interest
spreads. While by and large successful, this organization produced
an economy that was prone to crisis.

The crisis of 1997 was not the first, but had been preceded
by several macro-level crises and many instances of government

Figure 1. Corporate Finance: Leverage and Profitability

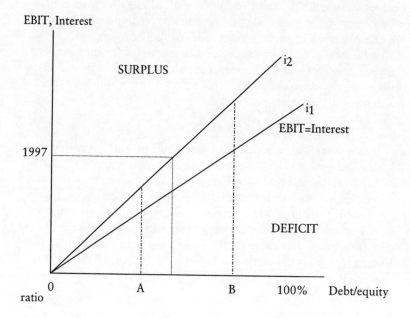

intervention in enterprise problems. To make the model work, until the early 1980s the government owned, and until the late 1980s controlled, the banks and directed credit to favored *chaebols*. Even after the banks were privatized, the government made clear that there was implicit credit insurance—that is, that the government would resolve problems on loans it sanctioned. Its low level of debt enabled it to serve as the ultimate repository of risk, a role that in western economies is held by stakeholders.

We may not have learned yet how to predict financial crisis, but in the last decade we have learned much about prevention and resolution. Crisis is not a matter of insolvency at the enterprise or financial institution level—insolvency can, and does, persist for years without crisis. Crisis is a liquidity problem; it arises at the firm or the country level when creditors refuse to roll over maturing debts. Most recent crises have started with foreign creditors, who tend to be more volatile in their behavior than domestic creditors, in part because governments cannot print foreign exchange to cover external liabilities.

Figure 2. Implications of Highly Leveraged Corporate Finance

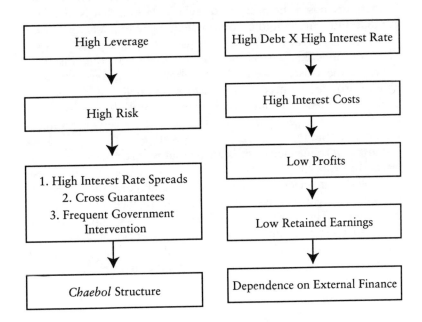

In most developing country crises, the overexposed debtor is the government. In the Asian crises, the defaulting debtors were enterprises that had borrowed abroad directly or through domestic financial intermediaries. The IFIs based their early advice to the Asian countries on what they had learned about crisis in Latin America in the 1980s and about enterprise adjustment in the transitional economies of Central Europe in the 1990s. This advice proved inappropriate to the different circumstances of Asia. The IFIs advised the afflicted governments to raise interest rates, to maintain foreign exchange reserves, and to force bankruptcy upon those companies that could not repay their debts. Higher interest rates reduced the ability of the highly leveraged corporations to pay their debts, however, compounding the problem at the corporate level. The Asian corporations differed from their Central European counterparts in other ways, too: where the capital stock of enterprises in the transitional economies typically was obsolete, enterprises in Asia commonly operated state-of-the-art plants. Few of these firms were value subtractors, raising the question of whether forcing bankruptcy was in fact the best solution.

The underlying problems of the Korean corporations were both financial and nonfinancial, and adjustment in both was needed. In Central Europe, a firm's inability to service debt usually indicated low pre-interest earnings relative to total capital; this was not the case with many of the highly leveraged Korean enterprises. The high corporate leverage and cross guarantees so common in Asia furthermore posed the problem of debt deflation; that is, the danger that illiquidity would become a chain reaction. When Daewoo collapsed in Korea, for example, a major run took place on a set of institutions known as investment trusts. In this instance, although the trusts' assets became illiquid the government was able to provide the necessary won to meet creditors' claims. The calling in of loans, laying off of workers, and closing of plants compounded the problem by adding domestic recession to international illiquidity.

How best to manage crisis is an art that we are just beginning to learn. To properly understand country risk, it is clear from these examples that macroeconomists must add corporate financial analysis to their studies of government finance and financial institutions. The crisis interventions and policy advice of the IFIs also must take into account the uniqueness of a country's financial structures. Until we understand more, the IFIs should be cautious in their advice and in the conditionalities they set for their assistance.

Globalization of Finance

In the 1970s, private international finance for developing countries consisted of syndicated bank loans to a small number of governments, mostly in South America, plus niche finance in selected countries by a few large banks. A substantial fraction of the syndicated loans were not repaid, creating the debt crisis of the early 1980s. That crisis slowed the globalization of finance in developing countries. Banks not only reversed the flow of funding, but institutions that had opened overseas branches cut back. The failure of the 1989 WDR to recognize that this was merely a temporary setback in the globalization of finance represents the biggest failure of the report.

By the early 1990s, the globalization of finance was surging forward once more, and private flows soon dwarfed official flows of money to the developing world. Not only did the capital flows become larger than in the 1970s, but the funding also went to more countries and to the private as well as to the public sector. Many different types of funding were involved, including equity funding. A small number of large financial institutions, banks, insurance companies, investment banks, and fund managers additionally have pursued a global business strategy, purchasing local institutions or setting up branches and subsidiaries in many of the middle-income countries, providing not just niche financing but also a full range of financial products. When the governments in Central Europe decided to sell their financial institutions, many of us wondered if any institutions at all would be interested in becoming owners. We never imagined the number of potential buyers that actually would come forward.

This phenomenon is not universal among financial institutions: it is primarily the larger firms and middle-income countries that have become part of the international financial system. Where quality investors can be found, as in Central Europe, privatization has enabled countries to transform their financial systems. The IFIs must, however, be careful in their recommendations for privatization of low-quality intermediaries in small countries: where there is little interest from quality investors the choice may be between privatization to gullible domestic investors, to unscrupulous businesses bent on insider lending, or to fly-by-night foreign banks. Globalization may offer a partial solution to this small-country problem. In small countries, banks that are part of global institutions can be supervised by the parent bank and portfolios can be diversified internationally. What could otherwise be an excessively large exposure can be manageable within the context of a larger institution.

The globalization of finance is far from complete. It will move forward at an uneven pace and there inevitably will be reversals. The disruptions in the Asian economies in 1997 and in Russia in 1998, for example, were initiated by the sudden outflow of foreign funds-possibly signifying a much deeper phenomenon. I suspect that there are limits to the extent to which different financial systems can manifest uniqueness. Corporations and economies that go beyond those limits ultimately will be brought into line by the international capital markets, rather than by the rules and loan conditionalities of the IMF, World Bank, and Basle Committee. Globalization has been and is likely to continue to be a dynamic force in finance.

Development of Financial Institutions

Two institutional subjects that would require elaboration in a new WDR on finance are the channels and instruments for term finance, and regulation and supervision.

In the unstable inflationary environment of the 1970s and 1980s, term finance was a problem, with the result that the financial scene became dominated by commercial banks accepting short-term deposits and making short-term loans. While this is still the dominant form of finance in developing countries, more countries have stabilized their macro economies and are providing an environment in which domestic term finance can develop.

The 1989 report covered capital markets, contractual savings institutions (pensions and insurance), mutual funds (investment trusts), and risk management through securitization and derivatives. A revision of that report today would need to expand on what was said in relation to these issues. In the last decade, pension reform has become an important issue for both industrialized and developing countries. Some countries now have introduced funded pension schemes, increasing the funds available for term finance. This development goes hand-in-hand with the development of the securities markets necessary to operate these funded pillars. Governments additionally are putting in place the necessary policies and are urging enterprises to reduce the leveraging of and dependence on short-term finance; the government of the Republic of Korea, for example, has insisted that the *chaebols* reduce their leverage ratio to two to one.

In the middle-income countries, all of the needed factors—demand, supply, policy, instruments, institutions, and macro stability—thus are coming together to make possible the development of longer-term finance. Unlike the nonmarket approaches of the past, this will be term finance based on market development.

In the late 1960s and early 1970s, the IFIs helped to establish and financed many specialized development banks. Financial arguments were put forward to justify these institutions—the absence of term finance was one notable argument—but these intermediaries also were useful to the IFIs, which could not themselves do retail lending, to channel loans to favored sectors such as agriculture. The experience with these institutions, particularly when government-owned, was disappointing. The banks often lent at subsidized interest rates to those with political influence, and these loans often were not repaid. Borrowers furthermore often used their loans for purposes other than those intended in the program.

The consequence of these abuses was a strong movement in the 1980s and early 1990s away from loans to this type of development bank. In the World Bank, such lending fell from around US$2 billion per year in the late 1980s to a few hundred million dollars per year in the late 1990s. A recent study since has revealed a return in the World Bank to this type of financing, hidden often in loans bearing different descriptions. The targeted sectors this time around are municipalities, housing, infrastructure, and micro borrowers.

Specialized institutions of this nature exist also in market-based financial systems, but while it is correct that investments in particular sectors are retarded by a shortage of funding, to believe that the problem can be rectified by money alone is naive. There are often good reasons why lending does not take place: a shortage of well-prepared projects; a lack of information about the borrower, meaning bankers are unable to assess risk and project quality; or difficulties in contract enforcement and risk diversification, for example. I worry that the lessons of the past are being disregarded by those who would substitute shortcuts for the patient development of institutions and infrastructure. These concerns were covered in the 1989 report; it simply needs updating.

Regulation and Supervision

Finally, a few observations on regulation and supervision. Much progress has been made in this area in the last decade. Most countries have new and better financial laws. Governments have strengthened the agencies responsible for onsite and offsite supervision, have added to staff, and have sent many abroad for training.

The Bank for International Settlements (BIS), International Organization of Securities Commissions (IOSCO), and International Association of Insurance Supervisors (IAIS) have drafted standards for the regulation of banks, securities markets, and insurance companies, and the developing countries have made progress toward the adoption of these regulations—although few have adopted them completely.

Financial supervision in general, and bank supervision in particular, are intensely political areas, however. Politicians and tainted managers have learned from Willie Sutton, the notorious U.S. criminal who, when asked why he robbed banks, replied: "Because that is where the money is." Money flows directly from financial intermediaries to line the pockets of politicians, to finance their political campaigns (almost no country is without a scandal in this area), and to reward their friends in the form of cheap loans. While the money that flows to politicians in practice typically is a tiny fraction of the bad portfolio, once institutions are corrupted control of the situation is lost. Some ministers of finance and governors of central banks fear that if the truth about the dire state of their financial institutions were to become public, the country would face either a run on the banks or a recapitalization cost that could not be met. Known cancers in banks thus go untreated, and when bankers see others getting away with bad practices, the cancer spreads.

On the technical front, major improvements have been made in financial supervision. Far less progress has been made on the political nature of the problem. While laws and regulations have been enacted, they are not enforced. In many developing countries, the last thing that politicians and corrupt businessmen want is a strong and independent financial supervisor. Finance is never clean, but when corruption goes too deep, development of the financial system is impossible. Reducing fraud in finance to tolerable levels is a major challenge.

Conclusions

I have six major conclusions to draw from my review of the 1989 WDR.

• In the last decade, the importance of financial systems to development has achieved widespread recognition-to the point, though I hardly dare say this, that we may today overemphasize finance. The effort in many small and poor countries to build securities markets is premature, for example, and the money that the IFIs have since the Asian crisis spent on country "vulnerability" studies is excessive, given that the financial shocks coming from these countries have proven too small to cause trouble outside their borders.

• Financial systems solve common problems, but solve them in different ways. These differences are important, and must be taken into account when implementing change and adjustment policies.

• Private flows of funds and financial services now dwarf public flows from abroad. For this reason, the discipline imposed by markets is likely to matter more than the conditionalities imposed by the IFIs.

• In the past, instabilities in public finance and financial institutions have caused crises. These instabilities will continue to be important, but economists must also pay attention to instabilities that arise in the financing of the corporate sector.

• Countries must continue the process of institution building. Donors and developing countries should be aware of the lessons of the past when considering shortcut solutions to intermediation problems.

• Political intervention in financial regulation is costly and has proven hard to prevent. We should look for market mechanisms that can supplement state supervision.

Allow me to conclude with two last paragraphs, drawn from the final chapter of the 1989 WDR and from its summary:

> This report has tried to specify the prerequisites for building an efficient financial system capable of mobilizing and allocating resources on a voluntary basis. Such a system would . . . probably make fewer mistakes and waste fewer resources than the interventionist approach.

> [To make a financial system work,] confidence is needed— confidence that the value of financial contracts will not be eroded by inflation and that contracts will be honored. . . . Countries need to create appropriate financial institutions, develop better systems of prudential regulation and supervision, improve the flow of financial information, develop human skills for managing complex financial operations, and promote good financial habits. None of this will be easily or quickly accomplished.

Note

1. There were other problems in Korea as well as that of high leverage. Years of expansion had led to euphoria. Overoptimistic assumptions about corporate sales led to overinvestment in certain business lines. Wages had risen, further squeezing profits. The won furthermore was tied to the U.S. dollar, which had appreciated; this, plus the higher wages, made exports less competitive.

Reference

Williamson, John. 1990. *The Progress of Policy Reform in Latin America.* Washington D.C.: Institute of International Economics.

From Good Bankers
to Bad Bankers

Aristóbulo de Juan

Introduction

CONTRARY TO THE THEORY THAT macroeconomic factors alone are responsible for all financial crises, this paper argues that bank mismanagement also is a major element in all banking crises, operating as crisis originator or as a multiplier of losses and economic distortions. It demonstrates the way in which good bankers, when in trouble, often become bad bankers through a sequence of deteriorating attitudes. The paper does not seek to pass judgment on the behavior of bankers, but merely describes and reflects on actions and attitudes that are repeated in the history of banking around the world, in industrialized countries as well as in developing ones.

The potential of poor management and ineffective supervision to harm a single institution or a section of a banking system is well understood, but they also can be a major factor in a general financial crisis affecting an entire system. Where good management may enable a bank to survive a crisis in reasonable health, bad management can lead to deeper crisis and the compounding of losses, through, for example, the misallocation of resources or by contributing to inflation via high interest rates. In short, both good banks and bad banks are observed in such crises. Applying only macroeconomic remedial action to a general financial crisis, without simultaneously addressing the institutional side of the crisis, can be ineffective or even counterproductive.

Effective banking supervision-regulation, supervision proper, and remedial action, from conventional enforcement to the restructuring of institutions—is essential to prevent or limit the damage that poor management otherwise could inflict. If good regulation, supervision, and remedial mechanisms are in place, bad management is less likely to exist; and if it exists, it is less likely to last. The deterioration of a situation can be stopped and reversed. Given the potential of deterioration to accelerate, the sooner remedial action is implemented, the better.

Good Management and Mismanagement

The first step toward an effective system of regulation and supervision is analysis of the managerial problems that lead banks to failure. In the United States, regulators use the CAMEL system (capital, assets, management, earnings, and liquidity) to rate banks on a scale of 1 to 5, or from "very good" to "failing." Each institution is periodically assessed by supervisors and scored in each of the five CAMEL areas for competence, leadership, compliance with regulations, ability to plan, ability to react to changes in the environment, quality of policies and ability to ensure that they are properly applied, quality of the management team and the prospects for management succession, and the risk of insider dealing.

If all banks were well managed—by the CAMEL definition, performed satisfactorily in all of the above areas—the potential causes of bank failure would be reduced to those of an economic or political nature. The need for regulation and supervision nonetheless would remain, for much the same reasons that traffic laws and police are needed even in a country of good drivers: banking, like motoring, can present risks to third parties.

There are essentially four categories of mismanagement: technical mismanagement, cosmetic mismanagement, desperate management ("*la fuite en avant*"), and fraud. Each does not necessarily progress sequentially to the next, but when technical mismanagement leads to losses or to the need for a dividend reduction, it frequently unleashes cosmetic and desperate management. Fraud may be present from the beginning, but for the purposes of this paper it is dealt with at the end, to reflect the dynamics that make good managers become bad managers. Illiquidity comes at the end of the process, by which time the bank may have lost its capital several times over.

It is a peculiarity of banking that insolvency invariably precedes illiquidity. This characteristic is a product of the size of portfolio that a bank typically holds, the leverage that it maintains, and its ability to raise money from depositors. It is one of the key differences between financial and nonfinancial firms, which may, in contrast, experience illiquidity while still solvent.

Technical Mismanagement

Technical mismanagement may occur when a bank is first set up and operating under new management, when control of a bank is acquired by new owners, or when an established bank fails to plan for changes or fails to acknowledge and remedy a deteriorating situation. It may be manifested in any of a variety of inadequate policies and practices, including overextension, poor lending, lack of internal controls, and poor planning in the areas of business and management.

Overextension. Overextension and quick growth are among the leading sources of failure. Overextension entails either the lending of money beyond the ability of the bank's capital to cushion potential losses, or the diversification of activities to geographical or business areas with which the bank is not familiar or in which it is ill-equipped to manage. Overextension often is identified with the seeking of growth for the sake of growth.

Poor lending. Poor lending policies also may prove fatal. At the heart of bank management is the obligation to ensure that funds entrusted to the bank are lent in such a manner as to generate an appropriate remuneration, and to ensure that all loans made are reimbursed to the bank. Policies or practices to avoid include the following:

• *Risk concentration,* or the lending of a large proportion of the bank's capital to a single borrower or group of borrowers or to a single sector or industry. Risk concentration often is the result of a banker miscalculating the health of a borrower or succumbing to pressure to support an unserviced debt with further loans. It frequently is mixed with connected lending (see below). Not all risk concentration leads to failure, but most bank failures are due in part to serious loan concentration.

• *Connected lending* describes loans made by a bank to companies wholly or partly owned by the banker or by the bank. Since ownership, especially in the case of bankers, frequently is indirect (i.e., is through subsidiaries or a decisionmaking relationship), the concept of connection, with its wider connotations, is used in preference to that of ownership. This form of lending frequently is fraudulent, and because of the tendency for connected loans to be made irrespective of the borrower's ability to repay, in most cases is high risk. Connected lending commonly is associated with concentration, default, and permanent rollover of loans. It, too, is evident in most bank failures.

In principle, there is nothing wrong with connected lending, provided that the borrower is treated as an ordinary third party. The inherent risks are significantly lessened if the borrower has shared ownership and shows proper internal controls. Connected lending is common among development banks, and also is practiced by commercial banks in industrialized countries such as Germany and Japan.

In practice, however, connected lending tends to be high risk, for the following reasons: (a) loans absorbing a high proportion of the bank's capital are made according to less rigorous criteria—for example, because of a parent-subsidiary relationship between the bank and the borrower; (b) the connected borrower's easy and systematic access to credit can cause managerial attitudes to deteriorate; (c) a cozy familiarity between the bank and the borrower can undermine the bank's supervisory role on the borrower's board, obstructing the flow of information and becoming an impediment to control; and (d) the bank seldom will recognize a loan as overdue or doubtful. In the case of state-owned development banks, short-term social objectives and political pressure also may lead to bad loans and losses, whether or not accounted for in the books.

• *Mismatching,* or lending at much longer term than that of the underlying deposits. Banks must constantly transform terms, because money is fungible and deposits stay longer with the bank than their legal terms would permit. Should the term of lending become stretched too far beyond the term of liabilities, however, perhaps because of forced rollovers, serious liquidity problems may arise. Even if a bank that had mismatched its assets and liabilities can solve its liquidity situation, it may in so doing have to pay excessive rates for its new funding. In a case where it operates with fixed interest rates, it may incur losses in the transformation. This is a modality of interest risk. Banks that operate in foreign currency face particularly serious additional risks, including transfer risk and rate-of-exchange risk.

Mismatching is not necessarily such a serious problem for a bank that operates with variable interest rates, even if meeting liquidity needs involves more expensive funding (provided this is at market rates). The borrower nonetheless may prove unable to pay high variable rates, especially in situations of high inflation. If the bank's funding is obtained at much more than the market rate, it will not be enough for the bank to have linked its variable lending rates to market, and losses will be incurred. If the mismatching is the result of continuous rollovers or debt rescheduling, the financing of nonperforming loans also may cause losses.

• *Ineffective recovery.* This frequently stems from conflict of interest between the bank and companies owned by the bank or its bankers. It also can be the result of political pressure on the bankers or of labor problems.

• *Overoptimistic assessment* of the borrower's prospects. This may include failure to assess all possible risks and inadequate assessment of management quality. Loans characterizable as overoptimistic often are made under political pressure.

Lack of internal controls. There are many areas in which the lack of internal controls can produce problems. The areas in which inadequate control is of most danger are those of credit review procedures, information systems, and internal audits, as follows:

• *Credit review procedures* should be in place to eliminate overoptimistic loans, excessive risk concentration, and inappropriate rescheduling. They also should prompt timely recovery action.

• *Information systems* should support the constant oversight of the business, and in particular should be able to provide management with early warning of potential problems, enabling remedial measures to be quickly taken.

• *Internal audits* should ensure that regulations and internal policies are properly applied throughout the bank.

Poor planning. True foresight is a rare gift, but a measure of foresight can be developed through the use of appropriate techniques. Poor planning, in contrast, is a matter not only of technique but also of attitude. There is a close relationship between poor planning and the age and interests of top management, an absence of teamwork, and the sort of complacent thinking that sees banking as a safe business that need never change. This complacency often is manifested in such aphorisms as "we have always done very well," "nothing serious ever happens," or "problems are solved by time."

In a context of economic upheaval or technological and structural change in banking, it is easy to blame the problems of an individual bank on external factors rather than on poor planning. Proper planning, however, that sees a bank follow its own trends and try to exploit future opportunities in the economy and on the markets, can enable the bank to minimize damage even in the midst of the most serious upheavals. Together with quick growth and bad lending policies, poor planning is the most frequent cause of bank deterioration.

The crossroads. Technical mismanagement, in conjunction with other macro or micro factors, can place a bank in a situation in which equity is eroded by hidden losses, real profits decrease or disappear, and dividends are threatened. Good supervision or a good board would at this point direct the bank to disclose the situation, change management, and inject new capital. Where proper supervision is absent, however, a very different situation can arise.

A drop in dividends is the signal to the market that a bank is deteriorating. The banker's instinct is to do everything possible to avoid a collapse of confidence and to keep control of ownership and management. This is the crossroads for the bank. If it does not take the right road, the bank will decline into cosmetic management and desperate management, sequentially or simultaneously. The culture of the organization will deteriorate quickly, the market will be distorted, and losses will soar. Insolvency can grow in geometric progression, leaving liquidation or restructuring of the bank as the only effective solution.

Cosmetic Management

Cosmetic management entails the hiding of past and current losses to buy time for the existing management team, to allow it to retain control while looking for solutions.

There are countless ways to hide the economic reality of a bank. Some of these involve use of the "upside-down income statement" technique. On a typical income statement, the first item is interest income and the last one dividends—i.e., the sum of all the items in between. When dividends are in danger, the banker may decide that they no longer can be considered a variable, but must become a fixed element. As such, dividends become the base on which the statement is built, with other figures manipulated to fit regardless of the reality of the situation (see Figure 1).

Once dividends have been determined, the first area a banker will manipulate to maintain those dividends is undistributed profits. This is not yet an accounting gimmick, but is the threshold to cosmetics, and should sound a warning to any careful analyst. The bank is sacrificing its equity capital for the sake of a good image. Still, investors will receive the remuneration to which they are accustomed.

Figure 1. The Upside-Down Income Statement

Model A (Upside Down)		Model B (Classic)	
	Dividends		Interest/income
+	Undistributed profits	-	Financial cost
+	Taxes	=	Spread
=	Net profits	+	Fees
+	Provisions	-	Overhead
±	Sundry income/expenditure	=	Operational profit
=	Operational profit	±	Sundry income/expenditure
+	Overhead	-	Provisions
-	Fees	=	Net profits
=	Spread	-	Taxes
+	Financial cost	-	Undistributed profits
=	Interest/income	=	Dividends

The next problem arises when it is no longer possible to further reduce undistributed profits. The banker at this point may manipulate net profits to increase them on paper, even if this means having to pay more taxes. There are four main ways to achieve this: (a) by provisioning less than required, through "evergreening" procedures or collateralization; (b) by considering uncollectable accruals as income; (c) by revaluating assets; or (d) by advancing the accrual of income and postponing accrual of expenditures.

Evergreening

The most serious problems of a bank are not in loans classified as overdue, as these are smaller loans that are being dealt with. The worst losses of a bank are hidden in the current, or "good," portfolio. A banker seeking to adapt provisions to a given level of profits and dividends will not classify a bad loan as overdue, doubtful, or a write-off, but automatically will reschedule the loan over long periods of time. Interests also will be refinanced.

This is a snowball process that can lead to disaster. Repeatedly rescheduled loans become increasingly difficult to collect, and a bank's failure to take effective recovery action serves to strengthen the borrower's bargaining position. A culture of nonpayment can develop.

The practice of automatically rescheduling bad loans is typical in cases where the bank or banker has stock in the borrower company or where the bank has concentrated disproportionate sums of money. A significant example of the latter occurred among lender banks substantially engaged during the 1980s in less developed countries (LDCs), when loans repeatedly were rescheduled without the necessary provisions being made.

Another common way of reducing the need for provisions is to make a bad loan look good by obtaining collateral. The collateral—for example, loans with prior mortgages, factories with business or labor problems, or real estate with limited development potential—frequently is insufficient to cover the debt or may be impossible to foreclose on, but nonetheless will appear on bank accounts as being worth the principal plus accrued interest.

While the borrower may have negative equity, current losses, or even negative cash flow, the bank will argue that it does not have to provision these loans, and that time in any case will solve the stressed situation of the borrower. The bank may even go so far as to say that it cannot make provisions for these and other bad loans beyond the limits the tax laws consider as expenditure. By this logic, the loans are not bad.

The desire to make loans look like evergreens not only leads the bank to provision less than it should, but also leads it to capitalize interest—that is, to account for refinanced interest as income. In practice, refinanced income represents increased losses. On the income statement, however, the bank's lower provisions and artificial interest accruals translate to better profits.

Where "evergreening" is insufficient to keep profits at the desired level, the bank can revalue fixed assets, be they real estate or stock. Some legislation permits banks to periodically revalue their assets in times of inflation, without additional tax implications. This enables a bank to increase the book value of its assets beyond their economic value, thus creating artificial additional income (the difference between the previous book value and the new one) and reserves (as a counterpart of the asset revaluation).

Worse than this is the practice of selling bank assets, on credit, to companies that are connected with the bank for a price above the book value of those assets. The positive difference is accounted for by the bank as income, but the negative difference is omitted from the buyer's balance sheet. Another practice is for a bank to account for foreclosures at the loan value, even if they are in reality insufficient to cover the loan in question.

Another maneuver to hide losses is to advance accrual of income and postpone accrual of expenditures. For example, fees normally should be spread over the operation term, but banks that are in trouble may account for them the day they are received. On the expenditures side, the banker may postpone accounting for commitments, such as payment of a purchase, to the time of actual payment, instead of making the entry on the day the contract is signed.

Desperate Management

When a bank becomes in danger of having to declare a capital loss or of having to pay smaller or no dividends, it may descend into desperate management. In addition to indulging in cosmetic management, the bank may at this stage start to engage in business that it hopes will buy time and, if lucky, make up for the deterioration it has already experienced. The most common practices followed as bank management grows desperate are speculation, paying above market rates for deposits, and charging high interest rates to borrowers.

Typical examples of speculative practices are the buying or financing of real estate in times of inflation, in the hope that prices will continue to increase and a profit therefore be made when the property is sold; using bank loans to buy land for real estate development; and buying stock under the assumption that it will deliver a short-term profit. Profit frequently does not materialize, however, because of changes in market trends or because of inaccurate estimates. For example, should adoption of a tight national monetary policy bring in deflation and adjustment, the market would become narrower and the value of real estate drop dramatically.

The net result of such speculation is that the bank's proportion of nonperforming assets becomes higher and higher, and its yield, which has to cover deposits, interest rates, overhead, and profits, continues to diminish. No matter how the cosmetics are applied, the problem now is real cash flow. As its cash flow suffers damage, the bank will begin to experience liquidity difficulties.

Struggling for cash, the bank will go to the market, offering high interest rates to attract depositors. If it can maintain an image of growth, the bank may be able to charge similarly high interest rates and still bring in borrowers; and with growth, its problems may disappear. All that the bank realistically can hope for, however, is cash, to cover interest to its depositors, to meet payroll, and to pay for other fixed expenditures. At this stage, the bank is taking deposits knowing they are unlikely to be repaid.

To the extent that the bank can still make new loans, the high interest rates it must charge to cover the remuneration paid to depositors create their own problems. The bank is now involved in a perverse process. Customers that are prepared to accept interest rates above the market standard typically are stressed borrowers or borrowers connected to the bank or its bankers, and typically they will hope not to have to serve their debt. They will likely also have negative equity. While the bank may show high spreads on its income statements, these will exist only on paper.

Fraud

The fourth category of mismanagement is fraud. Fraud—common when a bank is set up or acquired by speculators or businesses with self-interest at heart—may be responsible in part for setting in process the deterioration of management, by, for example, causing early losses. It also is an element of cosmetic management, to the extent that, in a business that is based on confidence, it is a way of hiding the truth. Of the four categories of mismanagement, this paper deals with fraud last, however, to emphasize the process of deterioration that can turn a good manager into a fraudulent one.

When illiquidity approaches and the end of a bank is near, the banker may become tempted to divert money out of the bank. This is most commonly achieved through self-lending to companies that are owned by or connected with the banker, and may be done through formal procedures that make it difficult for the bank to foreclose on the debt.

Another common last-minute fraud is to "swing" ownership of companies that are owned by the bank or the banker. If a bank-owned company is prosperous, the banker may purchase it for himself at a low price; if one of his own companies is in poor shape, the banker may sell it to the bank at a high price. All such transactions are of course "properly" materialized through fiduciaries, paper companies, and other methods, to escape supervision. The banker may attempt to rationalize such fraud by reasoning that he is in charge and that the situation is "all the government's fault."

A Few Lines on Culture Deterioration

Deterioration of the management culture is both a consequence of failure to resolve problems and a cause of longer-lasting problems. The example set by top management influences middle management and other organizational layers, with the result that if a bad management culture becomes entrenched it may be difficult to change without replacing several layers of the management hierarchy. This is one of the reasons why mergers are advocated as a solution to bank crises. Some features of a deteriorated management culture include the following:

- Paper is mistaken for facts and numbers mistaken for money.
- Hiding and cheating are common practice, and are even accepted as ethical.
- Where speculation is one of the few hopes for recovery, speculators become the ideal kind of managers.
- Promotion of managers is based on loyalty, not on competence.
- The sharing of information and teamwork gradually disappear.
- Internal audit activities are cut back, being confined, for example, to the investigation of minor problems in branch offices.
- Branch managers become "one-legged professionals," instructed to concentrate on the collection of deposits. Lending operations gradually become concentrated in the bank's headquarters and main branch office.
- The "need for prestige" leads to inflation in staff numbers, salaries, and overhead. Luxurious premises are standard.
- As a counterpart to the culture of nonpayment by borrowers, bankers develop the culture of nonrecovery.

The Role Of Banking Supervision

The types of mismanagement and fraud described in this paper may be contemporaneous or sequential. They can occur easily in countries where there is no proper regulation rendering them illegal or subject to remedy. Where proper regulation is in place, lack of adequate supervision may allow them to both take place and persist. The following are examples of ways in which a few aspects of mismanagement may be prevented, limited, or remedied:

Regulation and supervision of market entry by an institution such as the central bank or superintendency of banks could control bank ownership, reducing the danger of mismanagement through incompetence or deliberate abuse.

Requiring banks to send detailed balance sheets and income statements to the supervisory authority would enable supervisors to identify potential problems and take early remedial action. Requiring banks to disclose publicly their accounts in disaggregated form would enable stockholders and the public to identify and press for any necessary remedial action. The publication of externally audited accounts and assets additionally would make difficult the concealment of bad management practices.

The major risk of insolvency could be eliminated if banks complied with legislation to limit loan concentration and connected lending to a given proportion of capital. This would need to be closely monitored. Similarly, compliance with a minimum level of real equity capital versus assets could minimize the risks of overextension and protracted undercapitalization.

Rules for determining the classification of bank assets as good or bad, in conjunction with provision and accrual requirements, would support close monitoring of bank health and would enable the timely use of remedial action should problems arise.

In all cases, compliance with these terms and regulations would need to be effectively monitored and supervised. To support supervision and further deter mismanagement, appropriate penalties—such as fines, legal action, or the replacement of management personnel—should be established and implemented.

Last but not least, mechanisms to facilitate bank closure and restructuring could prevent deteriorating situations from spiraling into market distortions and losses.

Lessons to Be Learned

There are three primary conclusions to draw from this discussion. In summary, these are:

• Regulation and supervision will not cure all ills, but they are essential pillars of a strong financial system, able to limit the potential damage that mismanagement can cause and to make macro policies effective.

• Good regulation and supervision may be of no use if there are no mechanisms in place to prevent insolvency. Where insolvency cannot be remedied, the danger even exists that the supervisor might become corrupted, through being obliged to tolerate hiding.

• Bad management is a cause of or contributing factor in all banking crises. Good management, in contrast—while in the worst cases of economic upheaval capable of being overwhelmed—will minimize the harm done.

Impact of Early Financial Growth Strategies on Financial Structures and Problems in Three Asian Crisis Countries

David C. Cole

Introduction

MOST FINANCIAL EXPERTS, BOTH national and foreign, who attempted to deal with the recent financial crises in East and Southeast Asia came onto the scene in the late stages of the boom or the early stages of the bust. They may have browsed some of the outdated literature on the initial phases of financial development in the countries with which they were immediately concerned, but most of them had little if any detailed knowledge or personal experience of the conditions prior to the inception of rapid financial development, or of the key policies and policymakers that helped initiate that development.

Those experts with a more academic background may have recalled the passage from Shaw (1973) stating that in Korea, the "keys to increasing real money demand were found and used," or the enthusiastic section in McKinnon (1973) entitled "Financial Reform without Tears: Korea, 1964–70." But those who, in search of a quick historical review, picked up the Asian Development Bank's timely *Financial Sector Development in Asia* for its country

The author would like to thank Hugh Patrick for his comments on an earlier version of this paper.

studies on Indonesia (Nasution 1995), Korea (Nam 1995), and
Thailand (Vichyanond 1995) would have learned little about what
transpired before the 1980s.

As one who began some rudimentary research on the Korean
banking system as a private in the U.S. Army during the Korean
War, and then became deeply involved in the early stages of financial reform in both Korea and Indonesia, writing a paper in honor
of a long-time friend and colleague who was one of the early
researchers on rural financial markets in Thailand, it would seem
appropriate to delve back into the history of these three countries
in search of lessons for the future. I hope especially that we might
expose some early actions that may at the time have been judged
beneficial but which now might be viewed more skeptically, or that
we might find some assumptions or lacunae that later opened up
damaging cracks in the system.

The Korea Story

The Republic of Korea inherited a Japanese-style banking system
after the Second World War. In 1948, the newly independent
Syngman Rhee government took over ownership of all the former
Japanese banks and converted one of them into a central bank. In
1950, Arthur Bloomfield of the New York Federal Reserve Bank,
who was brought to Korea by the U.S. economic assistance program as one of the early international financial advisors, recommended privatizating all the commercial banks and strengthening
the independence of the central bank. This attempt to transform the
Korean banking system from a Japanese to a U.S. model was initially frustrated by the advent of the Korean War, and after the war
President Rhee, who was more interested in maximizing the inflow
of foreign aid than in building up the domestic financial system,
chose to retain firm control of central bank policy. He also gave
away some of the commercial banks to his cronies as rewards for
their support.

After the Park Chung-Hee government took power in 1961, the
commercial banks were repossessed by the government and, along
with some newly created development finance institutions, were
used to fund credit programs for small farmers, fishermen, and
industry. These programs, based mainly on credit from the central
bank, quickly led to accelerating inflation and a harsh confronta-
tion with the major aid donor, the U.S. government. A stern, U.S.-
dictated, IMF-style stabilization program in 1964 brought down
the rate of inflation and caused some improvement in the trade
balance, but it also forced a contraction in base money and money

supply, causing financial stress for many firms and a severe squeeze on the banking system.

Largely in response to these painful disruptions, the USAID mission under its new director Joel Bernstein sought technical assistance in formulating a financial recovery and development program that would support the long-term development of the Korean economy. Three of the leading financial economists of the time, John Gurley, Hugh Patrick, and Edward Shaw, prepared a report entitled *The Financial Structure of Korea* (Gurley, Patrick, and Shaw 1965) that not only contributed to a significant reorientation of Korean financial policies but also fed into Shaw's pathbreaking *Financial Deepening in Economic Development* (Shaw 1973).[1]

The main themes of *The Financial Structure of Korea* are familiar to anyone who has read *Financial Deepening:* avoid inflation, remove price controls on financial instruments, and permit competitive financial markets to mobilize and allocate savings. The message that sold most successfully to the Korean officials was not freeing up all interest rates, but simply raising bank deposit interest rates above the rate of inflation to provide incentives for Korean households and firms to move their savings out of goods and unorganized financial institutions into the banks. This message was bought by two key officials: Chang Key-Young, the Deputy Prime Minister and chief architect of Korea's economic policies at that time, and Kim Yung-Hwan, the head of the Finance Section in the Ministry of Finance, who some years later became Minister of Finance. It was implemented by a directive of the central bank at the end of September 1965, some two months after the Gurley, Patrick, and Shaw report was presented to the government.

As Princeton Lyman and I reported shortly thereafter (Cole and Lyman 1971):

> "No one involved in the so-called interest rate reform anticipated anything like the response that did occur. Total time and saving deposits increased by 25 percent in one month, tripled in one year, and doubled again the following year. . . . [T]he increases in these deposits in the two years following the reform were equal to 5 and 6 percent of GNP in the respective years."

Bank loan rates also were increased by central bank instruction, but still held below the highest deposit rates. Because all the banks were owned and strongly controlled by the government, they complied with these instructions quickly. Most of the new funds mobilized by the banks flowed into loans to exporters at highly subsidized interest rates. Approval of these loans was almost automatic upon presentation of an export letter of credit (L/C), so the banks had little opportunity for exercising any discretion or rent-extraction from the lending process. Bank regulators focused primarily on whether or not the loan applications were processed quickly and the goods actually shipped within the time limits of the L/C. The financing of capital expenditures in the exporting sectors was done mainly through rapid expansion of foreign supplier credits, with repayment guaranteed by the government-owned Korean banks.

Thus, the banking system was used by the Korean government in the latter half of the 1960s as a powerful instrument for promoting exports, with little concern given to the profitability of the banks. Throughout most of the Park Chung-Hee era the government was clearly the dominant partner in the so-called "Korea, Inc." Businesses that abused their borrowing privileges or crossed the government in other ways were likely to get their credit lines canceled, their requests for foreign loan guarantees disapproved, and their tax returns reaudited. Corruption was kept to a minimum as export growth was both the principal criterion for resource allocation and the measure of successful performance.

Emergence of the Chaebol

This pattern began to break down in the later stages of the Park regime. Three factors were particularly important. First, the exporting firms grew very rapidly and diversified into many types of production, transforming themselves into multiproduct conglomerates—the famous *chaebol*. Second, the government sold some of the banks. While it retained control over the selection of senior bank officers, gave strong guidance to most bank operations, and set restrictions on the concentration of ownership of financial institutions, the leading conglomerates nonetheless were able to attain controlling interests in most of the bigger banks. The entry of new banks, including foreign banks, was tightly restricted. Finally, in the 1970s the government shifted its emphasis to development of heavy and military-oriented industries. To do this it had to elicit the cooperation of the big industrialists, while assuring the financing of their new investments. These three factors shifted the balance of power first toward greater equality between the government and the conglomerates, and in later years, under weaker presidents, to clear dominance by the conglomerates.

In the early years of financial expansion, from 1965 to 1971, banks were the major accumulators and primary allocators of funds. The unregulated financial institutions, mainly urban moneylenders, nonetheless still played an important role redistributing funds at short term between surplus and deficit firms. Also, the finance departments of most conglomerates often played the role of intermediaries, obtaining credit lines or export credits from banks and using cash surpluses to fund suppliers or to place with the moneylenders.

After six years of rapid economic expansion the Korean economy began to show signs of overheating and imbalances. Exports were slowing down and firms were experiencing difficulties meeting foreign debt payments. The government's response was a conventional stabilization package, consisting of a 20 percent devaluation and tighter restrictions on domestic bank credit and on guarantees of new foreign borrowings.

These measures caused a severe liquidity squeeze in the Korean money markets, and forced a number of the *chaebol* to turn to the moneylenders for short-term accommodation. The government was unwilling to relax bank credit ceilings to relieve this pressure, but did devise an alternative scheme that had significant implications for the future growth of the financial system.

By administrative decree the government voided all existing debts to unregulated moneylenders and stipulated that all borrowers that registered their obligations would have those obligations transformed into long-term, low-interest-rate loans with two-to-three-year grace periods before any repayment of principal was required.[2] This measure transformed the short-term assets of the moneylenders into long-term claims, and rendered the moneylenders incapable of meeting their short-term—often overnight—liabilities. Many of the moneylenders were forced to close.

This massive debt restructuring, equal to about 40 percent of the total loans of the banking system, wiped out most of the value of the claims of moneylenders on their borrowers and of the claims of the myriad individuals and firms that had deposited funds with moneylenders. It did not affect foreign obligations except to the extent that foreigners were depositors with the moneylenders. The effect of the restructuring was to relieve the liquidity squeeze on the major corporations and sharply reduce the activity of the moneylenders.

As a substitute for the moneylenders, the government encouraged the development of various types of nonbank financial institutions, including investment finance companies, merchant banking companies, and mutual savings and finance companies. These institutions were supervised by the Ministry of Finance rather than by the central bank, and were subject to less restrictive interest rate controls and legal lending limits. Many of them came to be controlled by the *chaebol*, and were used to arrange both domestic and offshore financing.

Between 1980 and 1996, the relative shares of banks and non-bank financial institutions in deposits and loans shifted dramatically: the share held by the banks dropped from roughly two-thirds to one-third, and that of the nonbank financial institutions rose from one-third to two-thirds (Smith 1998). The nonbank financial institutions, and especially the captive merchant banks that raised most of their funds offshore, were important contributors to the financial crisis of 1997.

The Indonesia Story

Indonesia at independence inherited a Dutch banking system that was mainly designed to support the export of crops from Dutch-owned plantations. The Dutch system included an agricultural bank, a legacy of the "new enlightenment" era that was intended to provide financial services to small Indonesian farmers (Charlesworth 1959). During the Sukarno years the Java Bank was transformed into a central bank, Bank Indonesia, and several new banks were established by the government. These banks were all subject to strong government direction, and in the early 1960s were consolidated into branches of the central bank. Massive expansion of central bank credit from 1963 to 1965 resulted in hyperinflation of 600 percent per annum in 1966, and widespread loss of confidence in the currency and the banking system. The ratio of broad money, M2, to gross domestic product (GDP) declined from 10.7 percent in 1960 to 3.3 percent in 1966 (Cole and Slade 1996).

The new Suharto government announced a financial stabilization program in October, 1966 that had been worked out with the IMF and received strong support not only from the IMF but also from the U.S. and Japanese governments.[3] The program proved very successful; by 1969 the annual inflation rate had been brought down below 20 percent and confidence in the currency had been partially restored. In September 1968 the Indonesian "economic team" implemented a sizeable increase in bank deposit interest rates, largely upon my recommendation, and this led to a rapid increase in time deposits over the subsequent four years, bringing the M2/GDP ratio up to 15.2 percent in 1972 (Cole and Slade, 1996, p. 34).

This early growth in the financial system occurred mainly in the six state-owned commercial banks, which accounted for some 80 percent of total recorded bank assets. The central bank did little to encourage the private banks, which were mainly owned by ethnic Chinese; on the contrary, it suspended some of these banks and encouraged others to consolidate. No new bank licenses were granted at this time.

Many of the smaller private banks were little more than licensed moneylenders, in most respects comparable to the informal, unlicensed moneylenders in Korea. They often provided a front behind which their owners or large depositors made loans with their own funds to affiliated or well-known borrowers. One important way in which they differed from the Korean moneylenders, however, was that these Chinese-Indonesian banks had links to the financial markets in Singapore and Hong Kong, where they could place deposits and arrange loans for their clients. These private banks and their offshore correspondents thus served as the principal suppliers of financial services, especially to the ethnic Chinese business community in Indonesia. While their services were similar to those provided by the big moneylenders in Korea, the vortex of their operations was offshore in Singapore and Hong Kong rather than in the national money center.

The total value of financial assets actually available for use by firms and individuals in Korea and Indonesia probably was at least double the amount reported for the banking system. In Korea, domestic moneylenders accounted for most unrecorded activity; in Indonesia, offshore banks and domestic private banks primarily were responsible. An important reason for this difference is that Korea had strong controls on capital movements, whereas Indonesia largely eliminated such controls in 1970, at an early stage of the financial development process.

Between 1973 and 1983 the Indonesian financial system experienced little growth, as increased oil revenues initially were channeled through the state-owned oil company and later through the budget, and as foreign investors bypassed the domestic banking system to deal directly with Indonesian firms. Central bank controls on interest rates and credit ceilings resulted in negative real interest rates on bank deposits and slow growth of bank credit. Offshore financial centers continued to provide more flexible financial services.

Proliferation of Private Banks

Financial growth resumed after 1983, when both interest rate and credit controls were largely eliminated. The private national banks were much quicker than the state-owned banks to respond to these liberalizing measures, and within five years doubled their share of total bank assets from 11 percent to 22 percent. Over the same period, the total banking system grew by 170 percent, in nominal terms.[4] This expansion occurred purely through the growth of existing banks: there was no increase in the number of banks. How much of the expansion was due simply to a shift of assets from off-shore banks to domestic banks is not known.

The second major set of liberalizing measures was implemented in 1988, when restraints were relaxed both on the opening of new branches by private banks and on the licensing of new private domestic banks and foreign joint-venture banks. The new regulations called for the Indonesian Ministry of Finance and the central bank to cooperate on the authorization of new banks: the ministry had the licensing authority and the central bank was to evaluate the qualifications and financial resources of the new applications and give its approval of all applicants. This cooperation failed completely.

The reasons for the failure are complicated and subject to different interpretations. Here I present my own. The reforms of 1988 were promoted by the Ministry of Finance and generally resisted by the central bank. When the "economic team" led by Professors Widjojo Nitisastro and Ali Wardhana, and in this instance including the Coordinating Minister for Economy and Finance and the Minister of Finance, decided to push ahead with the reforms and recommend them to President Suharto, the leadership of the central bank, Bank Indonesia, adopted a passive-resistant, nonsupportive role. It did not seriously examine the qualifications of persons applying to set up new banks, nor did it determine whether the capital pledged to establish those new banks was actually available and was not just temporarily borrowed funds. So far as I am aware, during 1988–1993 it did not once recommend against the issuance of a new bank license. For its part, the Ministry of Finance did not reject any application that met the minimal technical requirements. Additionally, in 1989 Bank Indonesia implemented an extremely loose monetary policy that made possible a doubling of bank credit over the next two years.

The unrestrained increase in the number of banks and bank credit in 1989–90 provided the kindling for the crisis of 1997. To this was added the undermining of bank prudential regulation in 1991, when President Suharto ordered removal of the Managing Director of Bank Indonesia responsible for prudential supervision because he tried to enforce legal lending limits on Bank Central Asia, the largest private bank which had strong links to the President's family. Over the next six years, the major private banks essentially became unregulated Ponzi banks used by the President's family and cronies to mobilize funds at home and from overseas, with little concern for the cost of funds, the concentration of lending, or the prospects of repayment. Not the central bank, nor the Ministry of Finance, nor the "economic team," separately or together, was able to convince the President to stop this process. Foreign investors played into the process because they generally believed that any investment that had strong political backing from the President's family or friends would be rescued if it got into trouble. The state-owned banks, although they were a declining share of the total banking system, contributed to the process by channeling much of their credit to enterprises linked to the President. They had little choice as the tenure of their senior officers was dependent upon the President's continuing approval.

Thus a program of financial liberalization that was supposed to lead to a predominantly private financial system, subject to effective prudential supervision, led instead to a rapidly expanding and largely unregulated financial system that was captured and used by politically powerful interests for their own objectives.

The Thailand Story

Thailand's financial growth followed a very different path from that of either Korea or Indonesia. Thailand was never a colony, and thus did not inherit a financial system molded by a single colonial power. The banking system that evolved during the 20th century consisted of a mix of foreign and domestic banks that mainly were engaged in financing the export of rice. The domestic banks were mostly owned by ethnic Chinese who had settled in Thailand and sought to integrate within Thai society, and who dominated rice processing and exporting.

The central bank, the Bank of Thailand, was created by the Thai government in 1942 as a way of curtailing Japanese dominance over the Thai financial system (Doner and Unger 1993). This nationalistic beginning and subsequent strong leadership—especially that of Dr. Puey Ungphakorn—made the Bank of Thailand a dominant institution that strongly influenced the government's economic policies. It also helped the Thai central bank avoid many of the subsidized credit schemes and deficit financing responsibilities that plagued other central banks. Doner and Unger summarize the central bank's situation in the two decades after the Second World War as follows:

There were, in sum, few major pressures for preferential credit during the immediate postwar period. Central bank activities focused on controlling inflation and building up foreign exchange reserves. These efforts were facilitated by the Bank of Thailand's own leverage within the bureaucracy and the growth of an export-based commercial banking sector that itself constituted an important support for the political-military leadership.

The Bank of Thailand operated a multiple exchange rate regime until the mid-1950s that strengthened the central bank's position in several ways. By maintaining a low exchange rate on agricultural exports, the central bank essentially imposed a tax on agricultural producers. It also generated a surplus that was mostly retained by the bank, rather than being passed on to the budget. This surplus provided a mechanism for both building up foreign exchange reserves and mopping up domestic liquidity. Even after shifting to a single exchange rate, the central bank continued to maintain tight liquidity, while adding to its foreign reserves. It encouraged a substantial capital inflow by emphasizing Thailand's sound financial policies, which were supported by the IMF and World Bank. It also avoided subsidized domestic credit schemes for import-substitute projects, while supporting nonsubsidized, short-term credit for agricultural exports.

Entry of new banks was severely restricted. By 1971, there were 16 domestic banks and 14 foreign banks in Thailand (Skully 1984). The three largest Thai banks accounted for 50 percent of all assets of the domestic and foreign banks. Most banking activities were concentrated in the Bangkok area. As in Korea, the restrictions on the establishment of new banking institutions led to significant growth of nonbank financial institutions. These included both unregulated institutions, such as "chit" funds, and various regulated institutions. The most important of the regulated institutions were the finance and securities companies that emerged in the late 1960s to fill gaps in the banking system, and which "in the beginning . . . were allowed to operate loosely with neither specific licenses nor supervision" (Vichyanond 1995). These companies were placed under the regulatory supervision of the central bank in 1972, but this responsibility was not taken seriously until 1983, when a number of finance companies failed, threatening the stability of the whole financial system.

The Thai banking system remained highly regulated and shielded from both domestic and foreign competition until 1990, when a three-year financial reform plan was implemented. The first component of this plan called for deregulation of interest rates and management of the portfolios of financial institutions (Vichyanond 1995). The second component was the licensing of Bangkok International Banking Facilities, to encourage more competition in banking and greater inflows of international capital, and the third was the lifting in 1990 of foreign exchange controls on current account transactions and in 1991 on most capital account transactions. These measures contributed to a significant increase over the next five years in the market share of finance companies relative to that of the banks, and to the substantially greater exposure of finance companies to international financial markets.

Some Consequences of Differing Financial Development Strategies

Korea's and Indonesia's early financial development in the 1960s was promoted more by their finance and planning ministries than by their central banks. The ministries instructed (in Korea) and encouraged (in Indonesia) the central banks to set positive real interest rates on bank time deposits, and then provided guidance to government-controlled commercial and development banks to extend subsidized credits, often at negative spreads, to preferred borrowers. Thailand's central bank, while controlling all bank interest rates, managed to maintain positive real interest rates on both deposits and loans. It also managed to avoid most subsidized credit schemes. Thai banks never experienced the sort of sudden spurts of bank deposit growth that occurred in Korea and Indonesia in the late 1960s, but rather had relatively steady growth consistent with the central bank's stabilization objectives.

Korea and Thailand limited the entry of new banks and maintained strong controls on foreign capital movements. This provided protection to existing banks from both domestic and foreign competition. Indonesia, in contrast, in 1970 opened up access to offshore banks by removing capital controls, and in the 1980s relaxed restraints on branching by existing banks and on the entry of new private and joint-venture banks. As a consequence, Indonesian banks, especially the private banks, tended to be much more aggressive than the Korean and Thai banks in terms of mobilizing deposits, extending loans, and arranging offshore financing.

The restraints upon and noncompetitive nature of domestic banking in Korea and Thailand contributed to the growth first of unregulated moneylenders, and subsequently of the loosely regulated finance and securities companies that played such a major role in the recent crisis. Indonesia permitted more expansive domestic private banking and free access to offshore banking, so its moneylenders and finance companies were less important. The banking system in Indonesia expanded far too rapidly, however, especially after 1988, and the resultant abundance of funds and weak supervision made it vulnerable to exploitation.

Prudential regulation of banks in Indonesia initially was weakened by the failure of cooperation between the Ministry of Finance and the central bank to enforce regulations, and subsequently was undermined completely by widespread political interference. A number of politically powerful groups ultimately were able to use their banks like Ponzi schemes to mobilize funds at home and abroad and to channel them into their connected enterprises, with little concern for safety or soundness and little fear of regulatory interference. In Thailand, central bank regulation of banks was much more effective, but regulation of finance and security companies was weak. In Korea, central bank regulation of banks also was reasonably effective, but ministry of finance regulation of finance and securities companies was weak.

1997 Economic Crisis

Given these historical experiences, it was not surprising that in Indonesia the banking system was at the center of the financial crisis in 1997, while in Korea it was the merchant bank component of the finance and securities companies, and in Thailand it was more broadly the finance and securities companies.

As it turned out, the many new private banks that were established in Indonesia after 1988 were not responsible for the biggest financial losses. Instead, it was the older private banks that had either gained political influence or been taken over by influential groups, and the state-owned banks that had been compelled to make large "evergreen" loans to the influential groups that quickly turned sour when the crisis hit.

The fact that all of these banks, however, were part of the Indonesian payments system created an extraordinary problem for the authorities. Prior to the crisis only one insolvent bank had been closed. In the early response to the crisis, largely at IMF insistence, 16 banks were closed, but immediately thereafter the central bank was instructed by the President to prevent any further bank closures. The only way in which the central bank could accomplish this was to provide continuing liquidity support to all banks. This resulted in an explosion of central bank credit, which went mainly to fund massive deposit outflows that often were used to transfer funds abroad through the open capital account.

In Thailand, the collapse of the finance and securities companies was due both to overly rapid growth and to maturity and currency mismatches. The Thai central bank attempted initially to bridge these gaps, but when the costs escalated it was able to simply shut down the finance companies without forcing a collapse of the payments system.

Similarly, in Korea the focus of the problem was the merchant banks that had borrowed heavily abroad, on increasingly shorter terms, to finance domestic and foreign loans. This made it easier to negotiate quickly a multilateral debt restructuring with many foreign creditors, again without posing a threat to the domestic payments system. In both Thailand and Korea, the crisis was initially manifested in a loss of central bank foreign exchange reserves as the central banks attempted to cover the debt repayments of the finance companies and merchant banks. When the reserve losses became excessive, it remained possible to either shut down these institutions to prevent further payments or to restructure their offshore obligations to stop the capital outflows. While some banks in both countries were in difficulty, their problems could be dealt with without endangering the payments system.

Lessons for the Future

Perhaps the most important lesson from these experiences is that inadequate prudential regulation and supervision of financial institutions, wherever it occurs, can be very costly. Indonesia encouraged an open, competitive, internationally connected banking system, but failed to supervise it effectively, enabling many banks to become legal Ponzi schemes. Korea and Thailand kept tighter control and more effective supervision of their banks, but allowed—and even encouraged—finance and securities companies to expand and borrow heavily abroad. The absence of adequate prudential constraints meant that many of these institutions in time became hopelessly insolvent, at which point their owner-managers turned to liquidation of their assets rather than preservation of their capital.

In the early literature on financial liberalization there was a notion that, if markets were sufficiently competitive, owners that had a sufficient equity interest in their financial institutions would seek to manage those institutions so as to increase their equity over time, leading ultimately to a healthy, competitive financial system. The experiences of Korea, Indonesia, and Thailand suggest that there are many other conditions necessary to achieve such a system.

As one who sided with the ministries of finance and planning of both Korea and Indonesia in their efforts to encourage their central banks to remove the constraints on financial system expansion, in the expectation or hope that effective prudential regulation and supervision would soon follow, I feel some remorse. While it is not clear that the central banks in those two countries would have implemented policies conducive to healthy financial development, the Thai experience does suggest that central bank-led financial development can achieve reasonably good results. The dominance of the ministries of finance in Korea and Indonesia tended to undermine the stature of their central banks, however, conceivably making them more susceptible to being pushed around. As long as the ministries of finance and planning were able to provide strong protection and to avoid unsound policies, the central banks were relatively safe. But when that protection was removed or overpowered by strong political interests, the weakened central banks were unable to defend themselves.

Recent attempts to legislate strong, independent central banks may not be any more successful if the political will is not there. It may take someone like Dr. Puey to help get a central bank off on a sound footing, but even his successors had difficulty maintaining the dominant role of the bank, and especially in extending effective supervision over finance and security companies.[5]

These reflections lead me to suggest that perhaps the pace and structure of financial development needs to be linked much more closely to prior, or at least concurrent, development of effective prudential regulation and supervision covering all relevant aspects of the financial system. Some governments may find it difficult to implement rigorous prudential regulation and supervision, especially on a continuing basis. Political institutions may be weak or legal systems inadequate. To forge ahead with efforts to promote rapid financial development in such countries can be a risky proposition. While research has shown that financial development is correlated with economic growth, the costs of financial collapse, such as that experienced especially in Indonesia, need to be factored into the analysis.

Notes

1. Gurley and Shaw had recently published their seminal work, *Money in a Theory of Finance* (Gurley and Shaw 1960), which elaborated on their "Financial Aspects of Economic Development" (Gurley and Shaw 1955), published in the September 1955 *American Economic Review*. Patrick's article, "Financial Development and Economic Growth in Underdeveloped Countries" (Patrick 1966), spelling out the concepts of "supply leading" and "demand following" patterns of financial development, was published in *Economic Development and Cultural Change* in 1966, and the Gurley and Shaw article, "Financial Structure and Economic Development" (Gurley and Shaw 1967), appeared in the same journal the following year. Patrick's knowledge of the Japanese financial system contributed a strong awareness of the antecedents of Korea's institutions to the more general perspectives of Gurley and Shaw.

2. See Cole and Park (1983). Kim Yung-Hwan, who had helped introduce the deposit interest rate increases in 1965, was the designer of the moneylender decapitalization scheme in 1972, although he was at the time serving as Vice Minister of Commerce and Industry and was more concerned about rescuing the large corporate borrowers than protecting the financial system.

3. U Tun Thin was the key proponent of the stabilization program within the IMF, and on the Indonesian side, the team of economists lead by Professors Widjojo Nitisastro and Ali Wardhana was responsible for selling the program to Acting President Suharto and his cabinet.

4. Between the end of 1983 and 1988 the ratio of M2 to GDP increased from 19 percent to 28 percent.

5. The experience of another strong central bank leader, Governor Cuaderno in the Philippines, is not reassuring. Governor Cuaderno turned the Philippine central bank into an import licensing agency, and its weak position was unable to withstand the election financing demands of President Marcos in the early 1970s.

References

The word *processed* describes informally produced works that may not be commonly available through libraries.

Ariff, Mohamed, and Ahmed M. Khalid. 2000. *Liberalization, Growth and the Asian Financial Crisis: Lessons for Developing and Transitional Economies in Asia.* Cheltenham: Edward Elgar.

Bloomfield, Arthur I., and J. P. Jensen. 1951. *Banking Reform in South Korea*. New York: Federal Reserve Bank.

Charlesworth, Harold K. 1959. *A Banking System in Transition*. Jakarta: The New Nusantara Publishing Co.

Cole, David C., and Princeton N. Lyman. 1971. *Korean Development: The Interplay of Politics and Economics*. Cambridge, Massachusetts: Harvard University Press.

Cole, David C., and Yung-Chul Park. 1983. *Financial Development in Korea, 1945-1978*. Cambridge, Massachusetts: Harvard University Press.

Cole, David C., and Betty F. Slade. 1996. *Building a Modern Financial System: The Indonesian Experience*. Cambridge, England: Cambridge University Press.

Doner, Richard, and Daniel Unger. 1993. "The Politics of Finance in Thai Economic Development." In Stephan Haggard, Chung H. Lee, and Sylvia Maxfield, eds., *The Politics of Finance in Developing Countries*. Ithaca: Cornell University Press.

Gurley, John G., Hugh T. Patrick, and E. S. Shaw. 1965. "The Financial Structure of Korea." Seoul: United States Operations Mission to Korea (July 24, 1965). Processed.

Gurley, John G., and Edward S. Shaw. 1955. "Financial Aspects of Economic Development." American Economic Review 45:515–538.

———. 1960. "Money in a Theory of Finance." Washington, D.C.: The Brookings Institution.

———. 1967. "Financial Structure and Economic Development." *Economic Development and Cultural Change* 15:257–268

McKinnon, Ronald I. 1973. "Money and Capital in Economic Development." Washington, D.C.: The Brookings Institution.

Nam, Sang-Woo. 1995. "Korea's Financial Markets and Policies." In Shahid N. Zahid, ed., *Financial Sector Development in Asia*. Manila: Asian Development Bank.

Nasution, Anwar. 1983. *Financial Institutions and Policies in Indonesia*. Singapore: Institute for Southeast Asian Studies.

———. 1995. "Financial Sector Development in Indonesia." In Shahid N. Zahid, ed., *Financial Sector Development in Asia*. Manila: Asian Development Bank.

Patrick, Hugh T. 1966. "Financial Development and Economic Growth in Underdeveloped Countries." *Economic Development and Cultural Change* 14:174–189.

Shaw, Edward S. 1973. *Financial Deepening in Economic Development*. New York: Oxford University Press.

Skully, Michael T. 1984. *Financial Institutions and Markets in Southeast Asia*. New York: St. Martin's Press.

Smith, Heather. 1998. "Korea." In Ross H. McLeod and Ross Garnaut, eds., *East Asia in Crisis: From Being a Miracle to Needing One?* London: Routledge.

Vajragupta, Yos, and Pakorn Vichyanond. 1999. "Thailand's Financial Evolution and the 1997 Crisis." In Seiichi Masuyama, Donna Vandenbrink, and Chia Siow Yue, eds., *East Asia's Financial Systems: Evolution and Crisis*. Tokyo and Singapore: Nomura Research Institute and Institute of Southeast Asian Studies.

Vichyanond, Pakorn. 1995. "Financial Sector Development in Thailand." In Shahid N. Zahid, ed., *Financial Sector Development in Asia*. Manila: Asian Development Bank.

Risk Management and Stable Financial Structures for LDC, Inc.

Andrew Sheng and Yoon Je Cho

Introduction

THE CONVENTIONAL DEVELOPMENT ECONOMICS of the past focused mainly on generating economic growth through the mobilization of savings and the allocation of these savings among investment opportunities. The mobilization of savings involved the encouragement of external savings and the generation of domestic savings through tax incentives and interest rate policies. The allocation of these savings often involved direct government intervention in the investment process.

Some disastrous early results of this policy have given rise to a new wisdom that relies on the private sector to generate growth, with the government relegated to the role of regulating and supervising competitive markets, ensuring the existence of level playing fields, and removing obvious cases of moral hazard.

This new wisdom, however, neglects the importance of how investments are financed: it does not address financial structure nor does it address the implications of financing for the stability and long-term growth of the economy. While experience shows that

This paper was first circulated in 1993. The authors gratefully acknowledge the research assistance of Bo Wang and the helpful comments of Gerard Caprio, Alan Gelb, Thomas Hellman, Aslı Demirgüç-Kunt, Ross Levine, Anita Schwarz, Lester Seigel, and Dimitri Vittas.

imperfect governments are not good at picking the winners in long-term investments, there is nothing to suggest that imperfect private entrepreneurs working under an inappropriate financial structure would do any better. A stable financial structure is critical to the achievement of steady long-term economic growth, and this can only be achieved through effective risk management at the national level.

Many developing countries have experienced financial distress, both external and domestic, since the early 1980s. In the period 1982–90, more than 50 countries had to reschedule their foreign debt and more than 40 countries were involved in major domestic bank restructuring. The transition to a market economy subsequently saw many of the former socialist economies experience similar distress. The clear lesson that emerges is that when poor risk management leads a country into financial distress, the cost is enormous. Making up for the losses of the banking system, reestablishing the confidence and credibility of government policies and of the banking system, and recovering international credit standing take time, and in the process economic growth and welfare suffer. While some developing and transition economies have struggled since the 1980s, the countries that avoided major domestic financial instability and the rescheduling of foreign loans enjoyed interest rates significantly below the London Interbank Offer Rate (LIBOR), retained access to international financial markets, and benefited from substantial foreign investment flows (Demirgüç-Kunt and Detragiache 1992).

The path of economic transition involves a high risk of financial instability, especially for countries whose product and export markets are not well diversified. The developing economy typically does not have an institutional and legal framework capable of effective bank supervision, nor does it have deep capital markets to cushion shocks. Newly emerging enterprises in these countries are highly geared (i.e., have a high debt-to-equity ratio), they have low managerial and financial skills, and they are operating in a repressed financial market with a highly distorted interest rate structure. Their access to the international capital market is tenuous and their credit standing fragile, compared to those of Organisation for Economic Co-operation and Development (OECD) countries. In such a situation, relative price changes during economic transition can easily worsen bank loan portfolios. An initial small external shock can lead quickly to higher country risk premiums and can drastically curtail the availability of foreign capital. If policymakers have insufficient reserves and administrative capacity to contain the vulnerability, capital flight can ensue, creating an economy-wide crisis.

The perceived and actual risks of financial instability are thus substantially higher in developing countries than in industrial countries. This situation is likely to be accentuated over time, as the internationalization of banking and the liberalization of capital accounts increase the ease of capital flight and reduce the effectiveness of traditional macroeconomic management tools.

Within such an environment, governments may have to devote more attention to prudential risk management and to establishing stable financial structures. This may incur some short-term cost of forgone investment and other higher-profit opportunities.

From Corporate Finance to National Finance

Many economists have stressed the importance of the processes and institutions by which capital is allocated and the role of financial institutions in the selection or screening of investment projects and in monitoring (Bencivenga and Smith 1991; Diamond 1991; Gertler and Rose 1991; Levine 1992; Scharfstein 1992; Stiglitz 1989). Stiglitz (1989) emphasized that the way in which financing arrangements are made for firms affects the ways in which risks are shared between the firm and its investors and in which incentives are structured for the managers. A similar argument can be extended to the national level: the way in which a country finances its industries and development has significant implications for the way in which risks are shared and managed at the national level; it also has significant implications for the long-term economic growth of the country.

This paper argues that it is important for the long-term growth of an economy not only how much investment is mobilized and allocated, but also how investments are financed. The new paradigm suggested in this paper is that finance and development are inextricably tied into the question of risk management, not only at the firm level but also at the macro-national level. One of the hallmarks of this paradigm is that it holds that development is a function not just of promoting the right industries and allocating capital for high-return investments (let us call this asset management), but also of choosing the right financial structure (let us call this liability management) and of the related risks arising from the choice of liability mix. Traditional development economics focused mainly on the former, largely neglecting the implications of the latter for

the long-term growth of an economy. It has been argued by many
observers that the East and Southeast Asian economies that registered such rapid economic growth in the second part of the last century[1] achieved their success largely because they managed to pick
winners to finance through their policy-based lending. Prior to the
early 1990s, few observers pointed out that successful risk management by these governments also was a crucial element for the
long-term success of their economy.

Why Is Risk Management So Important?

Let us examine some simple heuristic examples to see why risk
management is so important in the long run.

Asset Management

The intuitive logic of this argument on the asset side is very simple.
Suppose there are two economies whose growth potential and
expected rates of return on capital investment are similar: that
have, for example, similar levels of education, wage rate, and technology. Country A has a more concentrated asset mix than country
B, and accordingly the risk, as measured by the standard deviation
of returns, is higher.

In period 1, both countries make the same amount of investments, financed identically, partly by domestic bank loans and
partly by foreign loans. Suppose in period 2 an external shock
affects badly the heavily concentrated industries in country A. As
a result, A's current account deficit deteriorates and ex post economic growth rate becomes lower than expected. A's banking system becomes loaded with substantial nonperforming loans, and
foreign debt may have to be rescheduled. In contrast, country B
may be able to achieve a growth rate more or less as expected,
because of the stabilizing effects of industries not affected by the
external shock (standard deviation of returns is low due to B's
diversification).

In period 3, country A will face difficulties of access to external
borrowing as a result of its poor economic performance. This will
force it to curtail or reduce its investment plan and depreciate the
exchange rate. Domestic inflation will rise. In addition, foreign
loans may cost substantially more than for country B. This suggests
that even where countries are operating under similar economic
conditions, over the long term a country with a more diversified

mix of assets will perform better than a country with a concentrated asset mix.[2]

Liability Management

On the liabilities side, suppose there are two economies with similar initial economic conditions and products and export mix, but with different financing strategies. In period 1, firms in country A finance their investment exclusively through bank loans while firms in country B finance theirs largely through capital and internal finance.[3] In period 2 an external shock occurs. Country A's banking system is more likely to be loaded with nonperforming loans, but country B's enterprise sector is cushioned by its capital base. The higher the corporate sector leverage in a country, the higher is the risk of instability of the financial sector.

In period 3, the loss of confidence in country A's banking system and the financial disintermediation will result in lower investment and growth performance. State rescues of ailing enterprises and banks have enormous fiscal costs,[4] and the stabilization efforts necessary to contain the inflationary consequences of fiscal bail-outs also can dampen economic growth. Bank restructuring and reestablishing depositor confidence take time, and domestic investment and economic recovery would suffer significantly in the interim.

A parallel can be drawn with financing at the national level. If we regard domestic financing as self-finance or equity capital, a country that finances its investment mostly with domestic savings is likely to absorb external shocks better than one with a high reliance on external debt. While the volume of investment may be constrained by the limits of domestic savings, the country as a whole may be less vulnerable to changes in international interest rates and to exogenous reduction in access to foreign funds than a country that is heavily dependent on foreign borrowing.

A country that relies mainly on foreign direct investment to finance its domestic investment may be able to achieve both higher and more stable patterns of growth, however, since foreign equity capital is another external shock absorber.[5] Accordingly, the total risk exposure of a country depends not only on its asset mix, but also on its liability mix. Other things being equal, the higher a country is leveraged, through either domestic or foreign debt, the more volatile will be its economic performance, and the more likely over the long term will be poorer economic growth.

Table 1 compares the growth performance through 1971–90 of 98 developing countries. Those countries with an average foreign debt–gross national product (GNP) ratio in excess of 50 percent are considered to be high-debt countries; those with a ratio of less than 50 percent are classed as low-debt countries. The table suggests that there is a correlation between debt ratio and growth perform-ance. (It does not imply there is a clear causality between the two variables.) It shows that the growth performance of high-debt countries was significantly poorer than the growth performance of countries with low debt. It also shows that high-debt countries experienced more unstable growth and significantly higher inflation rates than did the low-debt countries.

It is interesting to compare the different growth patterns achieved between two resource-rich countries: Malaysia and Ghana. At the point of independence in 1957, both countries inher-ited strong administrative machinery, high education levels, and high external reserves. Their major products and exports were, however, highly concentrated on commodities: Malaysia on rubber and tin, and Ghana on cocoa and gold. Beginning in the late 1960s, Malaysia adopted an export diversification strategy, introducing one major export product roughly every five years—timber, palm oil, oil and gas, and finally manufacturing—financed significantly by foreign direct investments. In contrast, Ghana diversified little. In 1965, 99 percent of its exports were concentrated on primary commodities; by 1989 this figure had improved only slightly, to 92 percent (Table 2). While it is true that the two countries undertook different historical paths and that other factors also affected their actual growth outcome, over the period 1965–89 Malaysia, with its

Table 1. Growth Performance of High-Debt v. Low-Debt Countries (1971–90)

	High-Debt Countries[1] *(38 countries)*	*Low-Debt Countries* *(60 countries)*
Average annual real GDP growth rate (%)	2.7	4.5
Standard deviation of growth rate[2]	16.8	1.7
Average annual inflation (consumer price index, as %)	56.4	16.8

1. High-debt countries are those whose average foreign debt during 1971–1990 was greater than 50 percent of their GDP; low-debt countries are those with a ratio of less than 50 percent.

2. Mean-adjusted standard deviation.

Source: The data underlying this and the other tables in this chapter are taken from various issues of standard World Bank and IMF statistical publications.

diversified economy, achieved an annual average growth rate of 6.9 percent, compared to Ghana's 1.4 percent.

As stated, there are other factors at play in the political economy of growth, but the point should be taken that different national risk management strategies—specifically, asset diversification and openness to foreign direct investment (liability management)—do matter in terms of long-run growth.

We also compared the growth performance of developing countries during 1965–89 for two groups of countries, based on the degree of diversification of their production and exports (Tables 3 and 4). The countries that significantly diversified their production and exports during the period experienced more stable and higher growth rates than those countries which did not. Again, this suggests a correlation between the two variables, rather than implying a causality.

National Risk Management

The concept of managing an economy like a corporate firm is not new. One remarkable feature of the high economic growth achieved by some of the East and Southeast Asian economies is that they realized that growth while maintaining low inflation. While explanatory variables such as well-educated human capital and

Table 2. Export Concentration, Growth, and Stability of the Economies of Ghana and Malaysia, 1963–89

	Ghana	Malaysia
Primary commodities exports as share	99 (1965)	92 (1989)
of total exports (%)[1]	94 (1965)	56 (1989)
Average annual growth rate	1.4	6.9
Standard deviation of growth rate[2]	4.1	0.5
Average annual inflation (consumer price index, as %)	45.3	4.6
Memo items:		
Per capita income (US$)		
1965	260	390
1989	330	2,160

1. Export of fuels, minerals, metals, and other primary commodities as percentage of total merchandise exports.

2. Mean-adjusted standard deviation.

Source: See note to Table 1.

outward-looking industrial and trade policies played their part in this, the "institutional" or "managerial" view adds the explanation that policymakers managed these economies (and their finances) as if they were single corporations: Japan Inc. or the Republic of Korea Inc., for example. Some observers argue that resource allocation in these economies is similar to that of large multinational corporations: although guided by market signals, their allocation of resources and risks among the different competing sectors is not necessarily made through market arrangements. What may be more significant in the economic management of these economies, however, is not the intervention in credit allocation, but how government absorbs the risks of the private sector, or co-insures these risks with the private sector, during the development process. In other words, the risk management strategies employed may have encouraged private sector growth without the usual negative effects of direct government intervention.

National risk management is a relatively new concept. Policymakers and regulators generally are comfortable with sectoral risk

Table 3. Production Diversification and Growth Performance of Developing Countries, 1965–1989

	Significantly Diversified Countries (36)[1]	Not Significantly Diversified Countries (40)
Average annual growth rate (%)	5.1	3.2
Standard deviation of growth rate	1.38	2.73

1. Countries that between 1965 and 1989 reduced by more than 5 percentage points the share of agriculture in total GDP.
Sources: See note to Table 1.

Table 4. Exports Diversification and Growth Performance of Developing Countries, 1965–1989

	Significantly Diversified Countries (31)[1]	Not Significantly Diversified Countries (37)
Average annual growth rate (%)	4.6	3.5
Standard deviation of growth rate	1.31	2.40

1. Countries that between 1965 and 1989 reduced by more than 10 percentage points the share of total exports accounted for by primary commodities.
Source: See note to Table 1.

management, particularly that with a focus on risk reduction or amelioration rules and regulations for the behavior of firms in a single sector or financial institutions, and on the containment of systemic risks. It is rare, however, for ministries of finance or central banks to see the big picture in risk management. For example, a common problem in many developing countries in the 1980s was the lack of coordinated risk management in terms of debt (liability) management versus reserves (assets) management. A ministry of finance would typically seek to minimize debt servicing costs by concentrating on low-interest-rate currency borrowing, subjecting the nation to substantial risks of high revaluation losses in the future. A central bank with responsibility for reserves management, in contrast, typically would concentrate on maintaining high liquidity, with consequent low yields; while this may mesh with the central bank's objectives, it may produce a currency mix that does not minimize the net foreign currency exposure of the nation as a whole.

There are several reasons for this oversight. The first is the segmentation of responsibility within government itself. The incentives within government require each ministry or agency to focus on its own objectives, even though these may be contradictory and suboptimal for the nation as a whole. The second is even more fundamental, and is related to the severe data inadequacies that the typical policymaker faces. The national accounts of most less-developed countries (LDCs) are by and large flow accounts, with almost no sectoral or national balance sheets.[6] The minister of finance cannot engage in asset-liability management like a corporate treasurer even if he or she wanted to, because the necessary information simply is not available. Most governments do not even maintain a balance sheet. Cash-based government accounting disguises the detrimental effects of off-balance expenditure and hides the consequences of large quasi-fiscal deficits.[7]

This lack of data means that in many cases where a government had absorbed substantial amounts of off-balance-sheet liabilities—such as deposit insurance, credit insurance for sectoral programs, or exchange rate guarantees—fiscal adjustments may not have been adequate. A major lesson learned in the 1980s was that in a financial crisis the government is responsible for all national debt, irrespective of whether that debt was incurred by the private sector. The Chilean crisis of 1982–1985, for example, required that the government fully guarantee all domestic deposits as well as the external debt of the private sector (Velasco 1991). This is highly dangerous for fiscal and monetary stability, because while recession drives down government revenue it at the same time means that the government needs larger resources to service its growing domestic and external debt, to cover private sector external liabilities, and to cover losses in a banking system that is subject to an implicit or explicit government deposit guarantee.

National Balance Sheet

It would be useful to develop a notion of a national balance sheet for the effective risk management of an economy. Just as corporate managers manage their risk by changing the structure of their assets and liabilities, policymakers may have to manage domestic and systemic risks through rules and regulations that shift the national asset-liability mix.

At a minimum, a national balance sheet should distinguish between four domestic sectors: government, enterprises, households and the financial sector, and the external sector.[8] The importance of sectoral balance sheets is that they show how different sectors finance their asset base, and how financial imbalances in one sector could trigger imbalances in other sectors. Indeed, the building of a stable financing structure (the liabilities side of the national balance sheet) has been a major preoccupation of recent financial sector reform efforts.

Market shocks that have occurred during the internationalization of banking and the global harmonization of banking and financial market regulation have enabled us to reach a better, though not yet complete, understanding of some of the risks in national asset-liability management. These risks may be broken down into the following categories:

- market risks (e.g., interest rates, exchange rates, and prices)
- credit or default risks
- regulatory risks
- liquidity risks
- fraud risks
- systemic risks.

Clearly, government has a major role to play in all of these categories, as either a market participant or regulator. For example, macroeconomic policies will have a major impact on relative prices (interest rates, exchange rates, and domestic prices). Relative price changes, combined with government action or inaction in the legal, accounting, and debt recovery framework, will affect sectoral solvency and hence determine the size of credit or default risks.

Arbitrary or sudden changes in government regulations, such as the closing of markets, imposition of exchange controls, or nationalization of banks, are major regulatory (sometimes called political) risks; similarly, macromanagement of liquidity has a significant influence on liquidity at the enterprise level. Enforcement of laws deters fraudulent behavior. Finally, only the government can insure against systemic risks or shocks to the economy as a whole.

National risk management in a fully open economy is complicated by the fact that the private sector can always hedge its own risks through capital flight—and mistakes in government policy can easily trigger capital flight. The flight of capital in turn complicates macroeconomic management, and reduces the ability of government to pay for losses in a crisis by taxing wealth and income.

Consequently, just as a firm needs a good understanding of its risk exposures, a policymaker must have the "big picture" of risk exposures in the national balance sheet if he is to manage these risks in such a way that external, political, or natural shocks do not jeopardize the economy's long-term growth. For various reasons, many East and Southeast Asian policymakers have tended to follow several basic rules of risk management in their national asset-liability management. These are not risk-averse strategies, but strategies to ensure that high risk taking is properly financed and managed.

Managing Financial Stability: Some Basic Rules

The rules of risk management can be summarized as follows:

- Establish fiscal discipline and price stability.
- Encourage asset diversification through industrialization and outward orientation.
- Avoid large sector financial imbalances, including excessive domestic and external borrowing, and develop financial instruments and institutions to cushion shocks.
- Establish the institutional and administrative capacity to assess and contain systemic risks.
- When the above conditions are not adequately met, retain some policy measures to handle the risk

Establishing Fiscal Discipline and Price Stability

With few exceptions, those developing countries that have experienced financial instability since the 1980s suffered badly in the face

of high inflation and volatile relative prices. Inflation distorts relative prices, turning real interest rates negative when they are controlled and adding high risk premium to interest rates when they
are liberalized. As a result, funds shift toward speculation in nontradables, investment horizons shorten, and financial disintermediation takes place.

High inflation also tends to make the exchange rate unstable,
leading to overshooting or undershooting of the exchange rate if
not carefully managed. Such market volatility can rapidly decapi-
talize firms, pushing them toward distressed borrowing, deterring
long-term investments, and reducing domestic production, thus
causing higher inflation. Price volatility also reduces the transparency of information, raising information search costs and creating opportunities for rent seeking. The cost of high market risk furthermore lowers long-term growth and efficiency.

In most developing countries, the main causes of high inflation
are large budget deficits. The existence of budgetary deficits raises regulatory risks—the risk that the government will seek to
finance itself through heavier taxation, inflation tax, or both.
Once the sustainability of government expenditure is questioned,
tax avoidance increases; and where the government's own financial discipline has been lax, it loses the moral authority to require
financial discipline on the part of the private sector—which furthermore has greater incentives for speculation and moral hazard
behavior (Sheng 1991).

Tax reform, expenditure control, and achieving price stability
therefore are essential to secure financial stability and enable the
robust growth of the financial sector. Fiscal discipline is the anchor
of financial sector stability. The East and Southeast Asian
economies that expanded so rapidly in general have maintained a
very prudent fiscal stance and maintained low inflation rates.

Asset Diversification

In terms of portfolio diversification, capital stocks in different
industries, investments in infrastructure, and foreign exchange
reserves may be viewed as alternative assets. Simple risk diversification theory suggests that risk is minimized when resources are
spread widely across assets that have a negative or low correlation
with each other. In a concentrated economy that depends on oil, for
instance, an example of a long-term investment strategy to reduce
risk would be one that specifies avoidance of investment in domestic assets, such as property or shares, that are correlated with the

fortunes of the oil market, and maintenance instead of high foreign exchange reserves.

Another way of looking at asset diversification is to view the overconcentration of ownership of resources, whether in the private or public sectors, as risk-prone in the long run. Resources therefore should be distributed across a competitive environment to minimize risk and achieve maximum efficiency. While there are risks associated with industrialization, the broadening of national output can widen the tax base, reduce production volatility, and reduce the current account position through the diversification of markets and export earnings. Trade protection policies generally should be avoided, as these expose the nation to higher risks in the long run by forcing the concentration of resources in inefficient import-substituting industries. The development of export-oriented industries, in contrast, is in the long term risk reducing, because increased foreign exchange earnings can sustain a higher level of external financing.

The fast-growing East and Southeast Asian economies rewarded export earners by permitting them to use foreign exchange to import technology and equipment, thus encouraging firms to become competitive at the international level. Many other developing countries, however, violated the basic rule of using external borrowing only to finance assets that earn foreign exchange (Fischer 1991), with the result that they were subject to severe foreign exchange constraints in times of worsening terms of trade.

Inducing foreign direct investment for the development of new industries is an effective way for a country to reduce its economic risk, enabling it to diversify its assets and share the remaining risk with foreign partners. Trade liberalization and foreign direct investment therefore are good policy measures for effective risk management and for the promotion of industrial growth within a neoclassical framework.

Figure 1, while not suggesting that private investment is the major source of growth, offers evidence that low levels of private investment are correlated with low levels of growth.

Building Stable Financial Structures

As discussed, national liability management can shape the financial structure. The "safest" liability is equity. For example, a firm that finances its investments wholly through internal equity would be better able to cushion itself against interest rate or other external shocks than would a highly leveraged firm. The risk of overdiversification of debt can be seen from the problems of borrowers in debt negotiations. The more creditor banks that are involved, generally the longer it will take to achieve debt resolution; and any delay in achieving resolution will worsen the financial position of the distressed borrower. An economy that relies solely on domestic saving is much less vulnerable to external shocks, but its growth may be constrained by limited domestic resources. The same debt versus equity issue that faces corporate firms thus also faces national economies.

Debt versus equity. Given different corporate objectives and changing market conditions, there is no single optimal structure of debt-equity ratio for a firm,[9] nor an optimal financial market structure for an economy. However, just as a firm builds up capital and liquidity as a cushion against unpredictable market risks, a nation should maintain a financial structure that can absorb shocks.

Equity capital has a distinct advantage over debt in that risk is shared between the user and the provider of capital, and there is

Figure 1. Private Investment and GDP Growth (1970–89)

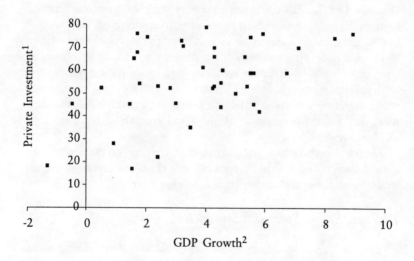

Note: For some countries the period covered is different due to data availability
1. Private investment as a percentage of the total gross domestic investment
2. Average annual GDP growth between 1970 and 1989.
Source: Pfeffermann and Madarassy (1991).

no fixed obligation to repay the equity holder.[10] Equity capital therefore is an important cushion to economic shocks and business cycles. The lessons of recent years suggest that excessive borrowing in one sector can rapidly destabilize the economy as a whole. Accordingly, building a strong equity base in the corporate sector, reducing credit concentration, strengthening capital adequacy and loan loss reserves in the financial sector, and improving public sector saving all are consistent tools of national risk management.

A nation can build up domestic equity capital in several ways; for example, through promoting retained earnings, by encouraging foreign direct or portfolio investment, or through privatization and building stock markets.

In Japan, the first large conglomerates were formed in the Meiji period from the privatization of state-owned industries in armaments, shipbuilding, steel, and mining. Here, as elsewhere in East and Southeast Asia, stock markets were not major players in capital mobilization for enterprises in the early stages of development. The successful economies of the region have tended to use a combination of low (but positive in real terms) lending rates, with tax disincentives against high dividends, to encourage the accumulation of retained earnings and corporate savings. On the whole, although perhaps with the exception of Japan and the Republic of Korea, these economies were open to foreign equity capital, which shared the risk of investment between domestic and foreign investors. They were especially welcoming to foreign direct investment for long-term industrial investment that introduced new technology, managerial skills, or new markets.[11]

Stock markets became more important as banking practices, law, and accounting became more established. Medium-sized and large firms turned to new equity, acquired at cheaper rates than bank borrowing, to expand production. Active stock markets create a new dimension of risk, however, by introducing the variable of public confidence; and when an economy is not yet stable, the rapid inflow and outflow of short-term foreign portfolio investment can complicate monetary control and magnify macroeconomic instability. If the domestic securities market is small, foreign portfolio investment in any case may not be a viable option for inducing foreign equity capital. In the early stages of development, a country consequently may have to rely mainly on corporate savings and foreign direct investments to develop the strong domestic equity base necessary to finance long-term investments.

Development of diversified financial instruments. Just as corporations and banks are concerned with their individual interest rate
risks, an economy also should be concerned with its interest rate
and the maturity structures of its domestic and foreign liabilities.
The soundness of "never borrow short to lend long" and "never
lend fixed rates and finance with variable rate" was clearly demonstrated by the U.S. savings and loan crisis, where fixed-rate, long-
term mortgage loans were financed with short-term, variable-rate
deposits. Sharp interest rate increases in 1981 decapitalized one
segment of the financial sector.

Many developing countries also have violated these rules by
using credit directives to banks to finance long-term investments
(infrastructure plus corporate investments) at fixed rates through
variable-rate short-term deposits, thus creating large maturity mismatches in their banking systems. The failure of many development banks was attributable to their practice of having a high concentration of risky loans at fixed rates, without a stable long-term
funding base. Inappropriate interest rate policies, directed loans,
and large interest rate and maturity mismatches were major causes of financial sector insolvencies in the 1980s. The striking ability of some East and Southeast Asian economies, such as Japan,
Singapore, and Malaysia, to sustain high fiscal deficits was due in
large part to the existence of strong contractual or postal savings
institutions.

Developing countries should seek to design their financial systems to include the diversified instruments and markets that are
able to transform and intermediate risks. The development of long-
term financial instruments and equity markets, either through the
development of a public securities market or the development of
institutions that provide equity capital, would help to contain the
risk of financial instability.

Management of foreign exchange risks. In recent years, many developing countries have made major errors in the management of their
foreign exchange risk. The four main errors are as follows:

• Many countries kept their currencies underdepreciated in
fear of the inflationary impact of depreciation. Underdepreciation
of the domestic exchange rate relative to domestic inflation
reduces competitiveness and encourages consumption and a major
shift toward nontradables, particularly speculation in property. In
such circumstances, abrupt exchange rate adjustments will inflict
severe losses on private sector firms that have external debt and

will strain the debt servicing capacity of the budget. Governments in East Asia and some countries of Southeast Asia generally have maintained fairly stable real exchange rates and have avoided using the exchange rate as an anti-inflation tool. Most have maintained high foreign exchange reserves relative to imports or to external debt.

• Governments have only belatedly tried to reduce currency mismatches by borrowing mainly in currencies of the country's export earnings. Initial borrowings in low-interest currencies have caused large foreign exchange losses for many borrowers, which have probably been larger in magnitude than the credit losses of the banking system.

• Unrestricted access to foreign borrowing by firms not used to foreign exchange risks may cause major problems. In the Chilean and Argentine banking crises of the 1980s, the lenders in essence forced the government to take over the external debt of failing private borrowers, with substantial fiscal impact. Almost all of the fast-grown East and Southeast Asian economies were reluctant to allow domestic firms unrestricted access to foreign borrowing until late in the sequencing of financial liberalization.

• Loading central banks with net foreign exchange liabilities presented those banks with the dilemma of setting an exchange rate to either balance the current account of the balance of payments or to preserve their own solvency. Allowing the exchange rate to depreciate would worsen the central bank's own financial position; to protect their own solvency, some central banks have felt compelled to allow an overvaluation of the exchange rate. The consequence of this has been massive relative price distortions in the economy. Throughout their rapid expansion, the central banks of most of the East and Southeast Asian economies maintained high foreign exchange reserves with no foreign exchange liabilities in their balance sheets other than reserve money, and they were therefore able to conduct exchange rate management in an autonomous and financially stable manner. The notable exception was the Philippines.

Institutional and Legal Framework for Bank Supervision

The strategies discussed above will reduce system-wide risks. The onus remains on banks, however, to also select sound and profitable borrowers and to monitor and enforce loan contracts. The business of banking and finance is essentially the business of public confidence: the public at large and market participants in particular expect effective official surveillance of a system in which credit and credibility are a unifying force (Corrigan 1987). The financial sector must be closely monitored and supervised by government.

An important function of financial sector supervision is the development of an institutional and legal framework for enforcing debt contracts, for measuring and reporting the solvency and efficiency of borrowers and lenders, and to ensure that systemic risks and sectoral imbalances are not such that the soundness and safety of the financial system are jeopardized. Where the financial sector may have to intermediate high risks, appropriate instruments and adequate capital should be put into place to support such activities. In short, national risk management is an important *raison d'être* of effective bank supervision.

Financial Sector Liberalization and Risk Management

Financial sector liberalization itself entails high risks. A major issue in the design and sequencing of economic liberalization is the need to engender change without creating instability. Economic liberalization involves changes in relative prices, and these can have large wealth and income distribution effects and can cause the rapid deterioration of net worth in some sectors. The use of sectoral and national balance sheets can help project the effects of such relative price changes and consequently identify the risks associated with price reforms.

A major lesson of recent financial sector reforms is that the fiscal costs of liberalization, in terms of actual as well as contingent liabilities, can be very large (Caprio 1992). Large sectoral wealth losses such as enterprise or bank losses are shifted to the budget, which may be incapable of digesting them without losing monetary and macroeconomic stability. Indeed, where national resources are insufficient or the institutional framework for prudential regulation inadequate to cushion such shocks, a country may have to take an approach by which distorting regulations are gradually removed, in parallel with the deepening of capital markets and the building of institutions and supervisory capacity. The proper sequencing is to first remove all distorting regulations that can be removed without causing major instability, and to remove all others as the market and institutional environments become sufficiently mature to cushion the impact of deregulation. In general, this has been the approach of the fast-grown East and Southeast Asian economies.

Most OECD countries opened their financial systems during the 1980s, when their financial markets were already diversified and mature. They had the institutional development and market depth to cushion the shocks arising from market liberalization, and as a consequence, their financial liberalization generally has been successful. They also have the capability to spread the costs of external shocks over time: most developing countries do not have this option. For example, while recent banking and savings and loan problems did not hamper U.S. access to the international capital market, the Republic of Korea, despite its remarkable economic success, has on occasion been on the brink of losing access to voluntary lending (Fischer and Reisen 1992).

The policymakers responsible for national risk management must have a clear understanding of the potential risk exposures in their economy and in the financial sector. This requires good accounting and reliable reporting of sectoral risks, including the provision of sectoral balance sheets and the reporting of net worth. By making the full costs of policy options more transparent, particularly below the line (or quasi-fiscal) costs of government guarantees on private sector risk-taking behavior, policymakers may be able to avoid the costs associated with taking short-run measures that have high long-run costs. For example, if policymakers do not foresee the immediate improvement of government finances, it may be premature to liberalize external capital transactions, since liberalization may put too much strain on scarce foreign exchange reserves, may worsen the national debt, may reduce the inflation tax base, and may further destabilize the economy.

Summary and Conclusions

This paper argues that national risk management is critical for the achievement of steady long-term economic growth. Neoclassical growth theory focuses mainly on making the right asset choice, and pays little attention to the implication of risks, uncertainties, and how investments are financed—i.e., on liability choice for the long-term growth of an economy. The experiences of many developing countries in the 1980s indicate that once a country fails its risk management and stumbles into financial distress, the resulting cost is enormous. Both economic growth and welfare suffer. In the long run, prudential risk management and the establishment of a stable financial structure are rewarded with steady and high economic growth.

For policymakers to manage risk effectively, they must have a "big picture" understanding of the national economy. Effective risk management at the sectoral level does not necessarily ensure effective risk management at the national level. Sectoral risk may be hedged against the risk of other sectors but national risk cannot be hedged, and therefore must be controlled by regulation and supervision. Just as a corporation controls firm risk through asset-liability management, a policymaker should apply national asset-liability management, using a national balance sheet that clearly identifies financial imbalances and the effects on sectoral net wealth due to changes in relative prices.

In general, the East and Southeast Asian economies that grew so rapidly in the latter half of the 20th century tended to manage their finances as if their economies were single corporations. They operated a strategy for asset diversification and a carefully managed financial structure that minimized systemic risks without retarding private sector risk taking. Their financial sector reforms consequently have been gradualist, but have been successful in attaining stable long-term growth.

Some general national risk management rules can be established, based partly on well-known corporate risk management rules:

• *Create price stability* (a stable macroeconomic environment) to reduce system-wide risks and uncertainties, and hence transaction costs, for private sector initiative. Fiscal discipline is a key anchor of price stability.

• *Asset diversification.* Using foreign direct investment, broaden the production and export (asset) structure through outward orientation to ensure competitiveness at international levels. Build up foreign exchange reserves when the domestic asset base is highly concentrated.

• *Liability management.* Reduce national and sectoral leverage by strengthening the capital base of corporations and banks, including through use of foreign direct investments; deepen domestic financial markets; improve debt management; and avoid large maturity, interest rate, and exchange rate mismatches.

• *Develop institutional and administrative capacity* to assess risk and to contain systemic risk.

• *Sequence financial sector liberalization measures* with a clear understanding of the risks involved; ensure institutional strength and fiscal resources are sufficient to manage the transitional process without causing macroeconomic instability.

In sum, the tortoise wins over the hare in the long run.

Notes

1. Including, for example, Japan, the Republic of Korea, Malaysia, and Singapore.

2. Brignoli and Seigel (1988) show that, even if the expected rate of return of assets is intertemporally independent, the assets with higher risk (standard deviation) will end up with lower growth in the long run.

3. Although domestic saving levels may be the same, country A savings are assumed to be in the household sector, which are on-lent via the banking system to the corporate sector. Country B savings are mainly in the corporate sector, or in household savings channeled through nonbank financial institutions (NBFIs) or the securities market for equity investment in the corporate sector.

4. In Chile, for example, the costs incurred over 1982–1985 have been estimated at 44 percent of the country's 1985 GNP (Fischer and Reisen 1992).

5. See Atiyas and Dietz (1991) on how firms with foreign equity are more resilient to financial distress in Colombia.

6. For example, the lack in many countries of national balance sheets, particularly of outstanding stock of foreign direct investment (FDI), would not facilitate a comparison of debt-equity structure across countries.

7. In other words, the nontransparency of government accounting does not assist enforcement of a hard budget constraint, with the result that governments easily can resort to off-budget expenditure and monetary creation to escape financial discipline.

8. From a national point of view, the national net wealth may be defined as the sum of domestic assets (land, equipment, and intellectual property) and financial claims on foreigners (including foreign exchange reserves), less external claims on the economy, including external short-term and long-term debt and foreign direct and portfolio investment in domestic corporations. Such a "net" national balance sheet would unfortunately not be able to distinguish the large internal sectoral imbalances that could jeopardize growth within an economy.

9. There is considerable discussion on the optimal financial structure at the firm level. The discussion in the finance literature on the optimal debt-equity structure can be broadly classified into four parts: (a) tax implications on the optimal capital (Miller 1977; Modigliani 1982); (b) the agency cost approach to optimal capital (Jensen and Meckling 1976; Diamond 1984; Jensen 1986; Hirshleifer and Thakor 1989; Harris and Raviv 1990; (c) the asymmetric information approach to optimal capital (Ross 1977; Myers and Majluf 1984); and (d) the industrial organization approach to optimal capital (Brander and Lewis 1986). See Demirgüç-Kunt (1992) for a survey.

10. Although equity capital has a distinct advantage over debt with respect to risk sharing, outside equity capital has a disadvantage with respect to incentive issues. Because entrepreneurs do not have a fixed commitment (and because they must share the returns to their effort with other shareholders), incentives are attenuated (Stiglitz 1989). Ex post, debt also could provide a certain degree of risk sharing through debt reductions and reschedulings.

11. See Caprio, Gelb, and Johnson (1989) for a discussion of the measures to promote foreign direct investment.

References

The word *processed* describes informally reproduced works that may not be commonly available through libraries.

Atiyas, Izak, and Mark Dietz. 1991. "Do Firms with Foreign Equity Recover Faster from Financial Distress? The case of Colombia." World Bank Industry Development Division. World Bank, Washington, D.C. Processed.

Bencivenga, V. R., and B. D. Smith. 1991. "Financial Intermediation and Endogenous Growth." *Review of Economic Studies* 58:195–209.

Brander, James A., and Tracy R. Lewis. 1986. "Oligopoly and Financial Structure: The Limited Liability Effect." *American Economic Review* 76:956–70.

Brignoli, R., and L. Seigel. 1988. "The Role of Noise in LDC Growth." Presented at Round-table Conference on Trends in International Capital Markets: Implications for Developing Countries; Oxfordshire, February 20–26 Processed.

Caprio, Jr., Gerard. 1992. "The Impact of Financial Sector Reform." World Bank, Washington, D.C. Processed.

Caprio, Jr., Gerard, Alan Gelb, and Melanie Johnson. 1989. "The Role of Foreign Direct Investment in Financing Developing Countries." World Bank, Washington, D.C.

Corrigan, E. G. 1987. "Financial Market Structure: A Longer View." Federal Reserve Bank of New York, New York.

Demirgüç-Kunt, Aslı. 1992. "Developing Country Capital Structures and Emerging Stock Markets." World Bank Country Economics Department, World Bank, Washington, D.C. Processed.

Demirgüç-Kunt, Aslı, and Enrica Detragiache. 1992. "Interest Rates, Official Lending, and the Debt Crisis: A Reassessment." World Bank, Washington, D.C. Processed.

Diamond, Douglas. 1984. "Financial Intermediation and Delegated Monitoring." *Review of Economic Studies* 51:393–414.

————. 1991. "Monitoring and Reputation: The Choice between Bank Loans and Directly Placed Debt." *Journal of Political Economy* 99(4):689–719.

Fischer, Stanley. 1991. "Issues in International Economic Integration." Keynote Address for the Ninth Pacific Basin, Central Bank Conference on the Globalization of International Finance, Bangkok. Processed.

Fischer, B., and H. Reisen. 1992. "Towards Capital Account Convertibility." OECD (Organisation for Economic Co-operation and Development) Development Centre, Policy Brief 4. OECD, Paris.

Gertler, M., and A. Rose. 1991. "Finance, Growth, and Public Policy." Working Paper Series 814, World Bank Country Economics Department. World Bank, Washington, D.C.

Harris, Milton, and Artur Raviv. 1990. "The Theory of Capital Structure." *Journal of Finance* 46:297–355.

Hirshleifer, David, and Anjan V. Thakor. 1989. "Managerial Reputation, Project Choice and Debt." Working Paper 14–89, Anderson Graduate School of Management at the University of California. University of California, Los Angeles, California.

Jensen, Michael C. 1986. "Agency Costs of Free Cash Flow, Corporate Finance and Takeovers." *American Economic Review* 76:323–39.

Jensen, Michael C., and William Meckling. 1976. "Theory of the Firm: Managerial Behavior, Agency Costs, and Capital Structure." *Journal of Financial Economics* 3:305–60.

Levine, Ross. 1992. "Financial Structures and Economic Development." Working Paper Series 849, World Bank Country Economics Department. World Bank, Washington, D.C.

Miller, Merton H. 1977. "Debt and Taxes." *Journal of Finance* 32:261–275.

Modigliani, Franco. 1982. "Debt, Dividend Policy, Taxes, Inflation and Market Valuation." *Journal of Finance* 37:255–273.

Myers, Steward C., and Nicholas S. Majluf. 1984. "Corporate Financing and Investment Decisions When Firms Have Information That Investors Do Not Have." *Journal of Financial Economics* 13:187–221.

Pfeffermann, Guy P., and Andrea Madarassy. 1991. "Trends in Private Investment in Developing Countries, 1990–91." National Account, IFC Discussion Paper 11. World Bank, Washington, D.C.

Ross, Stephen. 1977. "The Determination of Financial Structure: The Incentive Signalling Approach." *Bell Journal of Economics* 8:23–40.

Scharfstein, David. 1992. "Japanese Corporate Finance and Governance: Implications for the Privatization of Eastern European Enterprises." Massachusetts Institute of Technology, Cambridge, Mass. Processed.

Sheng, Andrew. 1991. "Financial Fragility and the Contractual Nature of Banking: Hard Contracts and Firm Regulations." World Bank, Washington, D.C. Processed.

Stiglitz, Joseph. 1989. "Financial Markets and Development." *Oxford Review of Economic Policy* 5(4):55–66.

Velasco, Andrés. 1991. "Liberalization, Crisis, Intervention: The Chilean Financial System, 1975–85." In V. Sundararajan and T. Bolino, eds., *Banking Crisis: Cases and Issues.* Washington, D.C.: International Monetary Fund.

Eggs in Too Few Baskets: The Impact of Loan Concentration on Bank-Sector Systemic Risk

Berry K. Wilson and Gerard Caprio

> Repeated patterns of risk concentration [by financial institutions] suggest either incomprehension or deliberate ignorance. Regulation may aggravate such patterns, if it constrains financial institutions to a narrow range of assets (Davis 1995).

Introduction

A GLOBAL PANDEMIC OF FINANCIAL CRISES has raised concerns over the risks of systemic bank failures, when the viability of an entire banking system is in doubt. Demirgüç-Kunt and Detragiache (1997) identify a wide variety of economic and financial market factors that are significantly related to the likelihood of a banking crisis. In contrast, this paper focuses on the role of lending concentration (i.e., limited diversification) as an underappreciated factor behind banking crises. Besides its potential role in systemic bank failure, loan concentration also questions the efficiency of the banking

This paper was first published in *Research in Banking and Finance*, Volume 2, 2002. It is reprinted here with the kind permission of Elsevier Science. Berry Wilson would like to acknowledge the research support of the Center for Global Finance of Pace University's Lubin School of Business.

sector and its effectiveness as a conduit for monetary policy in supplying credit broadly to the economy.

To examine the role of loan concentration, the study examines four major episodes of developing country crises that resulted in a banking sector crisis. First, the banking sectors of Chile and Mexico are examined before and after the international debt crisis of 1982. As a consequence of the debt crisis, the Mexican banking sector was largely nationalized. Second, during 1985–86 Malaysia suffered a sharp economic decline, resulting in a banking sector crisis. Finally, shortly after reprivatizing its banking sector during 1992–93, the Mexican banking sector was again in crisis following the 1994 peso devaluation.

Developing country banking crises have particular significance due to their often astronomical fiscal costs (Caprio and Klingebiel 1997; Lindgren, Garcia, and Saal 1996), with banking sector losses often 10 percent to 20 percent of GDP. Lacking the deep capital markets of industrial countries, developing countries turn to fiscal adjustment, inflation, and delayed loss recognition as financing choices for resolving crises. The consequent misallocation of resources, and a risk-aversion-driven credit crunch on the part of bankers (Bernanke 1983; Bernanke and Blinder 1988), can result in low productivity growth (Caprio 1997).

Section II of the paper reviews potential reasons for portfolio concentration. Section III then outlines the study's methodology used to benchmark banking sector performance. Section IV lists data sources and discusses the construction of real sector indexes and efficient frontiers. Section V follows with the presentation of study results. Section VI then summarizes our conclusions and makes policy recommendations. We argue that regulators should discontinue capital controls and other regulations that constrain, or even encourage, bankers to concentrate risks unnecessarily, and that positive incentives for portfolio diversification should be adopted in their place.

Reasons for Portfolio Concentration

Instances of loan-concentration-induced crises in industrial country banking sectors include the developing country debt exposures associated with the 1982 international debt crisis, and the Texas and New England real estate exposures behind the U.S. bank failures in the 1980s. In developing countries, exuberant property lending appeared in Malaysia in the mid-1980s, Japan in the late 1980s and early 1990s, and Thailand during its 1996–97 difficulties.

Why do bankers pursue portfolio concentration strategies? According to de Juan (1987), the common element is an inability to plan. However, a more comprehensive categorization can be made in terms of the following three hypotheses:

- *Ability to diversify.* Diversification opportunities will depend on local market structure and on capital controls that constrain bank lending. An industrial structure concentrated in a small number of commodities constrains diversification. For example, coffee and tea, whose prices are highly covariant, accounted for roughly 45 percent of GDP and 80 percent of exports in pre–civil war Rwanda in 1990. Nonetheless, diversification is possible if capital controls permit investment in foreign assets, or if local banks are branches or subsidiaries of foreign banks.
- *Portfolio theory.* Portfolio theory suggests that diversification across asset choices can reduce risk for a given level of expected return, resulting in an efficient allocation of scarce capital. An efficient-frontier analysis can identify the resulting risk and return tradeoffs. Banks might deviate from a purely efficient combination of assets for two potential reasons. First, banks may concentrate some portion of their loan portfolio to capture potential quasi-rents generated from the bank's information production. Second, banks may seek to maximize the value of underpriced government guarantees by concentrating in high-risk ventures—the well-known "gamble for resurrection" incentives of banks with low or negative worth.
- *Unintentional concentration.* Lending decisions may be subject to disaster myopia, where agents underestimate the probability of low-frequency events, perhaps due to instability in the underlying causal structure. Some authors argue that "collective amnesia" has resulted in periodic overexposures to sectors of the economy (Herring and Wachter 1999; Gutentag and Herring 1985; Kindleberger 1987). In this case, banks may have an "inability to plan," as discussed by de Juan (1987).

These three hypotheses can be potentially disentangled empirically, in terms of the actual portfolio choices of banks. First, a sufficient condition for rejecting the "ability to diversify" hypothesis is to compare bank portfolio choices relative to their opportunity set. Lack of diversification within their opportunity set would point to alternative explanations. Second, loan concentration to exploit sources of quasi-rents can be tested by comparing the risk and return performance of a bank portfolio relative to that of a purely passively managed portfolio. In this case, superior asset selection or market timing abilities should allow

the portfolio to generate positive risk-adjusted excess returns, as
with standard portfolio theory. Finally, a testable implication of
the myopia hypothesis is that banks lack market timing ability,
but otherwise make ex ante efficient investment decisions. In this
case, pre-crisis portfolio choices, which lie along the pre-crisis
efficient frontier, would nonetheless result in potentially large
post-crisis losses.

Methodology

Mutual funds play a capital allocation role that can be disinterme-
diative to traditional bank lending services. Asset diversification
and economies of scale enhance mutual fund intermediation. Much
like their banking counterparts, actively managed mutual funds
seek excess risk-adjusted returns through identifying mispriced
assets or correctly identifying market turns. In this context, the
investment performance of actively managed mutual funds has
been subjected to numerous studies, which benchmark their risk-
return performance relative to a hypothetical passively managed
mutual fund.

The present analysis views banks as analogous to an actively
managed bond fund, for the purpose of benchmarking their performance to that of a hypothetical passively managed bank.[1] Banks
leverage the limited upside potential of their loan portfolios with
low capital ratios, creating equity-like returns. As suggested by
portfolio theory, diversification and economies of scale are important risk-reduction tools for efficient intermediation. Our analysis
applies well-developed benchmarking techniques to evaluate banking sector performance during periods of economic stress.

Benchmarking allows the study to analyze the hypotheses raised
above concerning bank performance. As summarized above,
excessive portfolio concentration can arise (1) from the lack of
diversification opportunities; (2) from loan concentration to
exploit private lending opportunities that outperform public market investment opportunities; or (3) from the myopic underestimation of systemic risks.

To address these issues, the analysis first constructs sectoral
indexes from collected real sector stock market data, which serve to
proxy for the public market investment opportunity set of banks.[2]
The efficient frontier derived from the sectoral indexes represents
the maximum within-country diversification available to banks
(given optimum risk-return tradeoffs), and therefore yields a test of
whether banks are diversification-opportunity constrained.

The derived efficient frontier also allows the analysis to benchmark the excess risk-adjusted return performance of the banking sector. The quality of a bank's information production, in terms of identifying underpriced assets (venture capital and lending opportunities) and turns in the economy, will be reflected in the bank's ex ante asset allocation choices (cash, versus marketable securities, versus loans), as well as its ex post realized risk and returns. In this case, the sectoral market indexes represent the (public market) investment opportunity set, and the efficient frontier gives a passively derived benchmark for judging the success of the banking sector in exploiting private lending opportunities.

The analysis also divides the efficient-frontier analysis into pre-crisis and post-crisis segments to examine ex ante bank portfolio choices and to test the myopia hypothesis raised above. Note that since the efficient frontier is constructed passively (i.e., is not based on economic forecasts or probabilities), the benchmark itself is disaster-myopic. Changes in the risk and return tradeoffs realized by the banking sector pre-crisis to post-crisis, relative to changes in the benchmark frontier results, will reveal the extent of passive versus active management within the banking sector.

Data

To construct market-based measures of bank performance, stock market data are collected for each country and each crisis period. Both pre-crisis and post-crisis data are collected to assess the ex ante portfolio choices and the ex post consequences of those choices. Stock market data are collected for all companies listed on the particular domestic exchange, as reported in a local news source. Listed companies are then classified by industry, and are aggregated by industry to construct sectoral indexes. Sectoral returns are constructed as unweighted average of the stock market returns of firms in the particular industry.

Stock market data are collected covering four major banking crisis episodes. First, stock market data are collected for Chile from *El Mercurio*, covering the 1977–89 period. Mexican stock market data are collected from the Mexican newspaper *Excelsior* over the 1977–89 period, and from *El Financiero* for the 1990s. Finally, Malaysian stock market data are collected from the *Business Times* over the 1980–90 period. The 1980s data were collected quarterly, while the data used for analyzing the Mexican peso crisis were collected at higher frequency (weekly), due to the shorter time period involved.

Results

Study results are presented in this section. First, preliminary data on within-country asset concentration are presented and found to be a predictive factor in the occurrence of banking crises. Next, the analysis focuses on loan concentration in four specific banking sector crises.

Preliminary Cross-Country Evidence

A measure of industry concentration is constructed from export concentration data. Table 1 gives an export concentration index, listed separately for low-, medium-, and high-income countries.[3] Table 1 indicates that concentration is greater in low-income countries, with an index average about 2.5 times that of the wealthy countries. Thus export concentration tends to be an issue in most low-income and some middle-income countries.

The export-concentration index of Table 1 is added as an additional explanatory variable to the data and analysis of Demirgüç-Kunt and Detragiache (1997).[4] That study's bank crisis prediction model, which estimates the probability of a banking crisis using macro and institutional variables, correctly classifies 67 percent to 84 percent of the crisis cases (depending on specification, which includes predicting both the occurrence and the year of a crisis). The results of adding the export-concentration index show that greater export concentration yields a significantly (at the 1 percent level) greater likelihood, and greater cost, of a banking crisis.

While not a direct test of the impact of lending concentration on banking crises, the results of the analysis are sufficient to establish that (1) export concentration, as a measure of industrial concentration, potentially limits bank portfolio diversification in low-income and middle-income countries; and (2) that it is significantly related to the occurrence of banking crises.

Chile and Mexico: The 1982 International Debt Crisis

Banking crises followed the 1982–83 international debt crisis in both Chile and Mexico. In the case of Chile, the banking sector had just privatized in 1974. By November 1981, four banks and four finance companies were taken over by Chilean authorities, raising questions of weak regulation and supervision (Cortes-Douglas 1992).[5] As noted by de la Cuadra and Valdes-Prieto (1992), by 1984 60 percent of Chilean bank assets were controlled by the

Chilean government as a part of the nationalization of failed banks, with these assets subsequently fully reprivatized by 1987.

Figure 1 graphs the constructed pre-crisis efficient frontier, derived from the sectoral market indexes and covering the first quarter of 1977 through the third quarter of 1982. The graph indicates that Chile's banking sector realized low risk and low average returns over the period relative to the high pre-crisis growth rates of the real sectors of the economy, and lies below the efficient frontier. The results suggests underperformance by the banking sector, and a lack of broad involvement in Chile's real sector.

The post-crisis efficient frontier for Chile is graphed in Figure 2. The increased volatility of the banking sector is apparent in the figure. As well, the ex post inefficiency of the bank portfolio choices is apparent. Broadly, both figures suggest inefficient portfolio choices and the lack of involvement of the banking sector in broad sectors of the Chilean economy. As discussed by de la Cuadra and Valdes-Prieto (1992), loans in arrears (net of loan loss provisions) reached 57.5 percent of banking sector capital and reserves by September 1982, and 181.2 percent by September 1983.[6]

Figure 1. Chile Efficient Frontier, 1977Q1–82Q3

Mean Return %

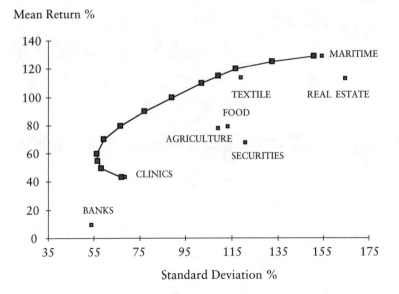

Standard Deviation %

Table 1. Concentration Index

Low-income	Concentration	Middle-income	Concentration	High-income	Concentration
Rwanda	0.505	Bolivia	0.318	Portugal	0.106
Ethiopia	0.557	Indonesia	0.194	New Zealand	0.174
Tanzania	0.248	Philippines	0.293	Spain	0.142
Burundi	0.667	Morocco	0.160	Ireland	0.125
Sierra Leone	0.586	Guatemala	0.219	Israel	0.256
Malawi	0.704	Papua New Guinea	0.465	Australia	0.196
Uganda	0.561	Equador	0.467	United Kingdom	0.063
Madagascar	0.285	Dominican Rep.	0.383	Finland	0.230
Nepal	0.519	El Salvador	0.238	Italy	0.056
Vietnam	0.308	Jordan	0.331	Kuwait	0.742
Bangladesh	0.246	Jamaica	0.406	Canada	0.125
Haiti	0.266	Paraguay	0.362	Hong Kong	0.152
Kenya	0.305	Algeria	0.546	Netherlands	0.061
Nigeria	0.934	Columbia	0.238	Singapore	0.183
Burkina Faso	0.623	Tunisia	0.209	Belgium	0.106
India	0.140	Peru	0.260	France	0.064
Togo	0.491	Costa Rica	0.303	Sweden	0.110
Nicaragua	0.289	Thailand	0.090	Austria	0.061
Zambia	0.787	Turkey	0.119	Germany	0.084
Ghana	0.465	Croatia	0.108	United States	0.080

Low-income	Concentration	Middle-income	Concentration	High-income	Concentration
Pakistan	0.228	Panama	0.422	Norway	0.366
Mauritania	0.605	Venezuela	0.555	Denmark	0.077
Zimbabwe	0.329	Iran, Islamic Rep. of	0.880	Japan	0.140
China	0.076	Brazil	0.089	Switzerland	0.102
Honduras	0.457	South Africa	0.378	United Arab Emirates	0.691
Senegal	0.258	Mauritius	0.332	Average	0.180
Côte d'Ivoire	0.368	Malaysia	0.156		
Congo, Dem. Rep. of	0.636	Chile	0.308		
Sri Lanka	0.232	Trinidad and Tobago	0.422		
Cameroon	0.485	Gabon	0.743		
Egypt, Arab Rep. of	0.361	Mexico	0.153		
Myanmar	0.282	Uruguay	0.176		
Average	0.431	Oman	0.824		
		Slovenia	0.083		
		Saudi Arabia	0.776		
		Greece	0.118		
		Argentina	0.153		
		Korea, Rep. of	0.109		
		Average	0.318		

Figure 2. Chile Efficient Frontier, 1982Q4–89Q4

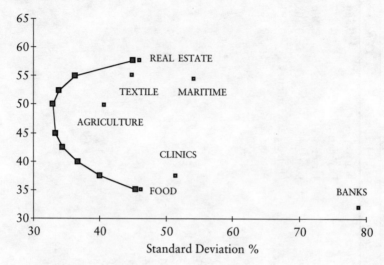

The pre-crisis and post-crisis efficient frontier results for Mexico are given in Figures 3 and 4, respectively. Note that as with Chile, the banking sector shows low realized risk and average returns pre-crisis, and lies below the efficient frontier. Post-1982 crisis, the banking sector was nationalized by the Mexican government. As a result, Figure 6 graphs the remaining portions of Mexico's financial sector, which includes brokerage and insurance segments.[7] The real sectors of Mexico's economy show strong positive growth rates over the period. The financial sector shows high volatility and inefficiency. Overall, the graphs suggest a lack of banking sector involvement in well-performing real sectors of the Mexican economy.

Malaysian Banking Sector Crisis, 1985–86

Malaysia underwent a sharp deflation in 1985–86, in part related to sharp declines in crude oil and palm oil prices. Over the period 1984–88, banking sector bad-debt provisions plus interest in suspense rose from 3.5 percent to 14.5 percent of total loans. Crisis-related financial sector losses amounted to 4.7 percent of GDP in 1986 (Sheng 1995). The financial sector crisis has been linked to concentrated lending in the property and development sectors.

Figure 3. Mexico Pre-Crisis Efficient Frontier,
1977Q1–82Q3

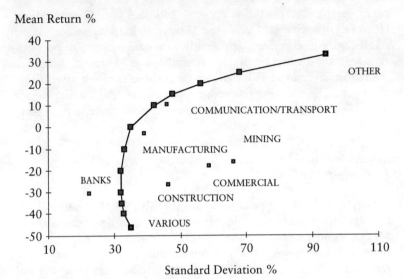

Figure 4. Mexico Post-Crisis Efficient Frontier,
1982Q4–89Q4

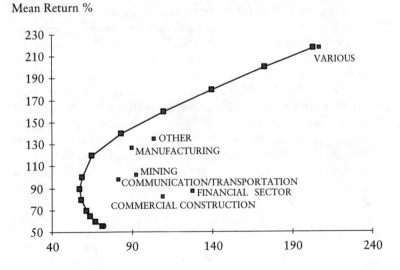

Figures 5 and 6 graph the pre-crisis and post-crisis Malaysian results, respectively. The pre-crisis results illustrate the relatively high volatility of the banking sector and its interior position, indicating inefficient portfolio choices and lack of diversification. However, note that post-crisis the Malaysian banking sector gained significantly in efficiency, apparently as a consequence of post-crisis reforms instituted by Malaysian authorities.[8] Figure 6 illustrates the reduction in asset risk that can be realized through asset diversification. The resulting risk reduction increases the lending capacity of the banking sector, given its scarce capital, thereby increasing the efficiency of intermediation.

Mexico's Post-Devaluation Banking Crisis, December 1994

Mexico devalued the peso on December 20, 1994. The resulting interest rate spike and high inflation caused a deep recession in Mexico's consumer sector that spilled over into the banking sector. Figures 7 and 8 give the pre-devaluation and post-devaluation results for Mexico, respectively. Both figures include a sectoral index, dubbed the "Sears index," which is constructed using returns taken from the market listing of Sears Mexican subsidiary. The Sears index is meant to proxy for Mexico's consumer sector. Figure 7 shows that the banking sector lies near the pre-devaluation efficient frontier. As Wilson, Saunders, and Caprio (2000a) show, Mexico's banking sector lending was concentrated in Mexico's construction and consumer sectors, with these sectors performing well pre-devaluation, given the support of a fixed peso exchange rate.[9]

However, the post-devaluation impact of the sectoral concentration can be seen in Figure 8. The banking sector, like the consumer sector proxy, shows poor returns, while most other sectors of the economy show strong recovery. The pre-devaluation efficiency of Mexican banking sector asset choices, and its post-devaluation poor returns related to Mexico's consumer sector, might be interpreted as evidence of a strong disaster myopia on the part of Mexican banks. As shown by Wilson, Saunders, and Caprio (2000b), Mexico's equity market showed a similar myopic response to the peso devaluation, with Mexico's broad stock market index showing an overall three-day positive average return in response to the devaluation announcement. In this case, it is difficult to distinguish whether the banking sector was just subject to poor market timing, or if indeed the probability of devaluation was myopically underestimated.

Figure 5. Malaysia Efficient Frontier, 1980–84

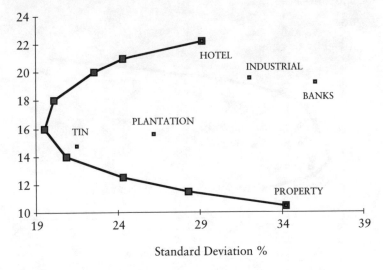

Standard Deviation %

Figure 6. Malaysia Efficient Frontier, 1985–89

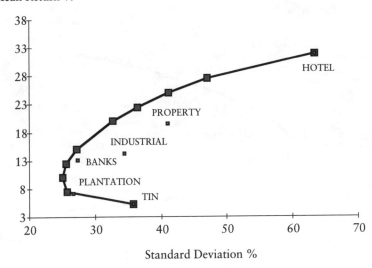

Standard Deviation %

Figure 7. Mexico Efficient Frontier,
June 1–December 19, 1984

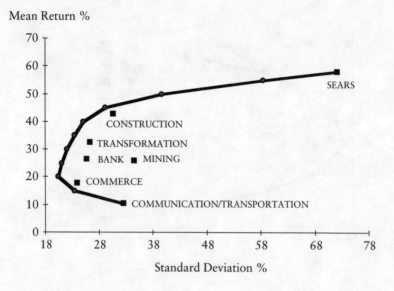

Figure 8. Mexico Efficient Frontier, December 20–31, 1984

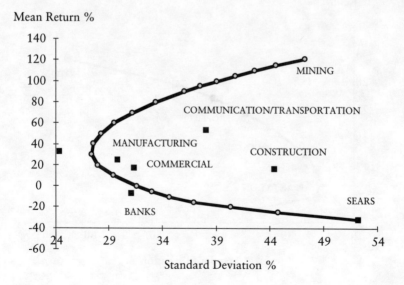

Conclusion

This study has investigated the role of loan concentration in four major historical banking crises. The study introduces an efficient-frontier analysis to benchmark the performance of the banking sector before and after each crisis, and to test three hypotheses concerning potential reasons for banking sector loan concentration. These hypotheses include: (1) the lack of diversification opportunities, as related to a country's industrial structure and capital controls that constrain diversification; (2) loan concentration to exploit quasi-rents derived from the information gathering and lending activities of banks; and (3) disaster myopia, leading to underestimation of the risk of structural economic shifts. The analysis constructs real sector indexes from stock market data to proxy for the investment opportunity set faced by banks. An efficient-frontier analysis is then used to benchmark banking sector performance relative to a hypothetical passively managed and leveraged bond mutual fund, to assess the extent of diversification and test whether banks realize superior returns.

In general, the study results reject the first hypothesis that banks are constrained by the lack of within-country diversification opportunities. If the banking sector is found to lie on the efficient frontier, then within-country opportunities to diversify have been exploited. However, overall the study results indicate that lack of diversification is a significant factor behind banking crises.

The analysis also tests whether loan concentration resulted in positive risk-adjusted excess returns, i.e., a positive investment Alpha, potentially related to the bank's information gathering and lending activities. The study results reject this hypothesis, since no evidence of excess returns was found. In general, banking sectors realized below market-risk-adjusted returns, both pre-crisis and post-crisis, except with the post-crisis results for Malaysia and the pre-devaluation results for Mexico. These results might indicate that capital controls and other historical factors constrained bank lending and diversification.

Some evidence of disaster myopia is found. In particular, Mexican banks pre-1994 devaluation grew their loan portfolios through consumer sector lending, a growth sector of Mexico's economy under the support of a fixed exchange rate. However, post-devaluation inflation and the resulting economic crisis decreased consumer sector spending, resulting in large banking sector losses. Mexican banks apparently did not foresee the devaluation or its impact on their loan concentration in the consumer sector.

The results of our analysis have implications for the role of bank
lending in economic development. The study results indicate that
loan concentration can create a crisis-prone banking sector. As a
part of prudential bank regulation, banking authorities need to collect data on the sectoral allocation of bank lending to detect
instances of undue loan concentration. As well, improved self-regulatory incentives might include higher capital requirements,
greater franchise value, and limits on explicit and implicit liability
guarantees (Caprio 1997; Calomiris 1997).

Notes

1. Banks and bond mutual funds potentially differ in that the latter specialize in holding corporate, municipal, and other forms of publicly issued
debt, while banks specialize in the origination and holding of private debt.
However, there is an active secondary market for bank loans, and closed-
end bank loan mutual funds participate as leveraged mutual funds in
investing in the primary and secondary U.S. bank loan markets.

2. Banks do invest in marketable securities as a liquid source of interest-bearing reserves. Loans are generally less liquid, and would be attractive to the extent that they offer sufficiently high risk-adjusted excess
returns that compensate for their lack of liquidity.

3. The export concentration index, from the United Nations Conference
on Trade and Development (UNCTAD 1996), is constructed as a
Hirschman index, which varies from 0 to 1 (with a level of 1 showing maximum concentration), using exports at the three-digit standard industrial
trade classification (SITC) level.

4. Demirgüç-Kunt and Detragiache (1997) define a banking crisis as an
event in which either the ratio of nonperforming to total assets exceeds 10
percent; the fiscal cost of bank rescues exceeds 2 percent of GDP; bank
runs lead to significant nationalization; or there are extensive bank runs
and extraordinary policy measures (deposit freezes, bank holidays, or
deposit guarantees) in reaction to a bank crisis. The explanatory variables
used include growth, the term of trade, real interest rates, inflation, a
measure of liquidity (M2/reserves), credit to the private sector as a share
of GDP, lagged credit growth, the presence of explicit deposit insurance,
and a general index of law and order (which captures both the efficacy of
the legal framework and may well be correlated with the "credit culture"
in a country).

5. At the time, Chile did have in place rules that required diversification
among debtors, although these were largely ineffective. In fact, many
Chilean banks made extensive loans to their owners, and an active market

in bank licenses developed to apparently exploit deposit guarantees (de la Cuadra and Valdes-Prieto 1992). For example, a 1981 investigation found that 45 percent of the loan portfolio of Banco de Santiago was loaned out to bank owners. Under new powers, authorities attempted to deconcentrate ownership of all banks down to the 25 percent of capital and reserves limit.

6. In 1983, the Chilean government took over eight banks, and also provided assistance to other Chilean banks in the form of forebearance and nonperforming loan purchases (de la Cuadra and Valdes-Prieto 1992).

7. As discussed by Nash (1995, p. 502), the government had granted private brokerage houses some banking functions, creating some degree of competition with Mexican banks.

8. Specifically, minimum capital adequacy requirements, limits on maximum equity holdings per individual shareholder, lending restrictions to single borrowers to prevent overconcentration, conflict-of-interest restrictions, establishment of board audits and examination committees, and improvement in on-site examinations were introduced.

9. Mexican commercial banks were privatized over 1992–92. In the short time period before the 1994 devaluation, Mexican banks expanded their loan portfolios through credit card, auto, and mortgage loans, which were growth sectors, given the support of a fixed exchange rate. However, post-devaluation inflation and the resulting economic crisis decreased consumer sector spending, resulting in large banking sector losses.

References

The word *processed* describes informally produced works that may not be commonly available through libraries.

Bernanke, B. 1983. "Non-Monetary Effects of the Financial Crisis in the Propagation of the Great Depression." *American Economic Review* 73(3):257–76.

Bernanke, B., and A. Blinder. 1988. "Credit, Money, and Aggregate Demand." National Bureau of Economic Research (NBER) Discussion Paper 2534. NBER, Cambridge, Massachusetts.

Calomiris, C. W. 1997. *The Postmodern Bank Saftey Net: Lessons from Developed and Developing Economies.* Washington, D.C.: The American Enterprise Institute.

Caprio, G. 1997. "Safe and Sound Banking in Developing Countries: We're Not in Kansas Anymore." World Bank Policy Research Working Paper 1739. World Bank, Washington, D.C.

Caprio, G., and D. Klingebiel. 1997. "Bank Insolvency: Bad Luck, Bad Policy, or Bad Banking?" In M. Bruno and B. Pleskovic eds., *Proceedings of the World Bank Annual Conference on Development Economics, 1996*, pp. 79–104. World Bank, Washington, D.C.

Cortes-Douglas, H. 1992. "Financial Reform in Chile: Lessons in Regulation and Deregulation." In D. Vittas, ed., *Financial Regulation: Changing the Rules of the Game*. EDI Development Studies. Washington, D.C: World Bank.

Davis, E. P. 1995. *Debt, Financial Fragility, and Systemic Risk*. Oxford: Clarendon Press.

de la Cuadra, S., and S. Valdes-Prieto. 1992. "Bank Structure in Chile." In G. G. Kaufman, ed., *Banking Structures in Major Countries*. Boston: Kluwer Academic Publishers.

de Juan, A. 1987. "From Good Bankers to Bad Bankers." World Bank Financial Sector Department. World Bank, Washington, D.C. Processed.

Demirgüç-Kunt, A., and E. Detragiache. 1997. "The Determinants of Banking Crises: Evidence from Developed and Developing Countries." World Bank Policy Research Working Paper. World Bank, Washington, D.C.

Guttentag, J. M., and R. Herring. 1985. "Disaster Myopia in International Banking." Brookings Papers on Economic Activity 31:1–53. Brookings Institution, Washington, D.C.

Herring, R. J., and S. Wachter. 1999. "Real Estate Booms and Banking Busts: An International Perspective." Wharton Financial Institutions Center Working Paper 99–27. Wharton Financial Institutions Center, Philadelphia.

Kindleberger, C. P. 1987. *Manias, Panics, and Crashes: A History of Financial Crises*. New York: Basic Books.

Lindgren, C., G. Garcia, and M. I. Saal. 1996. *Bank Soundness and Macroeconomic Policy*. Washington, D.C.: International Monetary Fund.

Nash, J. 1995. "Mexico: Adjustment and Stabilization." In T. Vinod, A. Chhibber, M. Dailami, and J. De Melo, eds., *Restructuring Economies in Distress: Policy Reform and the World Bank*. Oxford: Oxford University Press.

Sheng, A. 1995. *Bank Restructuring: Lessons from the 1980s*. World Bank, Washington, D.C.

UNCTAD (United Nations Conference on Trade and Development). 1996. *Handbook of International Trade and Development Statistics, 1983–1994*. New York: United Nations.

Wilson, B., A. Saunders, and G. Caprio. 2000a. "Mexico's Financial Sector Crisis: Propagative Linkages to Devaluation." *The Economic Journal* 110:292–308.

———. 2000b. "Financial Fragility and Mexico's 1994 Peso Crisis: An Event-Window Analysis of Market-Valuation Effects." *Journal of Money, Credit and Banking* 32(3):450–8.

Part II

International and
Intersectoral Linkages

Policy for Small
Financial Systems

Biagio Bossone, Patrick Honohan, and Millard F. Long

Introduction

IN FINANCE, BEING SMALL SELDOM IS efficient. Economies of scale of one kind or another prevail. This is a paper about policy for small financial systems. We argue that services within these systems tend to be limited in scope, expensive, and of poor quality. It furthermore is difficult to diversify risk and to maintain liquidity in small financial systems, and regulation and supervision are expensive. To some extent openness can offset the drawbacks of being small, but a small financial system seeking to achieve adequate opening without undue risk needs a carefully tailored policy design.

What Financial Systems Are Small?

About 60 countries worldwide have a financial system whose total size, measured in terms of M2 (the stock of money), is less than US$1 billion (see Figure 1 and Table 1). This is no larger than a small bank in an industrial country. Many of these countries have

The authors are grateful to Samir Abhyankar, Abayomi Alawode, Jerry Caprio, Massimo Cirasino, Tom Glaessner, Linda Goldberg, Hennie van Greuning, Bob Keppler, Jo Ann Paulson, John Pollner, Ann Rennie, and Christine Richaud for valuable information and helpful suggestions. Anqing Shi provided valuable research assistance.

Figure 1. Size of Financial System (167 countries)
M2 ($ billion)

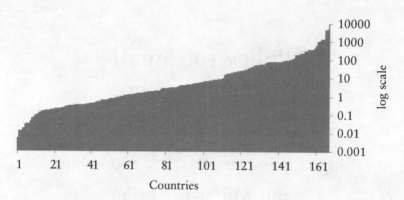

small populations, but the list also includes reasonably populous countries such as Sudan and Uganda; in aggregate, the population of these 60 countries is more than 200 million-greater than the population of Brazil, Russia, Bangladesh, or Indonesia.

One billion dollars is a low threshold. The issues raised here also affect larger financial systems, although to a lesser extent. As shown in Table 1, 118 countries, or about two of every three states worldwide, has a system whose M2 is less than US$10 billion. Again, this sum is exceeded by many hundreds of individual banks in industrial countries. The aggregate assets of the banking systems in these countries is US$600 billion. The aggregate population of these countries, which include Vietnam, Ethiopia, and Ukraine, each with a population of more than 50 million, is 800 million.

It is evident from Table 1 that most small financial systems are, naturally enough, found in small economies (as measured by aggregate GDP). For a few larger economies, such as the Ukraine, it is the shallowness of the financial system, resulting from inflation and/or financial repression, that keeps them below the line. With appropriate policies, the financial systems of these larger economies will deepen over time, and they will rise beyond the scope of our analysis. Most of these countries, however, are too small to have any realistic hope of developing a large financial system.[1]

The problem of size will not vanish simply as a result of financial development. On the contrary, technological trends are likely to raise the threshold size below which the issues addressed here are important. While domestic development may deepen some of the financial systems that today we consider small, the problem of insufficient absolute size is likely to grow.

The Role of Globalization and Financial Openness

Today's globalization of finance does not imply that borders no longer matter and that all financial systems, no matter how small, operate in a worldwide market. National borders remain important for financial systems. Finance is information intensive, and gathering information across borders is costly. The licensing and regulation of banks and other financial intermediaries usually is a national responsibility. Furthermore, securities markets, payment systems, and other elements of the financial infrastructure often are country-specific. Financial institutions often are constrained in cross-border deposit mobilization, borrowing, and lending by regulation as well as by information deficiencies. Finance is subject to a well-known "home bias" (Haque and Montiel 1991; Tesar and Warner 1992; Huberman 2000): only the largest firms have access to credit outside their country, with small and medium-sized businesses and households typically limited to the use of local financial intermediaries for loans and most other financial services.

We suggest in this paper that, as with trade, many of the disadvantages of small financial size can be mitigated through openness-that is, through integration into a larger system. With finance there are several dimensions to openness, such as cross-border trade in financial flows and services; foreign ownership of financial intermediaries; and regional/international cooperation in the establishment of financial infrastructure.[2] Each form of openness has its advantages, depending upon the problem to be resolved, and may be supplemented by other actions, such as the adoption of a common currency or the tailoring of prudential regulations to the circumstances.

Openness also has its disadvantages: it may, for example, increase the volatility of capital flows, it may reduce the quantity of investable resources, and it almost certainly will lead to a loss of autonomy and an increase in the dangers of contagion. Some dimensions of openness furthermore are not available to all countries; for example, small, poor countries may find it impossible to attract high-quality foreign financial institutions.

It is our impression, nonetheless, that most of the financial systems under discussion have not opened up enough.

Since the crises in Mexico, East Asia, and the Russian Federation, there has been much concern about instability in financial systems and about its potential to spread across countries.

Table 1. 118 Countries with Financial Systems (M2) of Less Than $10 Billion, 1999

	rank	M2 ($ millions)	GDP ($ millions)	Population (millions)
Afghanistan	72	2000		24.965
Albania	61	1335	2460	3.323
Angola	52	900	7662	11.659
Antigua and Barbuda	38	403	584	0.066
Armenia	10	143	1613	3.783
Azerbaijan	42	560	4399	7.619
Bahamas, The	75	2467	3750	0.289
Bahrain	87	4138	6097	0.619
Barbados	63	1382	2185	0.265
Belarus	71	1880	11420	10.265
Belize	31	327	618	0.228
Benin	41	489	2120	5.795
Bhutan	11	143	354	0.736
Bolivia	84	3695	7654	7.767
Botswana	56	1077	4729	1.51
Brunei Darussalam	107			0.308
Bulgaria	83	3391	10085	8.312
Burkina Faso	44	588	2146	10.946
Burundi	14	167	790	6.586
Cambodia	28	308	3044	10.517
Cameroon	59	1155	8379	14.072
Cape Verde	29	315	425	0.399
Central African Republic	18	194	1019	3.415
Chad	17	191	1603	6.776
Comoros	4	41	194	0.518
Congo, Republic of	33	337	2298	2.779
Costa Rica	86	3830	9290	3.508
Côte d'Ivoire	78	2685	10025	14.709
Croatia	102	7965	19081	4.494
Latvia	65	1520	5443	2.465
Lesotho	27	298	843	2.067
Liberia				2.886
Lithuania	70	1810	9585	3.701
Macedonia, FYR	45	600	2201	1.997
Madagascar	47	696	3422	14.122
Malawi	25	279	1965	10.276
Maldives	19	196	342	0.262
Mali	43	577	2391	10.301
Malta	92	5261	3280	0.376
Marshall Islands				0.06
Mauritania	12	158		2.392
Mauritius	82	3092	3917	1.145
Micronesia			213	0.111
Moldova	39	413	1857	4.319
Mongolia	22	209	906	2.569
Mozambique	49	719		18.527
Namibia	60	1322	3280	1.623
Nepal	69	1724	4433	22.613
Nicaragua	57	1151	1913	4.632
Niger	13	164	1540	9.657
Oman	93	5291	16154	2.312
Palau			129	0.017
Panama	97	6375	8700	2.717
Papua New Guinea	66	1522	4639	4.5
Paraguay	76	2627	8919	5.084
Qatar	95	5933		0.675
Romania	101	7746	31129	22.546
Rwanda	26	290	1843	7.895

(continues on next page)

Table 1. Continued

	rank	M2 ($ millions)	GDP ($ millions)	Population (millions)
Cyprus	104	8759	8204	0.747
Djibouti	30	317	500	0.636
Dominica	15	169	243	0.074
Dominican Republic	88	4157	14971	8.107
Ecuador	96	6095	17850	11.934
El Salvador	91	4990	11185	5.959
Equatorial Guinea	2	30	487	0.421
Eritrea				3.773
Estonia	62	1361	4540	1.448
Ethiopia	77	2668	6041	60.123
Fiji	51	877	2003	0.815
Gabon	50	782	5153	1.153
Gambia, The	9	113	407	1.18
Georgia			5244	5.427
Ghana	58	1154	6210	17.98
Grenada	24	267	295	0.099
Guatemala	85	3756	17471	11.221
Guinea	35	363	3688	6.926
Guinea-Bissau	3	30	266	0.692
Guyana	40	480	735	0.848
Haiti	55	1018	2989	7.478
Honduras	68	1723	4689	6.281
Iceland	79	2780	7265	0.272
Jamaica	81	2985	4135	2.57
Jordan	99	7206	7051	4.432
Kazakhstan	73	2000	22165	15.801
Kenya	89	4446	9596	28.043
Kiribati			55	0.083
Kyrgyz Republic			1764	4.635
Lao PDR	20	202	1096	4.849
Samoa	6	74	215	0.173
São Tomé & Príncipe	1	12	44	0.138
Senegal	54	968	4427	8.767
Seychelles	37	388	528	0.078
Sierra Leone	8	95	823	4.748
Slovenia	100	7299	17181	1.991
Solomon Islands	7	88	374	0.401
Sri Lanka	90	4708	14530	18.488
St. Kitts & Nevis	21	205	247	0.041
St. Lucia	36	376	598	0.159
St. Vincent & Grenadines	16	182	275	0.112
Sudan	53	917	9299	27.861
Swaziland	34	350	1242	0.952
Syrian AR	106	9000		15.000
Tajikistan			2000	6.017
Tanzania	64	1484		31.335
Togo	32	329	1365	4.347
Tonga	5	61	187	0.098
Trinidad & Tobago	80	2806	5822	1.307
Tunisia	105	8980	18214	9.28
Turkmenistan			4397	4.658
Uganda	48	705		20.317
Ukraine	98	6601	48701	50.355
Uruguay	103	8074	18778	3.222
Uzbekistan				25.046
Vanuatu	23	252	252	0.177
Vietnam	94	5758	24056	76.711
Yemen, Republic of	74	2260		16.304
Zambia	46	622	3558	9.445
Zimbabwe	67	1670	8906	11.484

Small financial systems can be unstable-and perhaps more so than larger ones-but because of their size are unlikely to have much impact on the world's financial system. In this respect, these countries are of little importance. The reverse, however, is not true. As these systems become more open, they will become also more susceptible to disruptions in the rest of the world's financial system.

Should Policy Be Different?

The optimal design of regulatory institutions and practices and of competition and entry policies varies with country size. Conventional financial sector policy thinking is implicitly calibrated on a large economy within which the fixed overhead costs of regulatory institutions are not a major consideration; within which there are sufficient intermediaries and markets are sufficiently competitive to enable the achievement of minimum efficient scale; and within which there is sufficient diversity of financial assets and prospects to allow risk-pooling. We argue here that some regulations need to be modified to make them appropriate for small financial systems.

Small Systems: A Problem For Finance

How Does Smallness Affect the Functioning of Finance?

In this section, we consider how small financial systems differ from larger ones because of their smaller economy, smaller institutions, and smaller borrowers. The discussion relies primarily on field experience and on a synthesis of the related literature; empirical research would be needed to confirm these impressions and in particular to quantify the importance of some of the issues raised.

Many, but not all, small financial systems are in small economies; this typically entails also that the financial institutions and the borrowing customers are small. Each aspect of smallness raises distinct issues. Small economies may be especially vulnerable to external shocks, and thus offer larger scope for the risk-pooling function of finance. Small financial systems are prone to a lack of competition and incompleteness, due to the high set-up costs of some financial services and markets. Financial regulation also is prone to high set-up costs. Small institutions cannot fully exploit the economies of scale offered by financial technology. Finally, small borrowers suffer from a lack of interest from and support of many financial services providers.

Small Economies . . .

. . . are volatile but not especially poor or slow-growing. It needs to be said from the outset that the size of a small economy does not necessarily translate to its being proportionately poor or slow-growing. This point has been empirically explored for micro states by Easterly and Kraay (1999). Whatever disadvantages smallness imposes, such as higher volatility from external terms of trade, are outweighed by advantages such as those of trade openness and, on average, a better educational system. On average, per capita income in micro states is 40–50 percent higher than in other countries.

Better overall economic performance by small systems does not, however, mean that their financial policy has been optimized. Finance would appear to help insulate small economies from external shocks, but the findings of Easterly and Kraay suggest that the volume of capital flows[3] to and from micro states, while somewhat higher as a share of GDP than in other countries, is insufficient to exploit the full potential for risk-diversification through financial flows.[4,5]

Terms-of-trade shocks are not the only sources of volatility in small economies. Such economies also may suffer from disproportionate supply-side shocks resulting from lower sectoral diversification, and perhaps also have a greater susceptibility to undiversified weather-related shocks and natural disasters. Like terms-of-trade shocks, the risks here cannot easily be diversified within the economy, but require diversification across borders. Figure 2 shows, for a variety of economic indicators, that volatility in economies with small financial systems is much higher than that for countries with large financial systems.

The kinds of financial arrangements that could help insulate national consumption from shocks to the volume of production or to the terms of trade include futures contracts in relevant commodities and exchange rates, and insurance against weather or natural disasters. They also include foreign holdings of local equity and other risk-sharing claims on local firms. As shown by Lewis (1996), economies with closed capital accounts suffer a higher volatility of domestic consumption.[6]

. . . are prone to lumpiness. The fact that investment in small economies is inherently lumpy also creates problems. One of the most important services of a financial system is to enable investors to overcome their inability to cover the cost of large investments by using external finance, applying the proceeds from the investment to service the obligation. In large economies, individual investments

Figure 2. Macroeconomic Volatility

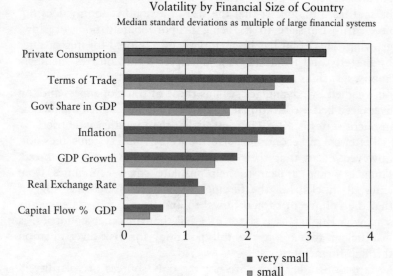

Volatility by Financial Size of Country
Median standard deviations as multiple of large financial systems

■ very small
□ small

Note: Systems with M2 of between $1 billion and $10 billion are regarded as small; those with M2 of less than $1 billion as very small.

are small relative to the savings pool; only the very largest investments require financing from outside the country. This is not true in small economies, where the lumpiness of the financing requirements of many different types of productive investment may pose problems.

This again argues for greater openness of capital flows, particularly for asset managers. However, countries worry, with justification, that capital flows may be asymmetric. International financiers have long been prepared to bear the cost of acquiring the information necessary for the appraisal for large projects-for example, Barings and J.P. Morgan led a huge effort in the 19th century to sell on the London market railway and other utility bonds from the Americas and elsewhere (Eichengreen et al. 1999)-but they may be less willing to bear the necessary cost of learning about potential borrowers whose business is likely to be small.

A final important aspect of finance in small economies is that borrowers and lenders are more likely to have some association, with the result that business dealing at less than arm's length-and even insider lending—is more difficult to avoid. This problem is difficult to overcome simply through openness, and may need to be managed through regulation and supervision.

Small Financial Systems . . .

. . . are likely to be less competitive. Smaller financial markets tend to have fewer institutions and tend to be less competitive. Would-be borrowers cannot shop among lenders, as there are few lenders that deal with any one type of client. The structure-performance hypothesis, according to which concentrated banking systems are more profitable, has been extended to an international comparison. This hypothesis argues that to maximize economy of scale some degree of uncompetitive behavior must be admitted. This trade-off is likely to be more acute in smaller financial systems (Honohan and Kinsella 1982).

Take, for example, interest rate spreads (see Box 1). Average quoted bank interest spreads are higher in small financial systems than in large ones, a point that appears to have gone unnoticed in the literature. Various factors might explain this, such as inherent cost penalties and high rents and taxation, both explicit and implicit. The effects are significant, potentially amounting to a few percentage points of GDP for smaller countries. Note that we are looking here at the effect of overall system size holding constant the level of per capita income.

Independent confirmation of the link between spreads and market size comes from the aggregation of data on average interest margins of the larger banks (as a percentage of their total assets), as recorded by the banking accounts database Bankscope. Figure 4 shows a fairly systematic decrease with market size. Note also that there is a corresponding decrease in unit costs, suggesting that not all of the difference corresponds to profit margins.

. . . are likely to be incomplete. Small markets are more likely to be incomplete in the sense that minimum-scale economies may preclude the existence of some financial services. Potential customers may simply be unable to get the services they need. Of the 60 or so financial systems for which M2 is less than US$1 billion, only three have organized securities markets that are members of the Federation International des Bourses des Valeurs (FIBV), and these three between them have only 16 listed companies. Only about one in two of the 60 financial systems in the range US$1 billion to US$10 billion have organized securities exchanges,[7]

Box 1. Bank Interest Spreads and the Size of the Financial System

One indication that small financial systems are less competitive than larger ones is obtained by looking at banking spreads. Box Figure 1 plots the quoted interest rate spreads (lending minus deposit rates) against the dollar value (measured in logs) of broad money for the 108 countries for which the data are available in *International Financial Statistics* for 1998. The scatter is wide, reflecting the many influences on spread as well as the imperfections of the data, but a downward slope is evident, suggesting that larger financial systems tend to have lower spreads and as such may be more efficient and competitive. (Note that the explanatory variable is not financial depth, normalized by GDP, but financial size.)

Box Figure 1. Interest Spreads and Size of Financial System for 108 Countries, 1998

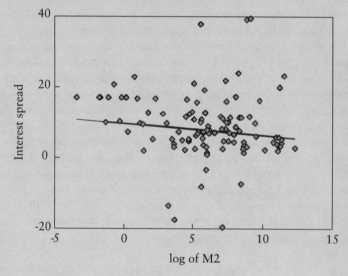

– Regression line (based on regression including gnp per cap)

continued

and bonds are traded on only about half of these. According to FIBV statistics, none of these exchanges includes futures or options trading. Several studies (e.g., Levine and Zervos 1998) establish the complementary importance of active markets for growth.

Box 1. *Continued*

Regression analysis confirms the visual impression: a negative coefficient is obtained on the scale variable. While this is not statistically significant on the whole sample, it is highly significant once we filter out the countries with negative spreads and those with spreads above about 2,000 basis points. This leaves between 80 and 90 countries, depending on whether the countries of the two CFA Franc Zones are included separately.

Financial size is correlated with level of development (per capita GNP), which in turn could be causally associated with lower spreads. To verify that the negative coefficient estimated for financial size does not simply reflect level of development, we included it in the equation. We also included the nominal deposit interest rate and recent inflation as control variables, to take account of the wider spreads that often are associated with higher financial uncertainty. The significance of financial size remains high (t-statistic = 2.4, implying statistical significance at the 2 percent level), and the economic significance of the effect also is high. The point estimates imply that a doubling of financial size would lower bank interest spreads by between 21 and 40 basis points.

These findings, though they can only be regarded as suggestive, raise the intriguing possibility that expanding the scale of a country's financial system, perhaps by entering into a financial union, could result in impressive gains in static economic efficiency. The predicted gain from quadrupling the effective size of a small country's banking system, when applied to aggregate balance sheets amounting to, say, 50 percent of GDP ranges from 2 to 4 percent of GDP per annum.

Ancillary financial firms such as credit rating agencies also are absent from many markets. Even where the various ancillary services do exist, scale economies mean that the cost of such overheads is higher or the quality of the service provided lower-or often both.

Overall, small financial markets tend to offer less comprehensive financial services. This could be partly alleviated by access to foreign financial markets or, for example, through establishing regional securities markets.

. . . and are more costly to regulate. The cost of achieving an adequate policy and regulatory infrastructure is almost certainly higher for small economies than for large ones, but this is hard to prove. Survey data for about 23 countries on the overall cost to the public authorities[8] of providing banking regulation and supervision

indicate that costs increase with the size of the system, but less than proportionately, suggesting substantial economies of scale (Figure 3).[9] (It should be noted, however, that these data do not address the comparative quality of regulation and supervision in the 23 countries. It is possible that the money spent by one or more countries was insufficient.) The policy capacity of a small regulatory system is likely to be more easily swamped by a large disturbance, and there is some indication that the cost of banking crisis may be disproportionately larger in small countries than large ones (Honohan 2000). If so, the economies of scale in supervision are even larger than indicated by these data.[10]

Small institutions and small borrowers. With few exceptions, small economies have small financial systems, and small systems tend to be composed of a small number of small institutions. At the institutional level, there has been considerable research[11] that supports the view that the potential economies of increasing the scale of small institutions are very great. In addition to the operational economies that come with larger scale, there is evidence that small institutions tend to be less well-managed and have higher default rates.

Figure 3. Supervision Costs in Relation to the Size of the Money Stock

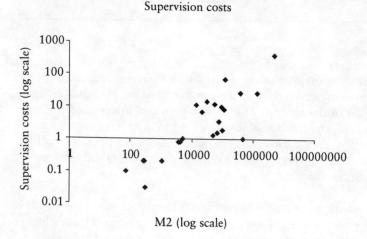

Supervision costs

Figure 4. Banking Data Based on Individual Banks'
Accounts (Source: Bankscope)

Share of foreign banks: smaller countries

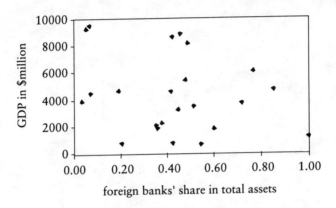

Concentration ratio: smaller countries

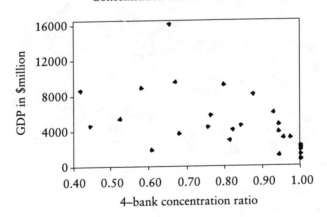

continued

Figure 4. Continued.

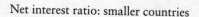

Net interest ratio: smaller countries

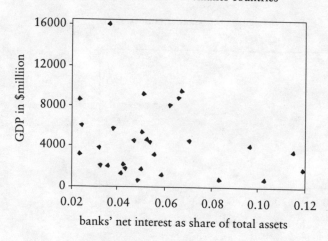

Overheads ratio: smaller countries

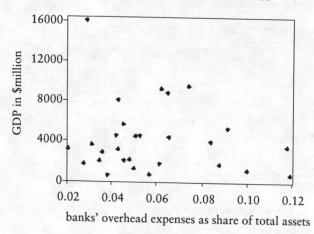

Furthermore, intermediaries within small economies must deal with small enterprises-for example, public utilities, transport and logistics firms, and retail and wholesale firms-whose size is limited by the size of the national market. Transaction sizes inevitably will be small, and intermediation costs therefore high.

Potential Solutions to Small Size

Different Forms of Financial Openness

There is a long tradition of exploration of the merits of openness for economies with small financial systems. We make no attempt here to summarize the literature on openness in all its aspects, but instead have selected six distinct areas in which policy can make a difference. These range from the micro to the macro, and from the passive removal of controls to the hands-on creation of regional institutions.

Although they may be the most important overall, we have placed the two macro policy issues, relating to liberalization of portfolio capital flows and to exchange rate policy, last in this discussion, to ensure due attention to less familiar but potentially valuable micro tools. These include allowing qualified foreign owners of financial intermediaries to carry out domestic operations, an initiative that can be very effective in achieving improvements and cost savings in the functioning of domestic finance. For securities markets, however, small size is a greater impediment, and one for which there is no easy solution. While the establishment of regional securities markets is receiving attention in several parts of the world, partly reflecting technological developments, the prospects of this strategy being adopted widely are not good. For individual firms, the solution may be to list on a larger, more developed exchange. In the areas of regulation, supervision, and other aspects of financial infrastructure, sharing on a regional basis may offer opportunities to achieve economies of scale. Finally, we consider whether opening small financial systems will require the tailoring of regulations to take into account their high fragility relative to that of larger systems.

The type of openness appropriate to a country depends upon the nature of the problem that the country faces. It should be noted that not all types of openness are suited to all countries.[12]

Possible Solution	Problem
Foreign ownership of intermediaries	Lack of competition; high intermediation costs; inadequate management and governance; inadequate supervision; missing financial products
Regional securities markets	Limited growth potential for and low franchise value of market intermediaries; poor risk diversification and high vulnerability to shocks; limited interest from foreign investors
Shared regional infrastructure or imported infrastructural services (including regulation)	Absence or low quality of some elements of infrastructure, due to high set-up costs; lack of competition; problems of ensuring operational independence of regulators
Tailored regulations	Normal regulatory parameters unsuited to small systems; high financial fragility
Open capital flows	Lumpy projects; inadequate diversification (risk, insider lending)
Common (or foreign) currency	High risk and cost on cross-border transactions

Solving the Problem of Small Intermediaries

Small banks and insurance companies in small financial markets have higher costs because of their size, and can offer only a limited range of financial services. The problem of small size is less severe for branches of larger, foreign intermediaries, however. But are foreign intermediaries interested in small, poor countries?

There is a long history of large banks opening branches in developing countries. Historical trading and colonial links explain the geographical specialization of many of these banks: for example, Barclays and Standard Chartered are major players in the former British colonies;[13] four major French-led banking groups feature in francophone countries;[14] and Citibank is an important player in parts of Asia and (like Fleet Boston) in Latin America. Small financial systems tend to have a higher share of foreign ownership. Figure 4 shows the percentage of banking assets that are held by foreign-controlled entities. This percentage clearly tends to diminish as financial system size increases.

Conversely, there also is the potential for small-country banks to expand into other countries. Although not widespread, there are some interesting examples of this phenomenon. HSBC grew from its roots in Hong Kong to become one of the world's leading banks. Arab Bank is another example.

Not all such expansions have been successful. The failures of BCCI and Meridien Bank were a blow to hopes of the emergence from developing countries of major regional banks, and the foreign expansion of Bangkok Bank has been interrupted by the Asian crisis. It is nonetheless inevitable that technology and increased financial depth eventually will enable other developing country banks to open branches abroad or buy foreign banks.

The wave of foreign acquisition. The movement of foreign banks into small markets has taken a different form in recent years. The privatization of banks and insurance companies, especially in transition economies, and fire sales of failed banks have provided great opportunities for intermediaries from advanced countries to acquire a preexisting branch network in other countries. The share of banking and insurance assets controlled by foreign banks has soared in several countries. Banks from smaller European countries notably have initiated major expansion strategies in transition and developing economies; these include ING bank of the Netherlands, which has become a significant player in East Asia; Kredietbank of Belgium; and Erste, Raiffeissen, and Bankaustria of Austria, which have acquired a high profile in several transition economies of Eastern and Central Europe.[15] In Latin America, it is Spanish banks, led by BSCH, that have made the largest acquisitions (IMF 2000). This new wave of entries shows the potential of cross-border banking, although it is true also that the supply of privatized banks has been so great as to cause something of a glut. Uganda, for example, failed to find a satisfactory buyer for the largest bank in the country, UCB.[16]

Do foreign banks behave differently? One concern that is commonly expressed is the danger that foreign-owned banks will neglect large parts of the local market. For example, in Africa banks of the former colonial powers have been accused of favoring large and foreign-controlled corporate customers at the expense of local entrepreneurs. While there is little systematic data available to support such accusations, this is a crucial issue: if foreign institutions are permitted to take over the financial system, will their business strategy mean that they contribute less to the local economy? If foreign banks suffered more than local banks from asymmetric information in lending to small local firms, this might be the case; but the favoring of large and foreign clients equally could reflect other deficiencies in the host economy's incentive structure.

Valuable econometric work has been done on the similarities and differences between the behavior of foreign-owned and domestic banks by Claessens and Glaessner (1998), d'Amato, Grubisic, and Powell (1997), Claessens, Demirgüç-Kunt, and Huizinga (2000), and Goldberg, Dages, and Kinney 2000. Their findings include, for example, that the presence of foreign banks can be stabilizing in a crisis, as demonstrated by the ability of foreign-owned banks in Argentina and Mexico to maintain better access to foreign funding in the Tequila crisis. Depositors also have been found to run to local branches of reputable foreign-owned banks in a crisis, even when the option has been available to them of shifting their funds abroad (Claessens and Glaessner 1998; d'Amato, Grubisic, and Powell 1997).

In non-crisis times also, healthy foreign banks-for example, in Argentina and Mexico-have contributed to a stable evolution of credit (Goldberg, Dages, and Kinney 2000).

Of most interest, however, is the impact of foreign entry on domestic banks. It appears that entry of foreign banks can make national banking markets more competitive, driving down both overhead costs and profit margins of domestically owned banks (Claessens, Demirgüç-Kunt, and Huizinga 2000).[17]

Finally, recent empirical research suggests that concerns may be unfounded that the increasing international integration of finance might skew access to financial services away from small and medium-sized enterprises (SMEs) (Clarke et al. 2001).

Experience in Eastern Europe. The experience of several Eastern European transition economies is relevant in assessing the practical potential of foreign ownership in banking. In Estonia, episodes of bank insolvency were followed by the entry of foreign banks, to the point where they now dominate the system. Major Swedish banks, already active in Finland and with regional ambitions in the Baltic area, acquired the bulk of ownership of the Estonian banking system. Through subsidiaries, they also dominate other less developed segments of the Estonian banking system.

The larger banking system of Hungary provides some additional lessons about the likely pattern of foreign entry. First, a correlation between the relative size of purchaser and target bank: The larger Hungarian banks, though small by international standards, were acquired by larger Western European banks; the smaller ones by medium-sized acquirers. Second, the appetite of foreign purchasers seems to be correlated with economic conditions; prior to 1995, sales of Hungarian banks were slow. Third, the financial success of the purchasers has not been a forgone conclusion: margins have narrowed substantially, and only some of the foreign banks have been successful. Fourth, not all of the purchasers were prime institutions, debunking the easy equation that foreign equals good. Overall, the transfer of the banking industry and other parts of the financial system-notably insurance, which is now about 90 percent foreign-owned-is seen as producing a marked improvement in the range and cost of financial services available to Hungarian firms and households.

Solving the Problem of Small Securities Markets

Small size has been even more of an impediment to the development of securities markets than it has of banking. The small markets that exist have few listings and lack liquidity, and trading in the best firms is migrating to larger markets. Small domestic securities markets have limited growth potential, and this discourages new intermediaries, especially foreign institutions, from entering the market.[18]

The arrival of the euro has complemented in Europe the formation of a single regional market for financial services, offering to European intermediaries a much broader and much less segmented operating space. This has helped accelerate the process of the international consolidation of securities exchanges in Europe through cross-border mergers and joint ventures. Is this a harbinger of things to come in the rest of the world?

In some circumstances it may be possible to overcome the difficulties of small size by joining together the markets of neighboring countries into a regional securities market. If the regional market can reach a critical size, it might become attractive to firms-including foreign firms-that are interested in investing in financial intermediaries. Foreign entry would in turn enhance the stability and efficiency of the local markets and institutions (Claessens and Glaessner 1998). Market regionalization also could help local financial intermediaries grow in size and achieve economies of scale.

Experience with regional markets is not extensive. A regional stock market, based in Abidjan, Côte d'Ivoire, covers the countries of the West African Monetary Union, but it is unclear if this can be seen as a significant success. The Eastern Caribbean Securities Exchange started operations in a small way in October 2001, and there also is an ongoing initiative to link a number of exchanges in the Middle East. Otherwise in only a handful of the emerging exchanges in small financial systems does the number of foreign companies listed account for as much as 5 percent of the total.[19]

The task of developing a regional exchange operating under common rules may be a little easier where the cooperating countries share a common legal heritage, but much of the needed legislation for making a securities market function is largely independent of the legal inheritance.

Depending partly on the pattern of technologically driven changes in cost structures, it remains to be seen whether there will be a significant role even for regional stock exchanges. An alternative and often more promising way for the shares at least of larger firms in small countries to find a wider market is through some form of limited listing, such as with depository receipts, on a larger stock exchange. The private placement of company shares with an emerging market fund offers a third way of opening access to the world pool of savings for equity issuers in a small country. Over the next decade, e-finance may present a fourth alternative. At this point, however, it is probably more important to emphasize development of the prerequisites of accounting and corporate governance that over time will enable companies to list on global markets.

Reducing Infrastructure Costs

Regionalizing the elements of financial infrastructure. Where feasible, a regional approach could enable some elements of financial infrastructure to be supplied at much lower unit cost. Neighboring countries could act together to build up common infrastructural components whose use they would share, or to standardize and link their existing components.[20] Such regional infrastructures could enable intermediaries in participating countries to sell and deliver their products and services anywhere in the region at no cost disadvantage to their competitors.

The creation of the single currency in the European Union has required member countries to integrate their domestic payment and securities settlement systems through the linking of domestic facilities and the sharing of technical and supervisory infrastructure. The resulting system integration has generated benefits for intermediaries and users across the region and has advanced the cross-border securities business.

Small developing countries might find it mutually beneficial to establish linked regional payments and securities settlement system facilities. This would require the establishment of common legal, regulatory, and supervisory arrangements necessary to make the linked/shared facilities work smoothly and efficiently. Success in such focused regional cooperation might also bring other politico-economic benefits.

Depending on geographic considerations, the most feasible approach to integration for a small country would be to link to a large neighbor, rather than attempt regional integration with several smaller countries. Other options include obtaining access to the infrastructure of a large neighbor or building up infrastructural components compatible with those of the neighbor, to enable the exploitation of scale economies.

Regulatory infrastructure. Savings can be made from information aggregation and standardization by regionalizing information-intensive supervisory functions. Cross-border banking certainly entails close international cooperation among regulators, and off-site supervisory functions entailing the collection, analysis, and elaboration of information from individual financial institutions also might be shared. In addition to the realization of scale economies in the use of scarce financial and human resources for processing information, gains could include the generation of directly comparable data on institutions operating across different countries; access to cross-country consolidated information to help institutions with significant cross-border positions identify risks; and use of more reliable vulnerability indicators incorporating cross-country risk correlations.

The case for establishing regional regulatory and supervisory infrastructure becomes compelling when countries open their economies to regional trade and when local financial institutions face stronger incentives to invest beyond their national borders (Folkerts-Landau and van Greuning 1997; see box 2). Cross-border financing may be furthered by adoption of a harmonized structure of national legislation, standard reporting and prudential requirements, and common measures for rules enforcement. A regional infrastructure with such characteristics would reduce the costs to market participants learning how to operate across national borders; would, through information sharing among national supervisors, strengthen defenses against the cross-border contagion of financial shocks; and would eliminate the incentives to regulatory arbitrage.

It also can be argued-although there is little concrete evidence to support this-that regional regulatory/supervisory organizations might be better shielded than national authorities from pressure to compromise prudential standards or to delay or deny action such

Box 2. Developing Regional Cooperation on Banking
Regulation and Supervision: The Potential Role of
the Private Sector

Different institutional approaches could be adopted to develop
regional cooperation on banking regulation and supervision. Where
the political will exists among national governments in a region to
move toward full-fledged cooperation, a regional public authority
could be established, within which each national government would
be represented and which would be entrusted with the responsibility
to determine prudential rules and regulations and to supervise their
adoption by individual banks throughout the region. The counterar-
gument to this arrangement is that it requires an abdication of national sovereignty: sanctioning a bank could have such serious adverse
implications for the economy in which it primarily operates that the
national authority might prefer to retain the freedom to weigh the
consequences of the sanction against the consequences of taking
lighter action.The jump to a regional, public sector solution therefore
might be politically difficult to achieve.

In the absence of government action, the market itself could play
a role by establishing a regional private sector authority, with public
functions. Reputable and sound banks could volunteer to submit their
operations to scrutiny by a private entity (much as they do for external audits), for clearing payments and securities transactions and for
acquiring and maintaining a credit rating. Individual banks could
agree to abide by a common code of conduct, including standards
based on transparent prudential criteria.

A private regional authority could be molded from within the
banking industry to act as a self-regulatory body (Bossone and
Promisel 1999) that would receive evidence from members of their
adherence to the code of conduct. It also should publish the results of
its findings. If the major players agree to adhere to the code, others
would be induced to conform. The mechanism could generate
stronger incentives for individual banks to improve their responsive-
ness to prudential requirements than unilateral national rules, which
might place banks at a competitive disadvantage.

Finally, the existence of regional private sector initiatives with public purpose could persuade, or even force, national governments to
develop regional cooperative strategies.

Source: Folkerts-Landau and van Greuning (1997)

as the changing of management, issuance of cease-and-desist
orders, or liquidation of problem institutions. This seems especially true for small systems in which regulators and regulatees are at

less than arm's length distance from each other. Regional organizations also might prove more effective in resolving "coordination failure" problems in the event of crises, when no individual national authority may be prepared to take the lead and act.

The prime example of regional regulatory authorities are the two CFA (roughly, "countries of francophone Africa") zones of francophone Africa, the performance of which has greatly improved since the reforms of the early 1990s.[21] Other initiatives for regional cooperation in banking regulation and supervision include the Common Monetary Area (CMA) that reunites Lesotho, Namibia, Swaziland, and South Africa; and the Eastern and Southern Africa Bank Supervisors (ESAF), comprising 13 members (Botswana, Kenya, Lesotho, Malawi, Mauritius, Mozambique, Namibia, South Africa, Swaziland, Tanzania, Uganda, Zambia, and Zimbabwe). The ESAF is a voluntary grouping of the bank supervisors in the region, who have chosen to operate as a regional subgrouping of the Basle Committee on Banking Supervision and to develop a common philosophy of financial regulation based on a market-oriented, risk-based approach. The CMA is a formal protocol that aims to include bank regulation and supervision in its goals of convergent monetary, fiscal, and exchange rate policies.

Importing Financial Infrastructural Services from Abroad

Where "going regional" is not an option, a small financial system may benefit from importing key financial infrastructural services from larger and more developed countries. So far there does not seem to be much evidence of this happening. This may in many cases be a rational way to move forward, not only for banks but also for specialized financial institutions such as insurance and securities markets.[22] Glaessner and Valdés-Prieto (1998) make such a case for pension services: Government could confine itself to mandating contributions, creating a collection system, and setting minimum standards for pension contracts, and then could license international companies to offer those contracts to local contributors. The small country that adopted such a practice would be de facto importing supervision services, while avoiding the need to develop much of the infrastructure that domestic securities markets require.

Regulation should enable residents to contract for investments in foreign currencies, and should allow domestic providers to subcontract internationally for specialized services, such as data processing; investment management; clearing, settlement, and depository facilities; and exchange facilities. Foreign providers should be granted remote access to domestic markets, allowing them to supply cross-border services to domestic users without the need for a physical presence in the country.

Measures such as these would place small systems in a position of great reliance on external supply, but they also would make domestic markets contestable, thus protecting local communities from the costs of monopolistic or state-driven solutions. Such measures also can enable a small system to benefit from better regulatory and supervisory infrastructure through indirect employment of the financial supervision, financial sector laws, and even civil laws of larger and more developed countries. For example, financial contracts could be signed under the jurisdiction of another country, and financial firms required to be branches of institutions licensed in well-supervised countries. In cases where consumer protection is a concern, such as in the life insurance business, the small system could require that the supplier be subject to the consumer protection law of a larger country.

The benefits of importing infrastructural pension and insurance services may in fact reach beyond the scale and network effects discussed, due to other factors that can negatively affect the cost and quality of production of such services in small financial systems. In particular, the latter typically suffer from higher factor mobility and higher concentration of wealth and ownership. Strong migration flows can produce unstable contribution/premium collection bases, and in less reliable actuarial tables the concentration of wealth and ownership in the hands of a few agents can limit the number of independent financial and political interests, causing arbitrary redistribution of income, poor industry governance and performance, risk of fraud, and loss of confidence on the part of service users.

Openness May Call for Tailored Regulations

Prudential rules. Because of their greater fragility, small financial systems may require policy instruments to steer them into zones of safe and sound finance. Honohan and Stiglitz (2001) assess the relative costs and benefits of five types of regulatory restraint frequently adopted by governments to achieve prudential bank behavior: restrictions on market entry, capital requirements, maximum deposit interest rates, ceilings on sectoral credit, and ceilings on portfolio size. The assessment concludes that capital adequacy requirements and entry restrictions may be the best options when international openness makes an economy susceptible to disintermediation.

POLICY FOR SMALL FINANCIAL SYSTEMS

In small financial systems the franchise value of incumbent intermediaries may be sensitive to new entry. Limiting entry will help
maintain the viability of local intermediaries, but may incur too
high a price if restrictions on entry reduce efficiency. Entry should
be open to domestic and foreign institutions, and should encourage
partnerships between resident and foreign investors. It should,
however, be restricted to those of good reputation, including existing owners and managers. Noncompliant subjects should be
opened to withdrawal of their license.[23]

Capital adequacy provides banks with a first line of reserves to
absorb losses. Local banks operating in small financial systems that
lack basic infrastructure could be required to maintain significantly higher capital ratios. Differential ratios also could take into
account the degree of financial product, sector, and geographic
diversification. This would introduce the incentive for such banks
to diversify their risk portfolio, to expand their scale, and to move
to regional or international integration. Tailoring capital adequacy
requirements to local conditions also would be in line with proposals to amend the 1988 Capital Accord as put forward by the Basel
Committee on Banking Supervision.

Types of pro-competition regulation can change with country
size. For example, the study by Glaessner and Valdés-Prieto (1998)
on pension reform in small developing countries identifies substantial economies of scale in the collection of contributions and in
the payment of benefits, and argues that these should be manda-
torily unbundled from other pension services. This would enable
the markets for trustees and investment management services to
remain competitive. (Interestingly, the study argues that this type
of pension design may be preferable to foreign firms providing all
pension services.)

Macro Solutions: Capital Account Opening and Exchange Rate Arrangements

It is worth mentioning here a few considerations concerning macro
solutions and their risks. There is an extensive theoretical and
empirical literature on the potential gains to a small country from
international trade in financial assets (recently reviewed in Stulz
(1999); see also Rodrik (1998)). Recent works have focused on the
volatility of portfolio flows and thus on the advantages of keeping
the capital market closed. However, the older tradition holds that
international financial integration increases the value of domestic
financial assets and lowers the cost of capital (Stulz 1999);[24] these

are effects that have been empirically documented (Henry 2000; Bekaert and Harvey 2000). With open capital markets, investments previously thought too risky become viable and can be undertaken without sacrificing consumption through foreign financing. The gains increase quite sharply as the size of the economy diminishes. Economies that are reasonably large but which have small financial systems also benefit substantially from access to international financial markets.[25]

There are potential downsides to the financial sector from opening the capital account, however. Quite apart from a possible increase in vulnerability to surges of speculative capital, there may be longer-run effects, including the following:

- A financial system may decline in size after being opened. The CFA countries have long had little financial depth; precautionary balances therefore are held outside the CFA, in a strategy that has been made easy by an open capital market. Similar behavior is reflected in the high dollarization of open economies such as Lebanon and the Russian Federation. In these cases risk-reduction through internationalization has reduced the size either of the entire financial sector, or of its domestic currency component

- International integration may reduce overall risk in the economy, but it also may render the domestic financial system more vulnerable. Financial institutions can seek to reduce risk by selling or trading financial assets, but this may not always be easy. In practice, the risk-reduction possibilities opened up by international financial integration are exploited more by nonfinancial than by domestic financial institutions.

The ease with which other regional solutions can be implemented likely would be enhanced by having a common currency. The common currency issue is highly relevant to small member states in Eastern Europe in the context of EU monetary union, as well as in Africa (Honohan and Lane 1999 and 2001). Adoption of a common currency or of a foreign currency can be a way of achieving network externalities,[26] but there are risks of some or all of the members of a currency union being caught in an overvaluation trap.

Concluding Remarks

Small financial markets are more likely than larger markets to have incomplete financial services, and more borrowers are likely to lack access to existing services. Those services that are available are likely to be of poor quality and expensive. Risk is less well diversified and supervisory institutions are less able to do their job. This raises the question of the extent to which these problems could be overcome through some form of openness.

Opening the economy to permit the importation of financial services from abroad can help resolve these problems. Much is to be gained from increased openness to foreign ownership of financial intermediaries; to regional solutions, in terms both of markets and financial infrastructure; and to importing elements of financial infrastructure from further afield. Regulations should allow residents to contract for financial services from abroad, should allow domestic providers to subcontract internationally for specialized services, such as data processing, investment management, clearing, settlement, and depository facilities, and exchange facilities; and should grant foreign providers remote access to domestic markets, allowing them to supply cross-border services to domestic users without establishing a physical presence in the country.

While these measures would incur greater reliance of the small system on external supply, they would make domestic markets more efficient and contestable, thus protecting local communities from the costs of monopolistic or state-driven solutions. These measures also could allow a small system to benefit from better regulatory and supervisory infrastructure by indirectly employing the financial supervision, financial sector laws, and civil laws of larger and more developed countries. For example, financial contracts could be signed under the jurisdiction of another country, and financial firms could be required to be branches of institutions licensed in well-supervised countries. In cases where consumer protection is a concern, such as in the life insurance business, the small country could require that the supplier be subject to the consumer protection law of a larger country.

Any move to greater openness may require prudential rules, competition policy, and liquidity management regulations to be tailored to suit the situation of the economy in question.

Notes

1. Some very small economies have developed substantial "offshore" financial services industries. Some of the most prominent of these, such as the Cayman Islands (population 35,000), are not sovereign states, and some are advanced economies (most notably Luxembourg). The growth of most offshore financial centers has been linked with tax avoidance, and to some extent with money laundering, but it is evident that the specialization of some small countries in the export provision of financial services nonetheless could be a lasting feature of the global financial system. It cannot, however, be a solution for all small financial systems: the presence of offshore finance often does not significantly contribute to the quality or depth of onshore finance in small poor countries.

2. We use the term *financial infrastructure* to refer to the complex of systems, actors, rules, and practices that define the field of action in which financial agents negotiate and perform financial transactions. Some of these are established and maintained by governmental bodies, reflecting their public good character; others are normally in the private sector. They include: (a) legal and regulatory frameworks (including contract enforcement mechanisms); (b) central banking services; (c) supervision, accounting and auditing rules, resources, and practices; (d) information provision (e.g., credit bureaus, rating agencies, and public registries); (e) payments and securities settlement systems; (f) exchange systems (e.g., trading and listing services, trading rules, and communication/information platforms).

3. Micro states have relied on capital controls to about the same extent as other countries, but their potential gain from financial openness is higher.

4. They also show that shocks to small economies are not highly correlated with the world business cycle, so that there is a definite potential for risk-pooling. To the extent that external shocks have a common regional component, the openness to financial flows would have to extend beyond the immediate region in order to provide the maximum benefit.

5. Financial openness is not a panacea for growth ailments (Grilli and Milesi-Ferretti 1995; Rodrik 1998), but nor is it systematically a conspicuous contributor to macroeconomic risk (Kraay 1998).

6. That the potential for risk-pooling may be considerable is suggested by analysis of risk-pooling between U.S. states. Observing that per capita state production in the United States varies nationwide, Asdrubali et al. (1996) examine the channels through which interstate risk sharing occurred in the country between 1963–1990. They find that 39 percent of shocks to gross state product were smoothed by capital markets, 23 percent by the credit markets, and 13 percent by the federal government. The remaining 25 percent remained unsmoothed. By repeating the analysis for

three subperiods separately (1963–70, 1971–80, and 1981–90), they observe a monotonic increase in risk smoothing by capital markets, possibly because of increasing financial innovation and better access to securities markets over time. They also find that credit market smoothing is less stable across subperiods and that it is considerably lower in states where shocks to gross state product are more persistent.

7. Several of these exchanges are very small-but note that the ratio of stock market capitalization to M2 is relatively high on average in the countries that do have an exchange. This is an artifact of our having selected the countries on the basis of having a small M2.

8. There are also private compliance costs, which are generally thought to be much higher than the official cost (one oft-quoted rule of thumb is that private costs can be four times those incurred by the regulator), but they are less likely to be subject to economies of scale. Franks, Schaefer, and Staunton (1998) estimated incremental costs for securities firms in the United Kingdom at £1,854 per financial sector employee, a figure that is broadly consistent within the range of 6–14 percent of noninterest expenses found by Hopkins (1992) for U.S. banking.

9. A log regression of costs on M2 gives an estimated elasticity of 0.689, with a standard error of 0.087, implying considerable economies of scale. According to the equation, 10 economies, each with an M2 of US$1 billion, will have more than twice the regulatory costs of a single US$10 billion economy. The projected aggregate regulatory costs of the 100 smallest financial systems, at US$53 million per annum, are almost US$20 million higher than they would be if regulatory costs were proportional to those of a US$10 billion economy. The source of these data is the DECRG-FI regulatory survey (Barth et al. 2001). This is based on the actual (not necessarily optimal) level of spending. Of course, actual spending may not be sufficient, and the shortfall may be greater for smaller systems.

10. Other aspects of financial policy also are subject to economies of scale, including monetary policy formulation, the cost of issuing and maintaining the circulation of currency notes, and the operation of a payments system.

11. Much of the empirical research that has been conducted by others on the problem of size in finance has focused primarily on institutional-scale economies in large financial markets. As a result, even those at the lower end of the institutions studied are by and large greater in size than those found in the economies under consideration. Furthermore, the studies have, for the most part, focused on advanced economies whose relative factor prices differ from those of developing economies in ways that could affect the outcome.

12. The existing pattern of real economy and financial sector activities will have an impact on the degree to which some of the policies are

needed. For example, if there is already a lot of cross-border financial activity, regional integration of supervision may be more urgent.

13. Barclays is present in nine African countries, all former British colonies: Botswana (present for 50 years), Ghana (80), Kenya (80), Mauritius (80), Seychelles, South Africa (5), Uganda (70), Zambia, and Zimbabwe (80). Standard Chartered is present in a different, but overlapping set of countries, all of which also were British colonies.

14. The BIAO, formerly the bank of issue in the French West African colonies, failed and was liquidated in 1990.

15. Not all of the cross-border expansion has come from industrial countries. OTP, the Hungarian savings bank, recently bought a bank in Slovakia.

16. Kono and Schuknecht (1999) show that formal liberalization of foreign ownership is increasing under the auspices of the World Trade Organization, and they argue that this is helping to limit the volatility of capital movements and of financial markets generally.

17. A note of caution is sounded by some who, while noting that assessing the credit-worthiness of small firms, especially start-ups, may be easier for foreign banks, it requires set-up costs (including the cost of relationship building) that might not seem remunerative for them. This perception of foreign banks is drawn from observation of their behavior in markets where they are niche players. It is an area which clearly needs more research.

18. Glaessner and Valdés-Prieto (1998) note that the small size of the market for pension services in small countries, in terms both of the number of active contributors and the level of wages, limits the interest of foreign firms in providing such services locally. With 200,000 to 400,000 active contributors and wage rates of about US$200 to US$400 per month, as in the Bolivian case that Glaessner and Valdés-Prieto observe, the flow of resources into the pension management business would be between US$2 million and US$10 million per year, depending on the commission rate. This clearly would limit the interest of major foreign companies in investing directly in the setting up of a local branch or agency.

19. Bermuda, Botswana, Kuwait, Namibia, Panama, and Zambia are examples, although in Zambia there is just one foreign company in a total of nine.

20. TARGET in Europe-the real-time gross settlement system for euro-denominated payments in the EU-is an example of a regional (cross-border) payment infrastructure built on different domestic payment systems, connected through a common interlinking component.

21. Despite the formal regional structure offered by the CFA franc zones-the initials stand for both financial cooperation and community in Africa-banking in the CFA appears to be largely confined by national boundaries. Bank groups operating in different countries do so through

subsidiaries whose relationships are primarily with head office in a third country, rather than with affiliates elsewhere in the zone.

22. The small volume and high cost of securities transactions generated domestically and the costly human capital necessary to set up securities markets led Costa Rica to subcontract to Chile's electronic stock exchange the pricing and trading of different kinds of domestic private and government securities (Glaessner and Valdés-Prieto 1998).

23. For a discussion of policy issues relating to reputation in finance, see Bossone (1999).

24. As to the size of such diversification benefits, Stulz (1999) quotes an average 30 percent gain in asset prices and a 100–300 basis point reduction in the real cost of capital. The scope for gains evidently will depend on the economic structure: an economy whose exports are specialized in one main product stands to gain a lot; a more diversified country may gain less. See also the evidence of an improved risk-return trade-off achieved by banks in larger geographical markets in the United States, as described by Hughes et al. (1999).

25. A closed economy may be less vulnerable to exogenous swings in foreign investor sentiment, but a small economy may be below the radar of speculators, and may not attract the more volatile type of portfolio flows (Honohan and Lane, 2001).

26. Reding and Morales (1999) show that a network of foreign (common) currency users reduces transactions costs for all prospective users of the currency, and that the strength of the network effects is increasing in its size, defined as the number of agents whose currency balances are larger than a given threshold.

References

The word *processed* describes informally produced works that may not be commonly available through libraries.

Asdrubali, P., B. E. Sørensen, and O. Yosha. 1996. "Channels of Interstate Risk Sharing: United States, 1963–1990." *Quarterly Journal of Economics* 111:1081–1110.

Barth, James. R., Gerard Caprio Jr., and Ross Levine. 2001. "The Regulation and Supervision of Bank Around the World: A New Database." In Robert E. Litan and Richard Herring, eds., *Integrating Emerging Market Countries into the Global Financial System.* Brookings-Wharton Papers on Financial Services. Washington, D.C.: Brookings Institution Press.

Bekaert, G., and C. R. Harvey. 2000. "Foreign Speculators and Emerging Equity Markets." *Journal of Finance* 55:565–613.

Bossone, B. 1999. "The Role of Trust in Financial Sector Development." World Bank Policy Research Working Paper No. 2200. World Bank, Washington, D.C.

Bossone, B., and L. Promisel. 1999. "Self Regulation in Developing Countries." World Bank Financial Sector Website Policy Note. World Bank, Washington, D.C. Available online at: wbwebapps2.world-bank.org/wwwfinance/html/self-regulation-in-developing.html

Claessens, S., and T. Glaessner. 1998. "The Internationalization of Financial Services in Asia." World Bank Policy Research Working Paper No. 1911. World Bank, Washington, D.C.

Claessens, S., A. Demirgüç-Kunt, and H. Huizinga. 2000. "The Role of Foreign Banks in Domestic Banking Systems." In S. Claessens and M. Jansen, eds., *The Internationalization of Financial Services*. The Hague: Kluwer.

Clarke, G., R. Cull, M. S. Martinez Peria, and S. Sanchez. 2001. "Foreign Bank Entry: Experience, Implications for Developing Countries, and Agenda for Further Research." World Bank Policy Research Working Paper No. 2698. World Bank, Washington, D.C.

d'Amato, L., E. Grubisic, and A. Powell. 1997. "Contagion, Bank Fundamentals or Macroeconomic Shocks: An Empirical Analysis of the Argentine 1995 Banking Problems." Central Bank of Argentina Working Paper No. 2. Buenos Aires: Central Bank of Argentina.

Easterly, W., and A. Kraay. 1999. "Small States, Small Problems?" World Bank Policy Research Working Paper No. 2139. World Bank, Washington, D.C.

Eichengreen, B., M. D. Bordo, and D. Irwin. 1999. "Is Globalization Today Really Different than Globalization a Hundred Years Ago?" National Bureau of Economic Research (NBER) Working Paper No. 7195. Cambridge, Massachusetts: NBER.

Folkerts-Landau, E., and H. van Greuning. 1997. "The Case for Regional Financial Market Infrastructure in Africa: How Africa's Financial Systems Could Move toward Greater Regional Integration." World Bank, Washington, D.C. Processed.

Franks, J. R., S. M. Schaefer, and M. D. Staunton. 1998. "The Direct and Compliance Costs of Financial Regulation." *Journal of Banking and Finance* 21:1547–1572.

Glaessner, T., and S. Valdés-Prieto. 1998. "Pension Reform in Small Developing Countries." World Bank Policy Research Working Paper No. 1983. World Bank, Washington, D.C.

Goldberg, L., B. G. Dages, and D. Kinney. 2000. "Foreign and Domestic Bank Participation in Emerging Markets: Lessons from Mexico and Argentina." *Federal Reserve Bank of New York Policy Review* 6(3).

Grilli, V., and G. M. Milesi-Ferretti. 1995. "Economic Effects and Structural Determinants of Capital Controls." *International Monetary Fund Staff Papers*, 42(3):517–551.

Haque, N. U., and P. J. Montiel. 1991. "Capital Mobility in Developing Countries: Some Empirical Tests." *World Development* 19:1391–1398.

Henry, P. B. 2000. "Stock Market Liberalization, Economic Reform and Emerging Market Equity Prices." *Journal of Finance* 55:529–564.

Honohan, P. 2000. "Banking System Failures in Developing and Transition Countries: Diagnosis and Prediction." *Economic Notes* 29(1):83–109.

Honohan, P., and R. P. Kinsella. 1982. "Comparing Bank Concentration across Countries." *Journal of Banking and Finance* 6:255–262.

Honohan, P., and P. Lane. 1999. "Pegging to the Dollar and the Euro." *International Finance* 2(3):379–410.

———. 2001. "Will the Euro Trigger More Monetary Unions in Africa?" In C. Wyplosz, ed., *The Impact of EMU on Europe and the Developing Countries*. Oxford: Oxford University Press.

Honohan, P., and J. Stiglitz. 2001. "Robust Financial Restraint." In G. Caprio, P. Honohan, and J. E. Stiglitz, eds. *Financial Liberalization: How Far, How Fast?* New York: Cambridge University Press.

Hopkins, T. D. 1992. "The Cost of Federal Regulation." *Journal of Regulation and Control* 2(1).

Huberman, G. 2000. "Home Bias in Equity Markets: International and Intranational Investment." In G. D. Hess and E. Van Wincoop, eds., *Intranational Macroeconomics*. New York: Cambridge University Press.

Hughes, J. P., W. Lang, L. J. Mester, and C. Moon. 1999. "The Dollars and Cents of Bank Consolidation." *Journal of Banking and Finance* 23:291–324.

International Monetary Fund (IMF). 2000. *International Capital Markets: Developments, Prospects and Key Policy Issues*. Washington, D.C.: IMF.

Kono, M. and L. Schuknecht. 1999. *Financial Services Trade, Capital Flows, and Financial Stability*. Geneva: World Trade Organization. Processed.

Kraay, A. 1998. "In Search of the Macroeconomic Effects of Capital Account Liberalization." World Bank, Washington, D.C. Processed.

Levine, R., and S. Zervos. 1998. "Stock Markets, Banks and Economic Growth." *American Economic Review* 88(3):537–558.

Lewis, K. K. 1996. "What Can Explain the Apparent Lack of International Consumption Risk Sharing?" *Journal of Political Economy* 106(2):267–297.

Reding, P., and J. A. Morales. 1999. "Currency Substitution and Network Externalities." University of Namur, Belgium. Processed.

Rodrik, D. 1998. "Who Needs Capital Account Convertibility?" In P. Kenen, ed., *Should the IMF Pursue Capital-Account Convertibility?* Princeton Essays in International Finance, No. 207. Department of Economics, Princeton University. Princeton, New Jersey.

Stulz, Rene. 1999. "International Portfolio Flows and Securities Markets." In M. Feldstein, ed., *International Capital Flows.* Chicago: University Chicago Press.

Tesar, L. L., and I. M. Warner. 1992. "Home Bias and High Turnover." *Journal of International Money and Finance* 14:467–492.

Dollarization, Private and Official: Issues, Benefits, and Costs

James A. Hanson

Introduction

THE TERM "DOLLARIZATION" HAS come to mean the widespread private holding and use of financial assets and liabilities denominated in any foreign currency, not just dollars. Dollarization has also come to mean the official adoption of a foreign currency, either as legal tender or as the basis of a currency board, with a legally fixed exchange rate and base money changes limited to purchases and sales of foreign exchange. Dollarization in both forms has seen an upsurge in the 1990s, demanding both an explanation and an interpretation of the issues that it poses.

The different forms of dollarization have similar implications for the financial system. The private and official motivations for dollarization also are similar: avoidance of the costs and risks associated with a volatile local currency. Dollarization generates its own costs and risks, however, both for the financial system and for the economy.

The author is grateful to Paul Beckerman, Gerard Caprio, Larry Hinkle, Patrick Honohan, Charles Humphreys, Steven Kamin, Larry Promisel, John Leimone, Richard Newfarmer, and Andrew Wolfe for helpful discussions and comments; to Bala Bhaskar Naidu Kalimili and Ying Lin for excellent research assistance; and to Elena Mekhova for excellent support services.

Dollarization: A Brief History
and Estimates of Current Magnitudes

In the decades after the Second World War, there was substantial de-dollarization in developing countries, notably among former British colonies that exited from their sterling currency boards and adopted their own currencies (Williamson 1995; Ghosh, Guide, and Wolf 2000; Hanke and Schuler 1994; Schuler 1992). Two important exceptions to de-dollarization were the two CFA Franc Zones in Africa, which remained linked to the French franc (see Box 2), and the Eastern Caribbean countries (van Beek et al. 2000). Typically, the new nations adopted an adjustable peg exchange rate regime, in line with the Bretton Woods system.[1] Many developing countries continued to use the adjustable peg system or variants of it, even after the Bretton Woods system broke up in the 1970s following the floating of the U.S. dollar and the massive speculative attacks on the currencies of the industrial countries. Some of these adjustable pegs remained constant for a long time. For example, the rate between the U.S. dollar and some Central American currencies was constant from before the Second World War until the 1980s, before falling victim to internal monetary instability (Edwards 1995). As international capital flows became larger, these long-term pegs tended to break down because of the so-called inconsistent trinity, or "trilemma," of a pegged exchange rate, an open capital account, and a monetary policy oriented toward domestic objectives (Obstfeld and Rogoff 1995). In 1997, the long constant peg between the Thai baht and the U.S. dollar collapsed in the Asian crisis.

Dollarization reemerged toward the end of the 1970s. Public and private external borrowing and deposits grew substantially, in effect shifting some financial intermediation into foreign currency and offshore. In Latin America, rising inflation was accompanied by increased holdings of foreign currency assets, first offshore, then onshore as regulations were eased on capital account convertibility (Savastano 1992, 1996). Other countries experienced asset and currency substitution to a lesser degree. Even where onshore foreign currency deposits were not allowed, foreign currency sometimes came to be used as a parallel medium of exchange and store of value.

Dollarization accelerated in the 1990s. In early 1991, Argentina adopted a currency board with respect to the dollar. And, while the break up of the Soviet Union led to the replacement of the ruble by many new currencies (de-dollarization), the accompanying political, economic, and financial turmoil led to substantial currency and asset substitution in favor of the U.S. dollar and the Deutsche mark (Sahay and Vegh 1996). Two of the new states, Estonia and Lithuania, soon also adopted currency boards linking their currencies to the Deutschemark and the U.S. dollar respectively. Legal dollarization more recently also has gained force. Bulgaria and Bosnia and Herzegovina adopted currency boards, and Ecuador, El Salvador, and East Timor (when it was founded) chose to officially designate the U.S. dollar as legal currency. (Box 1 shows the

---

Box 1. Developing Countries with No Separate Legal Tender or a Currency Board (date of adoption; currency link if other than US$)

Emerging Market Economies (5)

Bulgaria (1997; DM/euro), Ecuador (2000), El Salvador (2001), Panama (1934). Also Argentina (1991–2001).

Other Developing Countries (28)

Members of the two CFA Franc Zones (14, 1948[a], FFr/euro)
Central African Economic and Monetary Community:
Cameroon, Central African Republic, Chad, Republic of Congo, Equatorial Guinea, Gabon.
West African Monetary Economic and Monetary Union:
Benin, Burkina Faso, Côte d'Ivoire, Guinea-Bissau, Mali, Niger, Senegal, and Togo.

Members of Eastern Caribbean Central Bank (6, 1983[a])
Antigua and Barbuda, Dominica, Grenada, St. Kitts and Nevis, St. Lucia, St. Vincent and the Grenadines.

Other countries (8)
Bhutan (1974; Indian rupee), Bosnia and Herzegovina (1997; DM/euro), Djibouti (1949), East Timor (2000), Estonia (1992, DM/euro), Lesotho (1996[b], South African rand), Lithuania (1994), Namibia (1993[b], South African rand).

---

a. The CFA zones were preceded for many years by currency board arrangements, as was the case in countries that are members of the Eastern Caribbean Central Bank (van Beek et al. 2000).

b. Bhutan, Lesotho, and Namibia used the listed currency before their independence and it now circulates as legal tender.

Developing countries are those that supply country data to the International Monetary Fund (IMF) and are listed in the World Bank Debt Reporting System (World Bank 2000b), plus Antigua and Barbuda and Namibia.

Sources: IMF, *International Financial Statistics*; Ghosh, Guide, and Wolf 2000.

developing countries that have legally adopted a foreign currency or a currency board as of 2001.) The European Union's (EU) adoption of the euro in 1999 is certainly the most important case of "dollarization" ever, although, strictly speaking, the members did not adopt another country's currency but a currency union in which they all would have a role in making monetary policy.

Intellectually, too, legal dollarization has gained force. Some analysts argue that to avoid periodic exchange rate crises, countries must either legally fix their exchange rates or fully float them. This is the so-called bipolar view of appropriate exchange rate regimes, arranged along a spectrum of exchange rate flexibility (Hausmann 1999; Fischer 2001).

Whatever the exchange regime, the holding and use of foreign currency and foreign-currency-denominated assets is substantial. Various estimates suggest that between 30 and 70 percent of U.S. currency is outside the United States, most of it in $100 bills (Doyle 2000; Sprenkle 1993; Porter and Judson 1996).[2] Supporting these statistical estimates of high offshore currency holdings are surveys of U.S. currency usage that have found that individuals only held, on average, about 7 percent of the stock of cash in 1995, down sharply from the 15 percent held in 1986 (Sprenkle 1993; Porter and Judson 1996). Indirect estimates suggest businesses and illegal activities account for only about 8–10 percent of U.S. currency holdings (Sprenkle 1993).

Casual observation is supportive of these estimates: at the end of 2000, about US$550 billion of U.S. currency was in circulation (outside banks), of which about 60 percent was in $100 bills (Doyle 2000). If all U.S. currency were held only by individuals in the United States, this would imply each person was holding roughly US$2,000, including 12 $100 bills. This is far more than most people hold.

Germany, Japan, and Switzerland have even higher per capita stocks of currency outstanding than the United States—and almost one-third of German currency outstanding in 1999 was in DM 1,000 notes, each of which is equal to more than US$600 (Doyle 2000). Before the introduction of the euro, the Bundesbank estimated that some 40 percent of Deutschemarks were outside Germany, mostly in the Balkans and the countries formed after the Soviet Union disintegrated. Doyle's estimates suggest that the percentages of Deutschemarks and Swiss francs held offshore may be even higher than for the U.S. dollar: Rogoff (1998) argues that holdings of 30–40 percent offshore would be reasonable. If 30–50 percent of U.S., German, and Swiss currency were held offshore, it would represent 25–36 percent of the nonbank holdings of currency in the world outside of these three countries and Japan in 1999.[3]

The importance of currency substitution appears to be even greater in some countries. According to the U.S. Customs Service, cumulative shipments of U.S. dollars during 1989–1996 were: to Russia, about US$44 billion (equal to 250 percent of the domestic currency in circulation in 1996); to Argentina, US$35 billion (about 300 percent); to Bolivia, US$800 million (about 300 percent); to Uruguay, US$2 billion (about 440 percent); to Venezuela, US$1 billion (about 140 percent); and to Turkey, US$4 billion (about 100 percent) (Balino, Bennett, and Borensztein 1999). The recorded cumulative shipments during this period to these countries alone totalled about US$86 billion, or more than 20 percent of U.S. currency outside banks at the end of 1996. The shipment data, moreover, probably underestimate U.S. currency outflows (Porter and Judson 1996).

Foreign currency assets and liabilities also are large (Table 1). In many countries, domestic foreign currency deposits exceed 20 percent of deposits in commercial banks. The offshore deposits of residents in banks in the Organisation for Economic Co-operation and Development (OECD) and loans by OECD banks to the nonbank sector (much of them to governments) in many countries also account for more than 20 percent of domestic deposits, indicating a substantial shift of financial intermediation offshore. Moreover, these figures tend to underestimate offshore financial intermediation, because they exclude both the deposits in and loans by banks located in non-OECD financial centers, such as Hong Kong, Panama, Uruguay (for Argentines and Brazilians), or the Cayman Islands, and the deposits made in OECD banks by offshore residents using OECD addresses or agents.

Latin America has some of the highest rates of asset substitution. Even Brazil, Chile, and Colombia, which have banned onshore foreign currency deposits or attempted to limit onshore and offshore disintermediation by offering inflation-indexed deposits, have large offshore financial intermediation. In part this reflects the external financing of public sector deficits by the countries of the region. Transition countries also have high rates of asset substitution. In contrast, East Asian countries tend to have lower ratios of foreign currency deposits and lower ratios of offshore financial intermediation (although they are large offshore borrowers) than the Latin American and transition economies. This difference probably reflects higher domestic saving rates, more attractive monetary and

Table 1. Indicators of Asset Substitution in 1999

Onshore Deposits	Foreign Currency Deposits (%)	Offshore Deposits (%)	Offshore Loans (%)
Argentina*	62.3	24.3	44.0
Brazil*	..	9.0	19.0
Bulgaria*	53.3	32.1	14.1
Chile*	8.7	18.2	48.6
China*	7.9	0.5	1.4
Colombia*	..	33.8	56.8
Czech Rep.*	13.3	10.7	3.4
Ecuador*	56.4	37.1	29.8
Egypt, Arab Rep.*	24.5	6.6	10.9
Estonia	18.9	26.9	11.7
India*	..	3.2	7.6
Indonesia*	20.7	5.2	41.2
Jamaica	27.4	21.1	16.9
Hungary*	5.3	30.3	4.4
Lithuania	43.7	49.9	21.8
Malaysia*	..	4.9	5.7
Mexico*	13.4[a]	24.3	44.2
Nigeria*	..	51.1	26.9
Pakistan*	12.2	16.2	25.9
Panama*	100.0	386.3	416.4
Peru*	66.0	16.0	30.1
Philippines*	40.9[a]	9.3	18.9
Poland*	5.3	14.0	2.1
Russia*	40.4	54.1	23.2
South Africa*	..	6.5	13.2
Sri Lanka*	..	5.2	15.9
Thailand*	..	2.3	13.4
Turkey*	46.9	66.0	26.8
Venezuela*	..	131.2	74.8
Uruguay	81.0	35.7	21.9

*Emerging market economy
a. 1998

Sources: Bank for International Settlements; IMF, *International Financial Statistics;* Beckerman (2001); Honohan and Shi (2001); State Bank of Pakistan; Bank Indonesia.

financial sector policies, and a history of lower public sector deficits than in Latin American and in the transition economies (World Bank 1993).

India and China have banned or limited foreign currency deposits (although in India, nonresidents can make foreign-currency-indexed deposits) and generally have maintained lower rates of inflation than the Latin American and transition economies while financing their public sector deficits though the banking system. India's external borrowings have largely been from bilateral and multilateral sources, rather than from foreign banks or capital markets. The China data understate offshore deposits and loans, because they exclude data from Hong Kong.

Private Dollarization: Currency and Asset Substitution

Motivation

Currency substitution occurs when households and firms switch to foreign currency use because high inflation has increased the loss on domestic currency holdings. Foreign currency also may be held as a store of value when the domestic banking system offers low real yields or is weak. Other factors include tax avoidance and illicit activities.[4] Asset substitution occurs when households and firms diversify their portfolios to achieve a better risk-return profile relative to domestic currency assets. This diversification may occur offshore or onshore, the former serving as insurance against expropriation and weak financial systems, and often reflecting tax avoidance.

Theory predicts and experience confirms that dollar deposits tend to rise with inflation and exchange rate depreciation.[5] The motivations for asset substitution are more complex. Foreign currency borrowing often is tempting because it implies lower, less variable interest costs—but it also involves foreign exchange risk. For these reasons, governments often have used external borrowing to ease domestic fiscal and financial constraints, even when they have set limits on such borrowing by the nonpublic sector. In transition economies, weak banks and governance and corruption problems have been important motivations for asset and currency substitution.

It is not hard to explain the growth of currency and asset substitution in many Latin American countries during the 1970s and 1980s, as noted above. Rises in already high inflation, together with large government deficits, limits on domestic interest rates, unsustainable exchange rate regimes, encouragements to public and private sector firms to borrow externally, and the possibility of gains from bail-outs of firms indebted externally all contributed to large public sector external borrowings and large capital outflows (Dooley et al. 1986; World Bank 1985)[6] and to large offshore deposit holdings (Savastano 1992, 1996).[7]

The trends over the last two decades in different elements of asset substitution are shown for Argentina, Bolivia, and Peru in Figures 1a, 1b, and 1c, respectively.[8] The data are shown relative to GDP to illustrate the importance of foreign currency deposits in limiting demonetization and financial disintermediation; graphs in dollar terms would be similar.[9] For Argentina, Figure 1a also includes foreign currency holdings (up to 1996, the last available year) to illustrate the importance of both currency and asset substitution. The Argentina graph thus effectively assumes no growth in dollar currency holdings after 1996.

All three countries show a fairly steady upward trend in foreign-currency-denominated holdings relative to domestic-currency-denominated holdings during the 1980s and 1990s. This is broadly consistent with the various models of currency and asset substitution. However, there are some deviations from these trends that are not explained by changes in inflation.

One reason for these deviations from the trends is changes in the laws regarding holdings of foreign currency deposits onshore and offshore. The legal framework, as well as expected inflation and devaluation, affects holdings of foreign currency assets and liabilities (Savastano 1992). For example, domestic foreign currency deposits were allowed in Argentina (1978), Bolivia (1973), Mexico

Figure 1a. Argentina Deposits 1981–1999, % of GNP

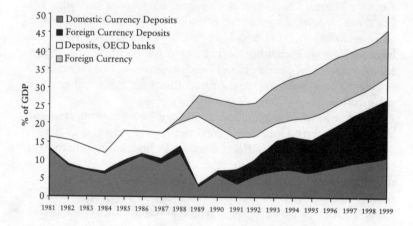

Figure 1b. Bolivia Deposits 1981–1999, % of GNP

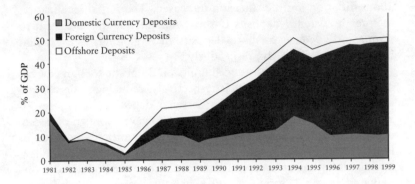

Figure 1c. Peru Deposits 1981–1999, % of GNP

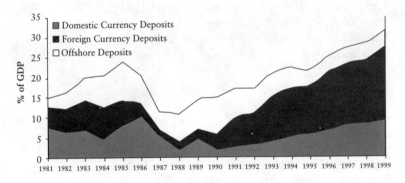

(1977), Peru (1978), and Uruguay (1970), albeit with restrictions. The hope was to reduce the growth in offshore deposits and to lower the high domestic interest rates that reflected concerns about devaluation—the so-called "peso problem." Other factors in the policy shift may have been economic ideology and concerns about the distributional aspects of the inflation tax in an economy in which capital controls are ineffective (see below). When foreign-currency-denominated accounts became legal, the public seems to have substituted them for domestic currency deposits. This substitution limited the reduction of total domestic deposits, as concerns about inflation and devaluation increased. The initial legalization of foreign currency deposits onshore nonetheless did not seem to significantly reduce offshore deposits in Argentina, Bolivia, and Peru (Figures 1a, 1b, 1c, respectively).[10]

Bolivia and Peru reintroduced limits on domestic foreign currency deposits in 1982 and 1985, respectively, reducing their volume and temporarily raising domestic currency deposits (see Figures 1b and 1c and Savastano [1992]). In Peru, however, foreign currency deposits offshore had risen before their limitation onshore. In Bolivia, Melvin and Fenske (1992) argue that the 1982 de-dollarization also stimulated capital flight and drove the dollarized economy underground. Soon after the new limits were imposed, domestic currency deposits collapsed in both countries as a result of increased economic and political instability. Such limits on foreign currency and assets generally are unlikely to be fully effective, particularly if prolonged financial instability creates strong incentives for holding foreign-currency-denominated assets (Dooley 1996; Ariyoshi et al. 2000). In the end, Bolivia (1986) and Peru (1988) eased restrictions on domestic foreign currency deposits. Thereafter, these deposits grew much faster than did domestic currency deposits.[11]

Is Dollarization Irreversible?

The return to monetary stability in Argentina, Bolivia, and Peru in the 1990s did not reverse currency and asset substitution, contrary to the prediction of the standard models and to the experience of some transition economies, notably Poland (Balino, Bennett, and Borensztein 1999; Sahay and Vegh 1996). In these three Latin American countries, foreign-currency-denominated deposits had a major role in remonetization as inflation fell (Figure 1). Within the growth of foreign-currency-denominated assets, the initial onshore foreign currency deposit growth seems partly to reflect declining offshore deposits, presumably because of greater confidence and the convenience of onshore deposits. Offshore deposits resumed their growth in both Argentina and Peru beginning in 1994.

Foreign currency also played a major role in the remonetization. In 1996, the sum of reported U.S. dollar currency exports to Argentina separately exceeded both offshore and onshore foreign currency deposits. From 1991 to 1996, Argentines also increased their holding of local currency, at about the same rate that their foreign currency holdings grew. The initial volume of local currency was much lower, however, and in 1996, foreign currency holdings were still more than triple local currency holdings. Bolivia and Peru have no annual data on currency imports from the United States, but the total export of U.S. dollars in the period 1989–1996 was large relative to domestic currency. In Bolivia, the total in 1996 was three times that of bank deposits. In other words, foreign currency holdings grew sharply in Argentina and Bolivia, even as remonetization and growth of domestic currency deposits occurred.

Various explanations have been advanced for the persistence of large and growing volumes of foreign-currency-denominated assets, even as stabilization has taken hold. One of these explanations is similar to the original explanations for currency and asset substitution: weak banking systems and illicit transactions, carried out in cash. For example, in Argentina, the banking system remained weak until the large-scale entry of foreign banks after the Tequila crisis (World Bank 1998). Bolivian links to coca and cocaine production continued during the 1990s, and numerous accusations of corruption have been made against the Argentine and Peruvian governments of the 1990s.

A second explanation for the persistence of dollarization relates to the history of inflation in these countries and their lack of a credible anti-inflation policy. Simply reducing inflation for a few years may be insufficient to restore credibility after the long history of failed Latin American stabilization programs. Individuals may choose to minimize risk by continuing to hold and use foreign currency assets. Local currency deposits in Argentina, Bolivia, and Peru tended to rise faster than onshore foreign currency deposits soon after stabilization, and spreads of short-term Argentine interest rates over U.S. dollar rates were small for much of the 1990s (Figure 3b); the various crises of the latter half of the 1990s were so frequent, however, that the rapid growth of dollar-denominated assets is not surprising. The experience with inflation in transition economies, notably Poland, is much shorter, and does not include the numerous failed episodes of stabilization that characterize Latin America's experience. Nonetheless, in Estonia and Lithuania, the growth of foreign currency deposits (relative to GDP) has resumed after the initial stabilization (Honohan and Shi 2001).

Another explanation for the persistence of foreign currency deposits relates to the large increase in capital inflows during the 1990s. Large capital inflows—including return-of-flight capital— may well have contributed to rising foreign currency deposits in Latin American economies in the early 1990s (Balino, Bennett, and

Borensztein 1999). Borrowers taking foreign currency obligations offshore may have wanted to hedge their obligations, or may have been forced to maintain countervailing balances.

A final explanation for the persistence of rapid growth in U.S. dollar deposits relates to the development of transactions networks using dollars that are costly to reverse.[12] There is no doubt that in many Latin American countries internal pricing in dollars and use of dollars for transactions have become accepted. Houses, apartments, offices, rentals, cars, other consumer durables, and imports have become priced in U.S. dollars in various countries in various combinations. Dollars became accepted in Lima supermarkets for articles priced in soles and in Buenos Aires generally, even for small transactions such as the purchase of a cup of coffee and taxi travel. Once such pricing rules develop, there is little reason for individuals to switch back to local currency pricing or to hold large volumes of local currency assets.

Dollars are fairly acceptable and widely available, although niches may remain for local currency use.[13] Deposits denominated in dollars may reflect inertia in converting to local currency in response to small (expected) differences in returns, but also may reduce transactions costs for conversion (for example, on monthly rent payments). In transition economies, such payments networks may be more limited; the availability of foreign currency also may have been limited by requirements for full surrender of export proceeds and limits on capital convertibility, for example, in Hungary, Estonia, and Poland (Sahay and Vegh 1996).

Benefits and Costs of Dollarization

The principal gain from currency and asset substitution is the protection it provides the public against monetary instability—that is, against inflation, exchange rate changes, and high real interest rates. The internal availability of foreign currency assets broadens the distribution of this gain. Currency represents the most important financial asset of many poor families, and their ability to hold and use foreign currency reduces the extent to which these holdings are taxed by inflation/devaluation. In Peru, for example, foreign currency deposits account for the majority of deposits even in the rural and urban cooperative banks, which are barred from operating in Lima. The internal availability of foreign currency assets extends the gains from currency and asset substitution well beyond those with direct access to offshore foreign currency assets and those willing to evade laws limiting foreign currency asset holdings.

The other side of this gain is the reduction in the government's ability to finance itself and to channel resources in the financial sector using seignorage (sometimes also called the inflation tax).[14] The inflation tax is a socially costly tax, both in terms of the resources spent trying to avoid it and its distributional costs. It nonetheless is an important contributor to government revenues in many countries. In economies with 5–10 percent inflation per year, the demand for "new" currency and other components of base money can easily be equivalent to 0.5–1.0 percent of GDP annually; in high-inflation countries, it is even more, given the inelasticity of money demand with respect to inflation. Taking into account economic growth, the demand for new base money can easily reach 1.0–1.5 percent of GDP annually, even where inflation is low.[15] Widespread use of foreign currency reduces the base for seignorage by reducing the public's demand for additional local currency and central bank monetary liabilities.[16] A government's attempt to rely on the same real volume of central bank finance, in the face of falling demand for central bank liabilities, will generate higher inflation (Fischer 1982). Moreover, this process can become cumulative, as higher inflation leads to an additional flight from local-currency-denominated assets. Governments in countries experiencing currency and asset substitution thus need to tighten their fiscal stance and develop government bond markets to finance their deficits and limit the risk of upward-spiraling inflation. The decline in seignorage due to increased currency and asset substitution may explain why developing countries are finding it more difficult to run large, noninflationary fiscal deficits than in the past.

The Impact of Dollarization on the Financial Sector

Asset substitution generates both problems and benefits for the financial sector. The demand for foreign-currency-denominated assets by citizens and foreign investors forces banks and other lending institutions to either bear foreign exchange risks or seek some hedge. The ability of banks to hedge by external placement of funds may be limited, and other types of hedging typically are unavailable in developing countries.[17] Because of risk aversion (and regulation), financial institutions in developing countries typically have responded to asset substitution by matching the currency composition of deposits with loans and other assets. Banks price loans and deposits in the two currencies to avoid open foreign exchange positions, taking into account competition from other banks, capital markets, and external lenders. The result typically is a large spread between the rates on local currency loans and deposits, partly reflecting the greater risks on such loans.

Bank matching of deposits and loans currency composition limits exchange risk, but probably increases credit risk. Borrowers, other than exporters, may not have assured sources of foreign exchange earnings. For example, a foreign exchange loan to finance an apartment house easily can become nonperforming if a devaluation occurs, even if the rent is denominated in foreign exchange. The renters are unlikely to have access to foreign exchange and the rent may increase substantially in local currency terms just at a point where aggregate demand for goods and labor may be falling. The deterioration of such loans, from both domestic and foreign banks, has been cited as an important factor in the 1997 Asian crisis and in Ecuador's problems (World Bank 2000a; Beckerman 2001). In Peru, the accelerated exchange rate depreciation in 1998–1999 caused the quality of foreign exchange loans to deteriorate faster than that of local currency loans. Of course, comparing credit risk in a dollarized economy with credit risk in an economy without dollars that has high, variable interest rates is not easy.

Asset substitution also provides some benefits in the financial markets. First, the availability of credit is greater with asset substitution than without, because the deposit base is larger. Second, the interest rate is likely to be much less, because it contains no premium for devaluation risk. Third, a foreign currency loan tends to have a longer effective maturity (in real terms) than a local currency loan—the higher interest rate on local currency loans (reflecting concerns over inflation and depreciation) means that more of the loan is effectively paid off early, and thus its effective maturity is shorter than that of a foreign currency loan. A borrower in foreign currency gains if no devaluation occurs; if and when devaluation does occur, the resulting increased cost is amortized over time—that is, the loan is, in effect, indexed to the dollar. Finally, the alternative to foreign-currency-denominated loans is the domestic currency loan, with floating interest rate, and such loans imply much higher debt servicing variability because local currency interest rates typically are much more variable than foreign currency rates.

These benefits are one of the justifications for allowing foreign currency deposits. Of course, borrowers may underestimate the risk of borrowing in foreign exchange, particularly if policy limits exchange rate movements. Those borrowers that are aware of the risk also may take foreign currency loans, in the expectation that they will be able to default should a sharp devaluation occur. Should a large devaluation in fact occur, the result in either case would be a financial sector crisis. These issues may partly explain the severity of recent financial crises (Caprio and Klingebiel 2002).

Public sector borrowers have been quick to take advantage of the benefits of foreign currency borrowing. Even small countries have resorted to external market borrowings, and have encountered good responses—both the Dominican Republic and Guatemala made large initial international bond issues during the fourth quarter of 2001, after the World Trade Center had been destroyed and when Argentina was facing a default. By borrowing externally, a government can take advantage of market infrastructure in the industrial countries without going through the costly and lengthy process of setting up a local government debt market. More important, foreign currency borrowing, whether onshore or offshore, avoids the devaluation premium.

As long as the exchange rate remains relatively constant, the budget benefits from the lower interest rate on borrowing in foreign currency. Governments have often taken advantage of this benefit (even when they have limited private external borrowing). For example, in early 1994, the government of Mexico converted its peso debt into dollars to reduce what it considered to be the excessive interest cost of its debt. If a devaluation occurs, however, the cost to the budget is large, as was the case in Mexico. Public sector borrowing in foreign currency thus raises the questions of whether the public sector is sufficiently sensitive to exchange rate risk and whether international financial architecture provides excessive protection to external lenders, thus increasing the supply of external loans to developing countries.

An obvious question is why countries in which currency and asset substitution is substantial do not simply adopt the foreign currency—that is, legally dollarize. The next sections discuss the issues surrounding legal dollarization.

Officially Adopting a Foreign Currency: The Choice of an Exchange Rate Regime

Robert Mundell's classic articles lay out the tradeoff between fixed exchange rates (through use of either a foreign currency as the medium of exchange or a currency board) and floating exchange rates (Mundell 1968). A floating exchange rate insulates GDP more against external demand shocks; a fixed rate more against internal demand shocks. Should a country's terms of trade fall, the fall in the supply of foreign exchange would depreciate the exchange rate, partially offsetting the output and employment effects of the initial shock on the export industry and encouraging production of import substitutes.[18] However, if the shock is a rise in the domestic saving rate or a fall in investment, the floating rate would tend to appreciate, adding to the initial shock. In such cases, a fixed rate would be beneficial.

Mundell applied this argument to the analysis of the optimum currency area (Mundell 1961). Countries that adopt a fixed rate between themselves and that experience demand shifts between each other would find monetary policy an ineffective response to maintain employment across the now single-currency area, and would need to rely on factor mobility to limit unemployment. In other words, the optimum currency area is one in which factor mobility between the members is high—that is, the members are actually "regions" in the language of international trade theory. Mundell's 1961 paper on optimum currency areas also raised concern about small countries attempting to maintain floating rates, both because of the balkanization of international currency markets and the difficulties of establishing competitive markets when the volume of currency trading was inherently small and therefore susceptible to destabilizing speculation.

Mundell's work is based on the idea of a fixed-price economy.[19] As McKinnon (1963) noted, an economy in which wages and prices are linked to world prices would not benefit much from a floating rate, nor would it have much demand for local currency. The different responses to shocks of the two exchange regimes are due to the presence of a nontradable goods sector with prices and wages not fully linked to world prices, a fact that also would explain the demand for local currency and assets denominated in local currency (Grossman, Hanson, and Lucas 1982). In such an economy, the financial sector could be dollarized more than the real sector. Adopting a foreign currency also would reduce transactions costs and eliminate the need for a central bank and the associated trappings of monetary policy and bank regulation (if foreign banks provided most of the banking services). Of course, fully adopting a foreign currency would eliminate seignorage.

These arguments suggest that optimum currency areas would involve small countries with trade oriented toward third countries, relatively low demand shocks from member countries, and relatively easy factor mobility between the member countries to offset any shifts in demand between the members. The two CFA Franc Zones and the Eastern Caribbean Central Bank, long-lived currency areas that account for more than half of the developing countries that have officially adopted a foreign currency, tend to satisfy these conditions (see Box 2 and van Beek et al. [2000]). Their member countries generally are small in terms of population or domestic financial sectors. Trade and tourism (in the eastern Caribbean), generally with nonmembers, play large roles in their economies; the

Box 2. The CFA Franc Zones in Africa

The origins of the CFA Franc Zones in Africa are more than a century old. They survived the colonial era to continue as monetary cooperation agreements after their separate components became independent countries, with some of the original countries dropping out, and some subsequently returning. (See Box 1 for the make-up of the zones in 2000.)

Broadly speaking, the two zones follow similar principles, notably:

• A ceiling on central bank credits to the member governments equal to 20 percent of budget revenue in the previous year. In addition, the member countries recently have been strengthening regional fiscal norms, including setting a zero primary fiscal deficit target, setting limits on the growth in the public sector wage bill, and addressing nonaccumulation of the payments arrears that in the past were a source of government finance.

• Free capital mobility.

• International reserves of at least 20 percent of base money. (International reserves are pooled in each central bank, with at least 65 percent maintained in the account of each central bank at the French Treasury.)

• Guarantee of convertibility of the CFA franc, at a fixed parity, through an unlimited overdraft facility of the French Treasury. This feature is obviously is not present in other currency unions.

Under the CFA arrangements, the CFA members had lower inflation than other sub-Saharan economies in the period 1973–1982; some evidence also suggests that they also grew faster than comparable countries in sub-Saharan Africa, despite the international turbulence in those years (Devarajan and de Melo 1987). This growth was based on strong export expansion but also involved rising wages and debt-financed public sector investment in uneconomic projects. When primary product terms of trade fell after 1982, the CFA countries' cost structure became uncompetitive because of the fixed exchange rate, the franc's 70 percent appreciation relative to the dollar, and depreciations by competitors; their exports stagnated and they lost market share (Devarajan and Hinkle 1994). In addition, some CFA

continued

Box 2. Continued

countries tried to delay adjustment by increasing borrowing, thus raising debt service to unsustainable levels.

Internal adjustment to the fall in export prices was made difficult by the rigidity of formal sector wages. Moreover, tightening fiscal policy by raising taxes would have been counterproductive while political pressures prevented layoffs of civil servants whose salaries accounted for most of spending. The financial system also was in disarray as a result of the drop in export profitability and the increasing burden of government debt (Honohan and Lane 2001).

In an attempt to ease the adjustment process, on January 12, 1994 the CFA rate was devalued by 100 percent, to 100 to the French franc. Prices rose 30–50 percent in 1994, but almost immediately the CFA countries returned to inflation rates that were lower than comparator countries; the cumulative rise in consumer prices had not caught up to the devaluation even by 2000. Moreover, both export and GDP growth rose sharply and relative to the comparators.

CFA Countries: Performance Indicators Relative to Comparator Countries 1992–1996 (% age p. a.)

	Average Inflation			Average Export Growth (US$)			Average Real GDP Growth		
	1992– 1993	1994	1995– 1996	1992– 1993	1994	1995– 1996	1992– 1993	1994	1995– 1996
CFA	-0.68	43.57	4.97	-7.21	0.49	17.25	-1.48	3.98	4.27
Comparators	23.96	27.28	22.33	-3.38	-2.27	2.78	-0.60	0.18	1.90

Note: Countries were included on the basis of data availability. CFA countries are Benin, Cameroon,*Chad,*Côte d'Ivoire,*Gabon, Mali, Niger, Senegal, and Togo. Comparator countries are Gambia, Ghana, Mauritania,*Nigeria, and Sierra Leone. Asterisk indicates that data were not available for the GDP comparisons.

nontraded sector is small. Although labor mobility may be legally limited within the zones, it probably is sufficient in border areas to offset demand shifts in border trade between the member countries.

These currency areas generally have not replaced the local currency, as Panama has done; rather, they have fixed the exchange rate of the local currency. The legal formation of the currency area thus did not eliminate the costs of exchanging currency for transactions with France (in the case of the CFA zones) and the United States (in the case of the Eastern Caribbean Central Bank), as is true for Panama and the United States, and some seignorage was retained.

More important, much of the trade and tourism of these currency areas takes place with the euro zone and the United States,
respectively, both of which limit labor mobility from the CFA zones
and the Caribbean. Demand shifts in the EU and the United States
against goods and service exports of the currency areas therefore
cannot easily be offset by labor mobility.[20] As discussed in Box 2,
the CFA Franc Zones devalued their currencies against the French
franc in 1994 to ease their adjustment process.

In adopting a fixed link to a foreign currency, countries are opting to forgo exchange rate changes as an instrument to counteract
external shocks. More than 100 developing countries, however,
have opted to retain the exchange rate as a policy instrument.[21] An
important reason would seem to be that variations in the exchange
rate can be used to help adjust to external shocks, as discussed
above. Although some of these countries are highly dollarized in
their financial systems (Table 1), their real economies probably are
less dollarized in terms of goods prices and wages.[22] A deterioration
in export prices or supply, for example, therefore can be offset partially by a depreciation, which raises export prices in local currency relative to wages and other local costs and thereby tends to
maintain the local currency value of exports. Depreciation also raises demand for import-competing and nontraded goods.

In Peru, for example, when unit values of exports fell sharply in
1998–1999 (and export supply fell because of weather conditions),
the exchange rate was allowed to depreciate nearly 30 percent
against the U.S. dollar. The consumer price index rose less than 10
percent from December 1997 to December 1999 and less than 4
percent in the following year, however, implying that a significant
change in relative prices occurred, despite the high degree of financial dollarization in Peru. Peru's case perhaps is somewhat unusual
(see also Hausmann, Panizza, and Stein [1999]):

> Countries that say they allow their exchange rate to float
> mostly do not—there seems to be an epidemic case of "fear of
> floating." Relative to more committed floaters—such as the
> United States, Australia, and Japan—observed exchange rate
> variability is low. The low variability of the nominal exchange
> rate does not owe to the absence of real or nominal shocks in
> these economies—indeed, relative to the United States and
> Japan, most of these countries are subject to larger, more fre-
> quent shocks to their terms of trade. . . . The low relative
> exchange rate variability stems from deliberate policy actions
> to stabilize the exchange rate. Reserve variability . . . is
> very high. Interest rate volatility (both real and nominal) is

significantly higher . . . [than for] the "true[r]" floaters. . . . [I]n most cases there is no correlation between commodity prices and the exchange rate—consistent with the view that the exchange rate may not be allowed to adjust in response to terms of trade shocks. (Calvo and Reinhart 2000).

Thus, many developing countries do not seem to have changed their behavior much from the Bretton Woods days of the pegged regimes—despite their claims of a more flexible approach to exchange rate management.

Why do countries with notionally flexible rates not allow more flexibility in their exchange rate? Concerns over financial sector stability in dollarized countries, maintenance of an attractive exchange rate for exporters, and credibility in policy seem the most likely answers. Once a country's banking system contains a large fraction of loans and deposits in foreign currency, the government obviously will be concerned that a depreciation would generate nonperforming assets and, possibly, bank runs. Similar pressures against devaluation exist when the overseas liabilities of the public sector and private sector entities are large. While the government may try to avoid devaluation by tightening money and by intervening in the foreign exchange market,[23] tighter money imposes higher costs on a different group of borrowers—those in local currency—and may increase banks' nonperforming loans. The decision of whether to try to maintain the exchange rate or to depreciate imposes different costs on different groups of borrowers, and may require a political tradeoff. The variations in the monetary/exchange rate policy followed by countries in East and Southeast Asia at different times during the 1997 Asian crisis probably reflect their recognition of this tradeoff (World Bank 2000a). Finally, it is worth noting that the pressures are not just against depreciation: real appreciation would hurt exporters, which may be an important pressure group. In sum, financial sector concerns and political economy pressures probably are major reasons for "fear of floating."

Maintaining credibility in monetary policy is another reason why countries may limit exchange rate movements. A floating exchange rate is a sensitive and easily sampled indicator of shifts in monetary policy. To demonstrate their concern for monetary stability, countries may try to limit exchange rate movements.

Attempts to defend a constant exchange rate raise three issues. First, the attempt to limit exchange rate variability tends to increase the variability of domestic currency interest rates (Calvo and Reinhart 2000; Hausmann, Panizza, and Stein 1999). Increased interest rate variability in turn would encourage dollarization through asset substitution—although dollarization would still be less than if a foreign currency were adopted. It is not clear if the greater interest rate variability that results from limiting exchange variability is a greater or lesser incentive to residents to support dollarization than is a truly floating rate with inflation or monetary targeting. A floating rate, in comparison to an exchange regime in which the country maintains a relatively fixed exchange rate, also may decrease the supply of external lending and may discourage demand for foreign currency loans.

Second, government attempts to fix the exchange rate would encourage unhedged foreign currency borrowing. They also would decrease the demand for private hedging services. This in turn would reduce returns to hedging services and discourage their development.[24]

Third, and perhaps most important, there remains the risk that countries would try to defend a peg even after the fundamentals have changed. This would lead to all the well-known problems of the Bretton Woods system: misaligned exchange rates, one-way bets by speculators against them, high domestic currency interest rates, incentives for excessive external borrowing to avoid high interest rates, and interventions in current and capital transactions to protect the peg. Excessive defense of an exchange rate peg thus would reduce the very benefits supposedly gained by not adopting a foreign currency.

Currency Boards

Benefits and Costs in the Search for Credibility

Most countries that recently have legally adopted a foreign currency appear to have done so mainly to generate quick credibility in monetary stability, without necessarily considering the relative size and frequency of the different types of shocks discussed above.[25] Most also adopted a currency by creating a currency board. Under a currency board, the exchange rate is fixed and the central bank cannot increase base money, except as the public exchanges foreign currency for local currency. In effect, the currency board forgoes the ability to use the exchange rate to offset foreign shocks in favor of obtaining credibility.

Argentina, Bulgaria, Ecuador, Estonia, and Lithuania all had experienced relatively high inflation, Argentina and Ecuador for many years, before legally adopting a foreign currency. All five countries quickly reduced inflation and broke inflationary expectations, Argentina perhaps most dramatically (Figure 2). Estonia also sought to emphasize its links to the EU by linking its currency to the Deutschemark; its performance was better than that of its Baltic neighbors (see Table 1 and Balino and Enoch [1997]). With the exception of Ecuador, which dollarized, these countries all adopted a currency board. As Ghosh, Guide, and Wolf (2000) summarize (see also Balino and Enoch [1997]):

> Modern currency boards have often been instituted to gain credibility following a period of high or hyper-inflation, and in this regard have been remarkably successful. Countries with currency boards have experienced lower inflation and higher (if more volatile) GDP growth compared to both floating regimes and simple pegs. . . . The GDP growth effect is significant, but may simply reflect a rebound from depressed levels.

The currency board yields the benefit of rapid reduction in inflation without large loss of output by speeding up the slow adjustment of inflationary expectations that usually accompanies stabilization. A currency board can provide instant credibility in monetary stability through the elimination of discretionary monetary policy and central bank financing of government deficits. It eliminates discretion in monetary policy by fixing the exchange rate and strictly linking the expansion of monetary liabilities to gains or losses in international reserves at that exchange rate.

Figure 2. Argentina Annual Inflation Rate, 1989–1995

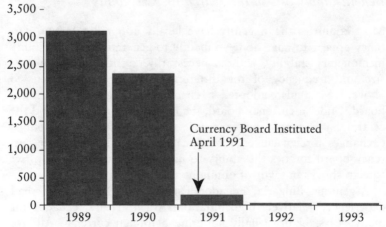

In contrast to a currency board, a traditional central bank can lend discretionarily to the government or to financial institutions. This increases aggregate demand, generating upward pressure on prices, wages, and the exchange rate. In many countries, persistent government use of expansionary monetary policies has led to high inflation and loss of confidence in monetary stability. Some countries have adopted currency boards specifically to counteract a history of such problems.

The currency board also ensures that a balance of payments deficit automatically will tighten monetary policy as the public exchanges local currency for foreign currency, and thereby will tend to close the deficit. The currency board thus guarantees that monetary policy will be directed toward maintaining the value of the currency—that is, toward correcting a balance of payments deficit (or surplus) rather than toward domestic monetary policy objectives—a guarantee that is critical to sustaining a fixed exchange rate (Obstfeld and Rogoff 1995).

An additional confidence-boosting feature of the currency board is its ability to provide convertibility for all its monetary liabilities (the money base).[26] International reserves are unlikely to be sufficient to cover bank deposits, however. In the event of a financial crisis or a crisis of confidence in the currency board itself, demands on the currency board for foreign exchange could become as large as deposits in the financial system—that is, could substantially exceed base money. A cumulative destabilizing process thus could develop in which conversion of domestic deposits to foreign currency, to take advantage of the fixed exchange rate, creates pressure for liquidity support of banks and a further loss of confidence in the maintenance of the currency board. The result is a feedback into further demands for foreign currency. Such a crisis developed in Argentina in 2001, when the public lost confidence in the ability of the government to service its debt (a substantial part of the banks' assets) and to sustain the currency board peg.

The adoption of a currency board or a foreign currency clearly requires the political will to give up discretionary monetary and exchange rate policy and inflationary finance of government deficits, as Williamson (1995) emphasizes. However, it also yields a relatively rapid payback, in terms of credibility, that translates into lower interest rates. In other words, the adoption of a currency board or a foreign currency changes the intertemporal tradeoff between stabilization and inflation. This change is not without cost: in giving up monetary and fiscal policy and linking itself to a foreign currency, the country leaves itself open to exchange rate misalignment and is unable to take action against recessions generated by lack of domestic demand. However, this cost is probably low, given that in the typical country adopting a currency board previous monetary and fiscal policy has led to chronic instability and foreign and domestic investors have lost confidence in the government's use of these policies.

This discussion of costs and benefits raises the question of whether a currency board (or adoption of a foreign currency) is needed to limit government borrowing as a source of inflation, or whether another approach could be used that is not linked to the exchange rate.

Fiscal Alternatives to Currency Boards, and Government Financing Issues

One possible alternative approach to currency boards has been to limit government domestic borrowing, the idea being that offshore lenders will provide fiscal discipline.[27] Such rules have proved difficult to enforce, however, and have the added detriments of encouraging foreign borrowing and preventing the development of a domestic government debt market.[28]

A second alternative has been fiscal responsibility laws to limit budget deficits. Such laws set a transparent target for budget making—say, less than 3 percent of GDP. In practice, though, these laws are hard to enforce, both because of budget slippage and, more important, because of difficulties in assigning responsibility and penalties for failure to meet the target.

A third approach has been to legally limit the central bank's credit to the that is, to focus on the lender rather than on the borrower. This approach is likely to be more effective because the central bank governor can be held responsible for making loans that exceed the legal limit. To be effective, however, such a rule also requires limits on central bank use of government debt for monetary policy purposes.[29] Even then, the central bank can make loans to commercial banks that permit them to buy government debt. Another potential flaw in this approach, from the standpoint of credibility, is that it could be superseded by another law more easily than it would be to go off a currency board. Nonetheless, a law limiting central bank lending to the government, combined with an independent central bank with responsibility for monetary stability, may be a substitute for a currency board in terms of limiting inflation from government deficits.

A strong domestic government debt market is a desirable adjunct to a currency board, and also is desirable in a country with legal limits on central bank finance of the government. Without access to seignorage, government deficits can be financed only by selling bonds domestically or by borrowing externally. Domestic debt sales reduce the currency risk and the risk associated with reliance on volatile international capital flows.[30]

Whether the loss of seignorage under a currency board is a benefit or cost is a complex question. The loss of the power to generate seignorage is, strictly speaking, a loss, but seignorage is a power that needs to be used sparingly, to keep inflation low, and losing it therefore may not be a great cost. Put another way, the costs of reliance on the inflation tax for deficit finance are high, in terms of distortions, resources devoted to avoiding it, and adverse distributional consequences, so giving up that reliance may not be a great loss. Moreover, currency and asset substitution tend to limit seignorage, even without a currency board.

The extent to which the currency board generates seignorage offshore also is a complex question. The public in the country with a currency board must be a net exporter or borrower offshore to increase its money base. However, the counterpart of the public's increased money holdings is increased international reserves, which usually are held as interest-bearing debt. Thus, the public in the country with the currency board effectively is exchanging goods or liabilities for interest-bearing assets that are held by their government.[31]

Financial Sector Issues under Currency Boards

A major benefit of the currency board—as long as it remains credible—is lower interest rates, as discussed previously with regard to asset substitution. Domestic interest rates decline because of the reduction in the expected rates of depreciation and inflation; they also decline because of reduction in the spread over international interest rates (see Figure 3, Balino and Enoch [1997], and van Beek et al. [2000]). The reduction in this spread presumably comes from greater credibility of the exchange rate and the corresponding reduction in concerns about failures of stabilization programs and sudden devaluation. (Failed stabilization programs and unexpected devaluation generate large spreads over foreign interest rates in developing countries from time to time—the so-called "peso problem.") The difficulties in reducing high real interest rates and spreads within conventional stabilization programs, and their impact on the fiscal position, have often led to failures of these programs.

It is important to note that a currency board eliminates neither the spread over international rates nor the widening of spreads in times of potential crisis. The risk remains that the country will go off the currency board, particularly should capital outflows under the currency board be tightening money at a time when domestic considerations would favor a more expansionary policy.[32] Foreign and domestic asset holders take account of this risk and thus demand higher risk premiums in such times. In Hong Kong, for example, the spread between foreign and domestic interest rates widened during the Asian crisis (Figure 3a). Similarly, in Argentina, the spread widened after the Mexican crisis (Figure 3b). The spread on peso instruments widened somewhat more than the spread in dollars, presumably reflecting the difference in the market's expectation of a devaluation alone and a devaluation combined with an elimination of domestic dollar accounts. In Argentina, the spread widened again toward the end of 2000, in both pesos and dollars, as expectations developed regarding the default risk of Argentine government debt and possible exit from the currency board. Both expectations were fulfilled in 2001.

As discussed, a currency board, strictly defined, implies no independent monetary policy, as is obviously the case if a foreign currency is adopted. In practice, countries with currency boards have not strictly followed this rule, but deviations at least have been relatively short and small: countries typically have attempted to tighten or loosen monetary policy by varying the reserve requirement, though the openness of the capital account limits the impact of this strategy.[33]

Countries with currency boards also must eliminate the lender of last resort function. Again, in practice, this has not always been the case. For example, in Estonia and Bulgaria, excess international reserves have been given to a "banking department" in the currency board, which can use them to provide liquidity to banks. Argentina took a number of actions to support its banking system when it was affected by Mexico's 1994–1995 crisis, eventually being forced to seek support from the International Monetary Fund (IMF) (Balino and Enoch 1997). Generally speaking, however, the extent of such lender of last resort arrangements is limited under a currency board; given the difficulties of carrying out the function in open developing countries, with their limited governance, this may be a good thing.[34]

The limits of the lender of last resort function and discretionary monetary policy raise the issue of the location of responsibility for other traditional central bank functions, such as bank regulation, bank supervision, and intervention and resolution of weak banks. These functions have accrued to the central bank as part of their lender of last resort and monetary policy functions, and because

Figure 3a. Hong Kong and U.S. T-bill Rates

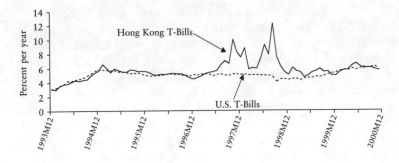

Figure 3b. Argentina and U.S. Money Market Rates

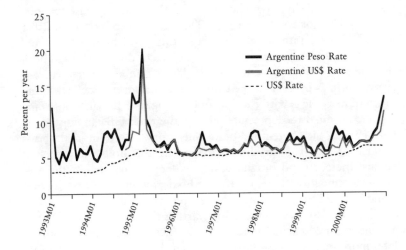

only central banks can quickly provide the resources needed to support liquidity-constrained weak banks. The currency board gives up these functions. If it were to retain an involvement in the traditional central bank regulatory and supervisory functions, concerns might increase that the currency board would be called upon to provide resources in the event of a banking crisis. This would reduce its credibility. Adoption of a currency board thus requires a reconsideration of the locus of financial regulation and supervision, and of the approach to and provision of resources for bank resolution.

Currency Boards and the Exchange Rate

The initial exchange rate is a critical issue in the setup of a currency board. All currency boards have begun with a fixed rate against a single currency. In theory, the rate could be fixed against a basket of currencies, thus providing some insurance against exchange rate misalignment, but this policy could lead investors and asset holders to question the computation of the basket. In theory, the rate could be adjustable, but in practice this would allow the government to create room for expansionary monetary policy by depreciating—an option that would reduce the currency board's credibility.[35] For these reasons, as well as simplicity, countries have linked their currency board to a single currency.

The choice of a currency for the link and the initial exchange rate thus are critical to avoid exchange rate misalignment.[36] Countries generally have chosen to fix their rate against the currency of a major trading partner. The main exceptions as of 2001 were Djibouti, Lithuania, and Argentina, which in 1991 fixed against the dollar because of its high degree of dollarization in both the real and financial sector and the lack of an alternative currency. Argentina's trade with the United States is not particularly large: much of its trade is with Europe and its neighbor Brazil, whose currency continued to depreciate against the dollar. Beginning in the late 1990s, the Argentine peso thus appreciated in real terms against its non-U.S. trading partners as the dollar appreciated against the euro and Brazil's currency depreciated against the dollar. Argentine growth also was hurt by declining export prices that could not be countered under the currency board.

There is also an argument for starting the currency board with an undervalued exchange rate. A currency board tends to stimulate more net capital inflows, which by increasing aggregate demand and inflation tend to appreciate the real exchange rate and reduce the current account position. Starting with an undervalued rate would tend to improve the current account initially, and thus might help establish credibility. It also would serve to increase the ratio of international reserves to the domestic money stock, even though such a rate ultimately may lead to higher and more prolonged inflation.

In recent years, interest has focused on ways to exit from a currency board—especially given Argentina's difficulties and exit (although Argentina's problems also relate to an excessive debt buildup relative to the tax base). Exiting is, first of all, a political issue: when economic performance is good, there is no incentive to

exit, but when performance is bad, attempts to exit are likely only
to add to the loss of confidence. In addition, the initial setup of a
currency board involves legal if not constitutional foundations, and
changing these foundations is likely to be time consuming and is
likely to cause capital outflow during the period of debate, as discussed above and as occurred in the case of Argentina. The final
issue is how to exit: as noted, some countries have shifted the peg
of the currency board, but returning to discretionary monetary policy is likely to raise even more concerns among investors.

Summary

Dollarization has grown sharply over the 1990s, with the increase
in international trade and financial flows generating more access to
foreign currency assets and loans, both onshore and offshore. The
U.S. dollar, Deutschemark, and Swiss franc currency held offshore
in 1999 may have been 25–36 percent of local currency outside the
United States, Germany, Japan, and Switzerland. Foreign currency
deposits exceed 50 percent of bank deposits in some developing
countries, and 20 percent in many others; in many countries, offshore deposits and loans range from 20 percent to 50 percent of
onshore deposits. Dollarization is particularly prevalent in Latin
America and in the transition economies, where monetary instability has been high.

The large volume of currency and asset substitution reflects the
attempts by individuals and firms to protect themselves against
monetary instability, political instability, and weak banking systems. Tax avoidance also plays a role in offshore deposits, and large
volumes of foreign currency are used in illicit activities, ranging
from corruption to narcotics. As the volume of currency and asset
substitution grows, the infrastructure for making transactions in
foreign exchange also seems to improve. The result has been that in
some Latin American countries with long histories of inflation,
even a return to monetary stability has not reversed dollarization.
In a few transition economies where experience with inflation has
been shorter, asset substitution appears to have reversed initially,
when monetary stability was restored and the banking system
strengthened. In some of these countries asset substitution is now
on the rise.

Currency and asset substitution involve both benefits and costs.
Dollarization allows domestic asset holders and borrowers to diversify risks and avoid the inflation tax that especially hits the poor.

However, in public finances it also shrinks the base for seignorage, meaning that countries either must curb their fiscal deficits or risk a spiral of higher inflation and further increases in currency and asset substitution.

In the financial sector, asset substitution tends to increase the availability of funds for intermediation in monetarily unstable economies and eases cash flow problems associated with the high and variable interest rates that prevail under inflation. Foreign currency loans, with their lower interest rates, have longer effective maturities than local currency loans. Borrowers pay only the cost of actual devaluations, and this cost, when it occurs, is in effect indexed in the amortization of loans over time. In contrast, local currency loans will reflect any expected inflation and devaluation upfront in their high interest rate. The variability of interest costs also is likely to be less on foreign currency loans.

Asset substitution also introduces a number of risks. Given the limited possibilities for hedging in developing countries, financial institutions may take unhedged foreign exchange exposure or, more commonly, will match liabilities and assets in foreign exchange. The fact that many of the borrowers in foreign exchange lack assured access to that exchange means that their borrowings entail substantial credit risk for the lender. These risks may be substantially underestimated, and it is important to ask whether the borrowers and lenders consider the possibilities of a general default and bailout. Given that governments are often major borrowers in foreign currency, their possible underestimate of currency risk and the possibility that the international financial architecture encourages excessive lending are important issues.

Whatever the balance of the costs and benefits of currency and asset substitution, efforts to curb these practices may be neither effective nor desirable, given today's globalizing economy. Relatively stable economies perhaps can restrict currency and asset substitution, de facto and de jure, and at limited cost to their citizens, while at the same time allowing the public sector and larger private firms to borrow offshore to reduce their costs and to diversify. Where inflation is high and banking systems weak, however, the incentives to avoid the inflation tax and to obtain more loans and lower-interest loans make currency and asset substitution difficult to resist. Chile, Colombia, and Brazil have sought to limit domestic asset substitution not only with legislation, but in part by creating indexed instruments—although these instruments, in effect a nondomestic-currency-denominated asset, have created their own problems in times of instability.

Inflationary economies often have allowed domestic foreign currency deposits to broaden the distribution of their benefits, rather than limiting those benefits to the public sector, which can borrow offshore, to individuals with access to foreign currency through trade and travel, and to those willing to break the law. Prolonged capital controls tend to be ineffective and have undesirable consequences for income distribution and governance, particularly in unstable economies where the incentives for dollarization are high.

Since 1990, eight developing countries have legally adopted either a foreign currency (East Timor, Ecuador, and El Salvador) or a currency board (Argentina, Bosnia and Herzegovina, Bulgaria, Estonia, and Lithuania). In so doing, they have joined the developing countries of the two CFA Franc Zones in Africa, the Eastern Caribbean Central Bank group, and Bhutan, Djibouti, Lesotho, Namibia, and Panama in dollarizing well beyond spontaneous asset and currency substitution. In legally adopting a foreign currency, these countries have given up discretionary monetary policy and the capability to manipulate the exchange rate to protect against international shocks. Their choice stands in contrast to that of the more than 100 developing economies that have opted to retain some degree of exchange rate flexibility—in some cases, despite having substantial foreign currency deposits onshore and offshore, and despite being engaged in substantial offshore borrowing. In practice, many of these countries use monetary policy to stabilize the exchange rate. This "fear of floating" is a policy that tends to offset some of the benefits of a flexible exchange rate, and which by stimulating expectations of a stable exchange rate also may encourage foreign-currency-denominated borrowing and limit the development of hedging facilities.

In most of the eight countries that recently have adopted a foreign currency or currency board, the choice of a fixed exchange rate and elimination of discretionary monetary policy seems not to have been based on a balancing of the costs and benefits related to the size and frequency of internal and external shocks, on country size, or on resource mobility as laid out in Mundell's classic work on optimum currency areas. In most cases, the decision seems to have been based on a desire to quickly establish credibility in monetary stability and thus to realize the benefits of that credibility—namely, lower interest rates and faster recovery than would be possible under conventional stabilization programs.[37] In general, these countries seem to have enjoyed these benefits. The cost of giving up discretionary monetary and exchange rate policy, furthermore, may

not seem to them too high, given their past experience with inflation, failed stabilization, and nominal exchange rate movements
that mostly were adjustments to inflation.

Currency boards and the adoption of a foreign currency not only
involve all the issues associated with currency and asset substitution, but also raise a number of their own issues. First, they may not
be necessary. Although there have been no controlled experiments,
it may be possible to obtain credibility by legally reducing excessive
central bank lending to the government (often a major source of
monetary instability) through central bank independence and limiting the central bank's support of government debt sales. This could
be done without abandoning the use of the exchange rate as an
external shock absorber. There are, however, many problems in
defining the limits to support of debt sales, just as there have been
problems using fiscal responsibility laws to limit government
deficits.

Second, while currency boards can sharply reduce interest rates,
they do not eliminate spreads over international rates. Spreads
remain large in the years before the board becomes well established, and also in times of crisis. Neither currency boards nor the
adoption of a foreign currency can reduce interest rates when concerns arise over excessive debt burdens, internal or external, and
defaults—junk bonds, after all, have higher interest rates than does
government debt. Argentina's recent history provides an obvious
example of this problem and raises the unexplored issue of the
potential of a currency board to create knife-edge problems, where
loss of faith in the banking system and the currency board lead to
increasing pressures on the board.

Third, the limits that a currency board or adoption of a foreign
currency places on fiscal deficits are even stricter than those created
by currency and asset substitution, making fiscal discipline and
development of a domestic government debt market even more
important. Reliance on variable offshore borrowing creates liquidity risk. The recent Asian and Argentine crises also raise questions
about the discipline provided by external lenders under the current
international financial architecture.

Fourth, the choice of the base currency and the rate at which to
fix initially are clearly important. And finally, a number of
observers have raised the issue of the process of exiting from a currency board once credibility has been restored. There is little political incentive to exit when economic performance is good, and periods of poor performance are exactly when the credibility of monetary policy becomes an issue.

In the financial sector, the adoption of a foreign currency or currency board limits the central bank's ability to exercise the lender of last resort function. Again, countries that have suffered problems arising from indiscriminate use of this function may not consider this limitation much of a loss. However, the central bank often plays an important initial role in dealing with financial sector crises because of its ability to issue a large volume of monetary liabilities. Adoption of a foreign currency or currency board requires that decisions be made about how to deal with a bank crisis, how to reduce its costs, and how to swiftly and transparently allocate those costs. The elimination of the central bank's monetary policy function furthermore raises the questions of whether the supervisory function should remain in the currency board and how it should be linked to any deposit insurance scheme.

Dollarization thus involves a complex mixture of costs and benefits. Although it creates a number of macroeconomic issues, private dollarization generates benefits to individuals and firms, and domestic availability of foreign-currency-denominated assets increases the access to those benefits. Moreover, attempts to restrict private dollarization currency controls may be hard to enforce and may generate corruption and adverse distributional shifts, particularly in unstable monetary environments. Public dollarization—the legal adoption of a foreign currency or a currency board—generates an even more complex mix of costs and benefits and thus is an even more complicated issue; its advisability depends very much on specific country conditions.

Notes

1. A few inflationary countries, notably Brazil, Chile, and Colombia in the 1960s, adopted crawling pegs.

2. These estimates of offshore currency holdings are indirect and are equal to the difference between the amount of U.S. dollar currency outside U.S. banks and the estimated currency held by U.S. residents. The large differences in estimates reflect differences in the approaches to estimating the currency holdings of U.S. residents.

3. Some of the offshore holdings of these currencies were in commercial banks.

4. In Bolivia, the use of dollars seems related to coca production (Melvin and Ladman 1991).

5. For the definitional distinctions between asset substitution and currency substitution in the literature see McKinnon (1996) and Mizen and

Pentecost (1996). Savastano (1992, 1996) and Calvo and Vegh (1992) develop and extend the basic currency and substitution model, examine the issues that it raises, and summarize some of the empirical regularities.

6. The availability of domestic assets paying realistic returns in Brazil and Chile seems to have deterred such outflows, at least initially, compared to Argentina, Mexico, and Venezuela. See Dooley et al. (1986).

7. Again note that offshore deposits tend to be underestimated. During this period, Latin Americans made significant deposits in Panama, and Brazilians and Argentines also made deposits in Uruguay, often using Uruguayan addresses or agents. Savastano's deposit figures (1992) for the 1970s cover only U.S. banks.

8. Data are from the Bank for International Settlements (nonbank deposits in OECD banks), Banco Central de la República Argentina, Banco Central de la República del Peru, *International Financial Statistics*, Beckerman (1987), and Kamin and Ericsson (1998). No Bank for International Settlements data exist on offshore deposits by Bolivia's non-bank sector in 1981 and 1982. The asset data are end-year and GDP data are for the corresponding year, to avoid problems associated with large devaluations at year-end. Savastano (1992) notes that major shifts in asset holdings also occurred within years, such as the increases in foreign currency deposits in Bolivia, Mexico, and Peru before large devaluations and the elimination of such deposits during the first half of the 1980s.

9. Exchange rates affect the relative values of local-currency- and foreign-currency-denominated deposits, whether the figures are reported relative to GDP or in U.S. dollars. Years of increasing undervaluation tend to produce rises in the ratio of dollar deposits to domestic deposits and to GDP, even if dollar deposits are roughly stable in U.S. dollars. With overvaluation, the reverse occurs.

10. Savastano (1992) argues that the introduction of foreign currency deposits eventually reduces the holding of domestic money balances by residents and introduces more instability in the demand for domestic money.

11. Note again that overvaluation or undervaluation of the exchange rate can affect the relative sizes of domestic and foreign currency deposits measured in the same currency. Also, legal restrictions on holdings of foreign currency assets may increase the underreporting of such assets.

12. See, for example, Guidotti and Rodriguez (1992), Kamin and Ericsson (1998), Redding and Morales (1999), and Uribe (1997) for discussions of this phenomenon and some empirical estimates, mostly of U.S. dollar deposit holdings.

13. Uribe (1997) and Redding and Morales (1999) demonstrate the possibility of multiple equilibria in the relative volumes of assets in the two currencies.

14. The word "seignorage," as used here, describes the ability of the government to obtain resources through its monopoly power of fiat

monetary issue (see, for example, the discussion in Fischer [1982]). In practice, seignorage occurs when the government spends issues of currency or funds borrowed from the central bank. In so doing, it thereby obtains goods and services without either taxing or selling bonds to the public; the public accepts these claims because they are legally defined as money; and, in the end, the public's saving to acquire the additional nominal amounts of (base) money to keep up with inflation and economic growth "makes room" for the government's purchases. The demand for additional money can come from real income growth or inflation (the latter is sometimes called the inflation tax). Seignorage largely reflects currency demand but the government also can earn seignorage from required reserves and liquidity requirements on deposits: for these items, the amount of the government's seignorage depends on the rate of return the government pays on them, compared to market rates.

15. See Fischer (1982) and Hanson (1995) for some estimates.

16. Seignorage may still be earned on the reserves that banks hold on their foreign currency deposits, but the amounts depend on the size of the required reserves, the remuneration on them, and the form in which the central bank holds the reserves, as noted above. Even if the central bank uses the banks' required reserves to hold international reserves, seignorage can exist, provided that the interest earned on the international reserves exceeds that paid on the banks' reserves.

17. See Mussa et al. (2000). Broadly speaking, hedging in developing countries is limited: the smallness of the market may lead to market power, constraints often exist on the ability of banks to do foreign exchange hedging, and residents with access to foreign exchange may choose to sell it directly or use it to self-hedge their own activities. Hedging therefore mostly depends on nonresidents and is discouraged by the difficulty of collecting on contracts in the context of the weak legal framework in most countries. Small offshore futures markets have existed in a few currencies in the United States, Singapore, and Hong Kong. Governments sometimes offer hedges, often at subsidized rates, but these have proved costly, particularly in crises (for example, in Thailand in 1997).

18. If export supply falls, the floating rate similarly provides more insulation than the fixed rate.

19. If wages and prices were completely flexible, there would be no difference between the fixed- and floating-rate regimes in adjusting to shocks. One way of looking at the difference between flexible and exchange rates is that they generate different short-run adjustment processes during the period when wages and prices are imperfectly flexible.

20. The two CFA Franc Zones receive preferential treatment of their primary exports by the EU, which to some extent limits the impact of demand shifts in the EU. The U.S.–Caribbean Initiative reduces tariffs against Caribbean exporters.

21. In the IMF's new terminology, this includes the developing countries within the following classifications: more conventional peg arrangements, crawling pegs, pegs within bands of various types, and managed or independent floats. Developing countries are defined in Box 1.

22. Prices in dollarized economies—especially prices of durable goods and housing—often are set in dollars. This policy affects the demands for local- and foreign-denominated currency and assets. However, the real question for the choice of exchange rate regime is the degree to which prices and wages are flexible, whatever their currency denomination. For example, a car may be priced in U.S. dollars in a dollarized economy, but that price may vary with changes in aggregate demand.

23. To avoid devaluation, a government may passively allow central bank sales of foreign exchange to reduce the money base, and it may try to reinforce this tendency through active policy measures, such as open market sales, higher discount rates, or higher reserve requirements. An obvious question is to what extent and for how long the government in a small economy with an open capital market can affect monetary conditions without allowing the exchange rate to move. This question is another version of Obstfeld's trilemma (Obstfeld and Rogoff 1995).

24. The question remains of whether the potential trading volume in foreign exchange in most developing countries is inherently too small to support effective markets for foreign exchange. This concern is one of Mundell's rationales for forming an optimum currency area.

25. El Salvador adopted the U.S. dollar after inflation had fallen and taking into account its highly dollarized economy. East Timor adopted the U.S dollar and Bosnia and Herzegovina (as part of the Dayton accords) adopted a currency board as simple, transparent monetary arrangements that did not require a large central bank.

26. This is because international reserves need to be at least as large as base money to start a currency board. In practice, most countries adopting a currency board have had international reserves that exceeded the money base by 25 percent or more.

27. Argentina's massive debt buildup and default in 2001 and the buildup of debt that preceded the Asian crisis have raised questions of whether offshore lenders provide sufficient discipline under the existing international financial architecture.

28. Indonesia had a government decree along these lines from 1967 to the mid-1990s, and ran up large foreign debts to bilateral and multilateral lenders to finance its deficits. The government also made large off-budget expenditures, so the system was not very transparent and thus not very credible. Although Indonesia's overall budget deficits, including the off-budget expenditures, were probably limited by the directive, inflation was in double digits in almost every year from 1973 to 1984.

29. For example, Peru's 1993 Central Bank Law prohibits Central Bank purchases of primary government debt issues and limits secondary market purchases, which presumably would be for monetary policy purposes, to 5 percent of base money in the previous year. In practice, the Central Bank has used its own debt for open market operations, as a domestic government debt market only began operation in 2001.

30. Sale of domestic government bonds is not seignorage, provided the purchase is undertaken freely. In such a case, the buyer is freely exchanging current purchasing power for the promise of a future income. However, regulations that make government debt more desirable, for example, that require holdings of government debt under liquidity requirements, contain an element of seignorage, since the interest rate paid by the government is reduced by the regulations.

31. Note that when a country adopts a foreign country's currency (as opposed to a currency board, seignorage is paid to the country issuing the currency. In recognition of this, South Africa pays Lesotho a sum in lieu of seignorage. Note also that in a currency union, such as the EU or the unification of East and West Germany, the unifying parties forgo their seignorage but agree on the division of the seignorage earned by the joint currency as well as on the rules for monetary policy.

32. Changing the exchange rate in a currency board regime is far more difficult, and costly, than changing an adjustable exchange rate peg, but it can occur. By legally adopting a foreign currency this risk can be reduced, but as experience shows, the risk remains that the deposits can be reconverted into a local currency.

33. In December 1994, as the crisis in Mexico led to capital outflows from Argentina and to banking sector problems, Argentina lowered the reserve requirement. Contrast this with 1992, when the country let interest rates rise when outflows developed. Eventually, Argentina was forced to respond to the 1995 crisis by tightening money and entering into an IMF program.

34. In the 1997–1998 Asian crisis, massive central bank support of financial institutions contributed to exchange rate pressures and the large overhang of government debt (World Bank 2000a).

35. Osband and Villanueva (1993) raise the possibility of using a decelerating crawling peg to start the currency board. This would allow the government to obtain additional reserves from the capital inflows that follow the formation of a currency board. However, such a crawl would raise concerns about monetary policy, especially given the failures of the schemes to reduce inflationary expectations in the Southern Cone of Latin America in the late 1970s and early 1980s with preannounced, declining rates of depreciation (the "tablitas," discussed in Corbo and de Melo [1985] and Balino and Enoch [1997]).

36. Occasionally, the base currency or the exchange rate in a currency board has been changed. The Eastern Caribbean Currency Authority, the predecessor to the Eastern Caribbean Central Bank, shifted the base currency from the pound sterling to the U.S. dollar in 1976. In 2001, Argentina added the euro to the computation of the exchange rate for the current account. The CFA zones devalued their exchange rate against the base currency (see Box 2), and Djibouti devalued twice.

37. Some of the countries also appear to have wanted to limit the costs involved in establishing a full-scale central bank.

References

The word *processed* describes informally produced works that may not be commonly available through libraries.

Ariyoshi, A., K. Habermeier, B. Laurens, I. Otker-Robe, J. Canales-Krijenko, and A. Kirilenko. 2000. "Capital Controls: Country Experiences with Their Use and Liberalization." International Monetary Fund (IMF) Occasional Paper 190. Washington, D.C.

Balino, T., A. Bennett, and E. Borensztein. 1999. "Monetary Policy in Dollarized Economies." IMF Occasional Paper 171. Washington, D.C.

Balino, T., and C. Enoch. 1997. "Currency Board Arrangements, Issues, and Experiences." IMF Occasional Paper 151. Washington, D.C.

Beckerman, P. 1987. "Inflation and Dollar Accounts in Peru's Banking System, 1978–1984." *World Development* 15(8):1087–106.

———. 2001. "Dollarization and Semi-Dollarization in Ecuador." Policy Research Department, Policy Research Working Paper 2643. World Bank, Washington, D.C.

Calvo, G., and C. Reinhart. 2000. "Fear of Floating." National Bureau of Economic Research (NBER) Working Paper 7993. Cambridge, Mass.

Calvo, G., and C. Vegh. 1992. "Currency Substitution in Developing Countries: An Introduction." *Revista de Análisis Económico* 7(1):3–27.

Caprio, G., and D. Klingebiel. 2002. "Episodes of Systemic and Borderline Banking Crises." In D. Klingebiel and L. Laeven, eds., *Managing the Real and Fiscal Effects of Banking Crises.* World Bank Discussion Paper 428. World Bank, Washington, D.C.

Corbo, V., and J. de Melo, eds. 1985. *Liberalization with Stabilization in the Southern Cone of Latin America.* Special issue of *World Development* 13(8).

Devarajan, S., and J. de Melo. 1987. "Evaluating Participation in African Monetary Unions: A Statistical Analysis of the CFA Zones." *World Development* 15(4):483–96.

Devarajan, S., and L. E. Hinkle. 1994. "The CFA Franc Parity Change: An Opportunity to Restore Growth and Reduce Poverty." *Afrika Spectrum* No. 2.

Dooley, M. 1996. "A Survey of Literature on Controls over International Capital Transactions." *International Monetary Fund Staff Papers* 43(4):639–87.

Dooley, M., W. Helkie, R. Tyron, and J. Underwood. 1986. "An Analysis of the External Debt Positions of Eight Developing Countries through 1990." *Journal of Development Economics* 21(2):283–318.

Doyle, B. 2000. "Here Dollars, Dollars . . . Estimating Currency Demand and Worldwide Currency Substitution." International Finance Discussion Paper 657, Board of Governors of the Federal Reserve System, Washington D.C.

Edwards, S. 1995. "Exchange Rates, Inflation and Disinflation." In S. Edwards, ed., *Capital Controls, Exchange Rates and Monetary Policy in the World Economy.* Cambridge: Cambridge University Press.

Fischer, S. 1982. "Seignorage and the Case for a National Money." *Journal of Political Economy* 90:295–313.

———. 2001. "Exchange Rate Regimes: Is the Bipolar View Correct?" *Journal of Economic Perspectives* 15(3):3–24.

Ghosh, A., A. Guide, and H. Wolf. 2000. "Currency Boards; More than a Quick Fix?" *Economic Policy* 31:270–355.

Grossman, H., J. Hanson, and R. F. Lucas. 1982. "The Effects of Demand Disturbances under Alternative Exchange Rate Regimes." *Oxford Economic Papers* 34:78–91.

Guidotti, P., and C. Rodriguez. 1992. "Dollarization in Latin America: Gresham's Law in Reverse." *International Monetary Fund Staff Papers* 39(3):518–44.

Hanke, S., and K. Schuler. 1994. *Currency Boards for Developing Countries: A Handbook.* San Francisco: International Center for Economic Growth.

Hanson, J. 1995. "Opening the Capital Account: Costs, Benefits, and Sequencing." In S. Edwards, ed., *Capital Controls, Exchange Rates and Monetary in the World Economy.* Cambridge: Cambridge University Press.

Hausmann, R. 1999. "Should There Be Five Currencies or One Hundred and Five?" *Foreign Policy* 119:65–79.

Hausmann, R., U. Panizza, and E. Stein. 1999. "Why Do Countries Float the Way They Do?" Research Department, Inter-American Development Bank, Washington, D.C. Processed.

Honohan, P., and P. Lane. 2001. "Will the Euro Trigger More Monetary Unions in Africa?" In Charles Wyplosz, ed., *EMU: Impact on Europe and the Developing Countries.* Oxford: Oxford University Press.

Honohan, P., and A. Shi. 2001. "Deposit Dollarization and the Financial Sector in Emerging Economies." World Bank Policy Research Working Paper 2748. World Bank, Washington D.C.

IMF (International Monetary Fund). Various issues. *International Financial Statistics*. Washington, D.C.

Kamin, S., and N. Ericsson. 1998. "Dollarization in a Post-Hyperinflationary Economy." Board of Governors of the Federal Reserve System, Washington, D.C. Processed.

McKinnon, R. 1963. "Optimum Currency Areas." *American Economic Review* 53:717–25.

———. 1996. "Direct and Indirect Concepts of International Currency Substitution." In P. Mizen and E. Pentecost, eds., *The Macroeconomics of International Currencies: Theory, Policy, and Evidence*. Cheltenham, U.K.: Edward Elgar.

Melvin, M., and K. Fenske. 1992. "Dollarization and Monetary Reform: Evidence from the Cochabamba Region of Bolivia." *Revista de Análisis Económico* 7:125–38.

Melvin, M., and J. Ladman. 1991. "Coca Dollars and the Dollarization of South America." *Journal of Money, Credit, and Banking* 23(4):752–63.

Mizen, P., and E. Pentecost. 1996. "Currency Substitution in Theory and Practice." In P. Mizen and E. Pentecost, eds., *The Macroeconomics of International Currencies: Theory, Policy, and Evidence*. Cheltenham, U.K.: Edward Elgar.

Mundell, R. 1961. "A Theory of Optimum Currency Areas." *American Economic Review* 51:509–17, as reprinted in Mundell (1968).

———. 1968. *International Economics*. New York: MacMillan.

Mussa, M., P. Masson, A. Swoboda, E. Jadresic, P. Mauro, and A. Berg. 2000. "Exchange Rate Regimes in an Increasingly Integrated World Economy." IMF Occasional Paper 193. Washington, D.C.

Obstfeld, M., and K. Rogoff. 1995. "The Mirage of Fixed Exchange Rates." *Journal of Economic Perspectives* 9(4):73–96.

Osband, K. and D. Villanueva. 1993. "Independent Currency Authorities: an Analytical Primer." *International Monetary Fund Staff Papers* 40(1):202–16

Porter, R., and R. Judson. 1996. "The Location of U.S. Currency: How Much Is Abroad?" *Federal Reserve Bulletin* 86:883–903.

Redding, P., and J. Morales. 1999. "Currency Substitution and Network Externalities." University of Namur, Belgium, Department of Economics. Processed.

Rogoff, K. 1998. "Blessing or Curse? Foreign and Underground Demand for Euro Notes." *Economic Policy* 28:261–304.

Sahay, R., and C. Vegh. 1996. "Dollarization in Transition Economies: Evidence and Policy Implications." In P. Mizen and E. Pentecost, eds.,

The Macroeconomics of International Currencies: Theory, Policy, and Evidence. Cheltenham, England: Edward Elgar.

Savastano, M. 1992. "The Pattern of Currency Substitution in Latin America: An Overview." *Revista de Análisis Económico* 7(1):29–72.

———. 1996. "Dollarization in Latin America." In P. Mizen and E. Pentecost, eds., *The Macroeconomics of International Currencies: Theory, Policy, and Evidence.* Cheltenham, U.K.: Edward Elgar.

Schuler, K. 1992. "Currency Boards." Ph.D. diss. George Mason University, Fairfax, Virginia. Available online at www.erols.com/Kurrency/Webdiss1.htm

Sprenkle, C. 1993. "The Case of the Missing Currency." *Journal of Economic Perspectives* 7(4):175–84.

Uribe, M. 1997. "Hysteresis in a Simple Model of Currency Substitution." *Journal of Monetary Economics* 40:185–202.

van Beek, F., J. Rosales, M. Zermeno, R. Randall, and J. Shepard. 2000. "The Eastern Caribbean Currency Union: Institutions, Performance, and Policy Issues." IMF Occasional Paper 195. Washington, D.C.

Williamson, J. 1995. *What Role for Currency Boards?* Washington, D.C.: Institute of International Economics.

World Bank. 1985. *World Development Report: International Capital and Economic Development.* Washington, D.C.: World Bank.

———. 1993. *The East Asian Miracle.* Washington, D.C.: World Bank.

———. 1998. "Argentina Financial Sector Review 17864–AR." Washington, D.C.: World Bank.

———. 2000a. *East Asia: Recovery and Beyond,* Washington, D.C.: World Bank.

———. 2000b. *Global Development Finance 1999.* Washington, D.C.: World Bank.

Policies to Promote Saving for Retirement

Dimitri Vittas

Introduction

The main focus of this paper is the promotion, organization, and regulation of funded pillars. The paper does not examine the case for a multipillar structure, nor does it seek to assess the relative importance of different pillars.

During the 1990s nearly a score of countries, mainly in Europe and Latin America, undertook major reforms of their pension systems. Most of these reforms were in the direction of multipillar systems, the advantages of which were first articulated by Swiss experts in the early 1960s (Helbling 1991). Multipillar structures have long characterized some of the Organisation for Economic Co-operation and Development (OECD) countries, especially Switzerland and the Netherlands in continental Europe and most Anglo-American countries around the world. In the 1990s the

This is a revised and expanded version of a paper that originally was presented at a conference organized by the European Federation for Retirement Provision and the U.K. National Association of Pension Funds in Estoril, Portugal in October 1995. Variations of this paper subsequently were presented at conferences and seminars in various countries around the world. The author is indebted to Estelle James, David Lindeman, and Roberto Rocha for their comments and suggestions.

171

World Bank publicized the benefits of multipillar pension systems
for developing countries also, through the publication and dissem-
ination of a policy research report (World Bank 1994) and through
its operational work around the world (Holzmann 2000).

Contrary to some claims (Orszag and Stiglitz 2001), beyond
sharing a multipillar structure the reform programs of different
countries are far from identical. They exhibit many differences in
the relative importance of different pillars, in the way in which the
public and private pillars are organized, and in the way in which
the transition is structured and financed. There are, however, a few
basic features that the reform programs share in common. All such
programs involve (a) the restructuring and downsizing of traditional social security systems that operate as unfunded (or partially
funded) public pillars; (b) an expansion of the role of funded private pillars; (c) a willingness to allow large foreign financial institutions to play a central part in the management of accumulated
assets, often in joint ventures with large local groups; and (d) the
creation of a more robust and effective regulatory and supervisory
framework.

The financial pressures caused by demographic aging often are
used as an argument for moving from unfunded to funded pension
systems. However, demographic aging will also cause financial
pressures on funded pillars. Pension contracts are long-term contracts spanning 60 years or more, and are by definition intergener-
ational contracts whether they operate through government agencies or through financial markets.

The argument in favor of multipillar structures that underlies the
approach of this paper is based on the premise that the evaluation
of the merits and demerits of different pension pillars suffers from
what may be called "empirical agnosia." This concept is different
from "ignorance," which refers to something that some people
know but others do not. The term "agnosia" refers to things that
no one knows. Given the long span of pension contracts, one would
need data covering in excess of 100 years to be able to assess the
relative merits of each pillar. The insuperable problem that causes
the agnosia lies in the fact that technology constantly is in a state
of flux. Production technology and electronic, regulatory, financial,
and especially medical technology all would undergo radical
change over such a long period. In the unlikely event that they ever
become available, long-term data thus would be very difficult to
interpret. Empirical agnosia suggests that despite its likely costs,
diversifying across providers may be a more efficient policy, since it

would protect against the effects of a complete failure of one or other of the pillars.

It is important to emphasize a number of key points regarding pension systems:

• The primary purpose of pension systems is to pay adequate, affordable, and sustainable benefits. This encompasses both social equity and redistributive issues, since pension benefits cannot be considered adequate if they fail to address the subsistence needs of pensioners. Other considerations, such as the minimization of labor market distortions, the development of long-term savings, the deepening of capital markets, and the promotion of economic growth, are important but secondary.

• Public pillars, funded or unfunded, are needed to offer basic benefits that are independent of the performance of financial markets. Financial markets suffer from prolonged, persistent, and large deviations from long-term trends and cannot be relied upon as the sole provider of pension benefits.

• Funded pillars provide benefits that are based on long-term capital accumulation and financial market performance. They should be privately managed to minimize dependence on funded public pillars and to avoid government domination of the economy and financial markets.

• Since both public and private pillars are needed, arguing that public pillars have lower administrative costs is of little relevance. What is important is to seek arrangements that minimize the costs of both pillars while promoting higher efficiency.

• Both public and private pillars can be organized in many different forms. The structure of pension systems in different countries reflects local and historical conditions. Local conditions also shape the structure and objectives of pension reform, including the organization and financing of the transition from one system to the next. What may work well in Chile or Mexico may be totally unsuitable for Greece or Slovenia, Egypt or Tunisia. The cost of transition, the demographic structure of a country, the state of development of its financial markets, and the political acceptability of pension reform all are important variables that must be taken, and are taken, into account in shaping pension reform programs.

The paper is organized around 10 basic questions regarding the promotion of funded pillars and policies to promote saving for retirement. Most of the discussion covers the accumulation phase of pension systems, but some reference also is made to the problems that are likely to be faced during decumulation. The first question addresses the needs to provide for compulsory participation and to offer tax incentives; this is followed by a discussion of different ways in which compulsory provision and the offer of tax incentives can be structured. The remainder of the paper focuses on the different ways in which funded pillars can be organized. The paper highlights the different approaches used around the world. It also makes a number of practical suggestions regarding the implementation of policies that seek to promote retirement saving by encouraging participation in funded pillars and by ensuring the safe and efficient management of accumulated assets.

Why Compel and Induce?

Why should governments be concerned whether or not people save enough for their retirement? In any society that emphasizes personal responsibility, the decision on how to allocate one's income should be a personal decision. Out of compassion, a society could provide social assistance to those who reach old age with inadequate financial means for subsistence and survival. But why should governments wish to encourage saving for retirement that could provide higher levels of income in old age than those obtainable from social assistance?

The answer is that such policies are popular with the public, for three reasons. First, they protect society from those who, in the expectation that they will be catered for when they reach old age, fail to save. This might be called a "weak moral hazard," since society's willingness to take care of the homeless and destitute old cannot be taken for granted. The growing number of poorly catered for homeless people in most high-income countries, not to mention the large numbers of beggars in poor countries, should cast considerable doubt on the relevance of this argument. Second, such policies protect a substantial minority, or perhaps even a majority, of workers from their own shortsightedness. Third, they protect farsighted workers from footing the bill for the myopic ones (James 1998).

Whether or not people generally are myopic in their saving behavior should be empirically verifiable, but there are no hard data to enable such verification. In the absence of hard facts, one must fall back on intuition and inference from observed behavior. Young people observably are more myopic than the old: biologically, infants clamor for instant gratification and the young are impulsive, while the very old contemplate death and the afterlife. Intuition suggests that the young have a higher discount rate than the old.

Poor people also tend to have a high discount rate. Forcing poor people to save raises some important issues. How fair is it to compel poor people to reduce their already low level of consumption to fund their future retirement needs? At the extreme level of abstraction, depriving poor people of the ability to meet their basic needs may cause their death, thus negating any concern about their possible future destitution. At a less extreme level of abstraction, poor and even middle-income people have immediate housing, education, and healthcare needs that are more pressing than their future retirement needs. Measures that would require compulsory participation in retirement saving therefore must be properly calibrated.

Libertarian economists who favor freedom of choice argue that high discounters should be allowed to save less and suffer the consequences of their choices when they reach old age. The problem with this argument is that the discount rate changes with age: many people regret later in life their failure to save more when they were younger. Furthermore, many people like the discipline that is entailed in nondiscretionary long-term contractual savings plans.

Where their promises have been credible and generous, social security and occupational pensions[1] have enjoyed a high degree of popularity; the growing dissatisfaction with social security around the world stems from the fear that the value of benefits will not be sustained. In many developing countries, the existence of widespread evasion undermines the argument that social security is popular, but widespread evasion may be the result not of unpopularity but rather of faulty design and poor administration. Experience from the United States and other industrial countries suggests that a well-designed, efficiently administered, and credible social security system will be popular.

Similarly, growing concern about occupational pensions derives from the realization that they depend on the integrity and solvency of the employer. As employers increasingly are being seen to change their pension plans in response to circumstances, it is evident that these factors no longer can be taken for granted.[2] These problems suggest, however, the need to change the form and modalities of retirement saving, not a need to do away with compulsion.

Compulsory provision for retirement can be justified by reference to the myopic behavior of a substantial minority of people and the need to protect both these people and the public at large from their shortsightedness. But how much compulsion is appropriate?

In most countries, participation in a social pension system involving some redistribution, and therefore sharing of costs, is compulsory, but participation in private pension plans is voluntary or quasi-voluntary.

Clearly, ensuring a minimum pension level offers greater justification for compulsory provision than does ensuring a pension level that implies maintenance of a preretirement standard of living and a high replacement rate of preretirement earnings. But as the real value of social security pensions declines, the case for compulsory participation in private pension plans that promise a modest but satisfactory overall replacement rate becomes stronger.

If the principle of compulsory provision is accepted, why are tax incentives also desirable? Tax incentives may provide a powerful inducement to promote compliance and thus may encourage long-term saving for retirement purposes. Tax incentives also could be used for other objectives, such as saving for housing, education, and medical care. Whatever the objectives and modalities of saving, a combination of compulsion and inducement is likely to be more powerful than either one in isolation.

How to Offer Tax Incentives?

The social desirability of long-term saving for retirement, the need to overcome the shortsightedness of a large minority of people, and the need to encourage compliance are the main justifications for the use of both compulsion and inducement. However, the more interesting question is not why, but how to impose compulsion and offer inducement. This paper discusses first the modalities of tax incentives and then considers the implications of compulsory provision.

In analyzing the tax treatment of retirement saving, a distinction usually is drawn between regimes that exempt contributions and investment income but which tax pensions (the EET, or exempt-exempt-tax, regime) and those that tax contributions but exempt investment income and pensions (the TEE, or tax-exempt-exempt, regime). These two regimes have different cash flow effects because of differences in the timing of tax payments, but their long-term impact can be the same.

Many countries use the TEE concept for compulsory social pension systems and the EET approach for voluntary company or personal pension plans. Switzerland is a notable exception, as it applies consistently the EET approach to both social and occupational pension plans.[3] It is also worth noting that there are countries with a TTE regime (tax contributions, tax investment income, exempt pensions), such as New Zealand after 1988, when fiscal benefits on occupational pension plans were removed; others with an EEE regime, such as Singapore; and still others with a TTT regime, such as Russia (for some pension plans in the early 1990s).

Most countries that operate an EET regime impose limits on the two Es. First, upper limits are placed on the rate of tax-exempt contributions that can be made to pension plans. Second, there is a ceiling on eligible earnings (although South Africa and Switzerland are notable for the absence of any such ceiling).

Most countries exempt investment income from income tax. Because the assets commanded by pension funds have increased dramatically in recent years, some countries have, however, imposed limits on the exemption of investment income (Davis 1995). In Denmark, this takes the form of upper limits on real rates of return; that is, any investment income in excess of a specified limit of real returns is liable to tax. The Netherlands subjects to tax any investment income arising from surplus assets in overfunded plans. The Dutch approach makes more sense than the Danish approach, although it faces the difficulty of identifying the level of overfunding, which can be controversial in defined-benefit plans. Several countries, including Australia, South Africa, and Sweden, impose tax on investment income at a reduced rate.

Many countries also allow partial commutation of pension benefits into a tax-free lump sum, with the result that pension benefits are only partially taxed (producing a situation in which the tax regime arguably is "eet" rather than "EET").

An EET regime that provides tax exemption of contributions at the marginal tax rate avoids the double taxation of retirement savings, but it offers a tax deferral benefit that has greater value for high-income workers—and the more progressive the scale of income taxation, the greater the income disparity between active working and passive retirement life. To mitigate this problem, the tax exemption of pension contributions could be limited to the basic rate of tax, thus eliminating the favorable treatment of high-income workers.[4]

Even if limited to the basic rate of tax, an EET approach entails no benefit for non-tax-paying workers, however. A more equitable solution would be to replace tax exemption with a credit transfer system that would offer the same tax incentive to all workers, either in the form of a direct government contribution to the retirement saving accounts of individual workers or as a form of negative income tax linked to saving for retirement.

The Czech Republic uses a plan that comes very close to this approach. The government makes a contribution that matches the contribution made by participants in pension plans, up to relatively low limits. Despite the small amounts involved, participation in this voluntary pension pillar in the Czech Republic has been remarkably high. By failing to link the government subsidy to a minimum contribution rate, however, the Czech scheme has encouraged small amounts of saving rather than adequate saving for retirement. The average contribution rate is less than 3 percent (World Bank 1999). An easy way to correct this plan would be to require a saving rate of at least 10 percent of a worker's earnings for the payment of a given amount of credit transfer. In the Czech Republic, penalty-free withdrawals from these subsidized accounts initially were allowed after just 15 years, but this was changed to 25 years in 2000. Allowing withdrawals only on retirement would be more consistent with the objective of promoting retirement savings.

A government co-contribution to the compulsory private pension pillar was envisaged in Australia in the early 1990s, but the plan was abandoned when a new government was elected in the mid-1990s. The co-contribution was scheduled to be gradually phased out as incomes reached average earnings. The Mexican government, as part of the pension reform program implemented in 1998, deposits one "indexed" peso a day to each retirement saving account under its compulsory system. This may explain the high ratio of contributors to affiliates, which exceeds 75 percent in Mexico against less than 50 percent in Argentina and Chile. In the United States, payment of a matching contribution by employers provides a strong stimulus to voluntary participation by workers in company-sponsored 401(k) plans.

In the United States, the much-discussed government co-contribution to "universal savings accounts" could be described also as a credit transfer system. This approach would eliminate the preferential treatment of tax-paying workers; it also could contain the tax cost of these exemptions or could achieve greater redistribution in favor of low-income workers for a given tax cost. From a social point of view, it would be superior to the other approaches as it would encourage saving by low-income workers.

Compliance by middle-income and high-income workers might decline under such a regime, but then high-income workers are among those workers least likely to require either compulsion or inducement to save for their old age. A government nonetheless could allow tax-exempt contributions by middle- and high-income workers within a specified band of income—i.e., could adopt a

CEET regime, offering a credit transfer (government co-contribution) to all workers, exempting contributions within a specified band of income, exempting investment income, and taxing pensions. This would encourage participation by both low-income and high-income workers, and would avoid or at least reduce the problems of regressivity of alternative approaches.

Tax incentives have opportunity costs for the government, and their use may be ineffective if they lead people to shift their savings to tax-favored forms without producing any overall increase in long-term savings. Moreover, visible tax incentives, such as the credit transfer involved in a CEET regime, may give rise to more objections than indirect, less visible ones, such as tax exemptions. Despite such objections, there can be little doubt that tax incentives are powerful tools in encouraging participation in pension plans and thus in promoting compliance.

Who Should Be Compelled?

Once a decision is taken in favor of compulsory provision, several important policy questions arise. Who should be compelled? What form should compulsory participation take? How much should be saved for retirement purposes? What type of benefits should be provided? Who should manage the accumulated funds? What types of regulation would be necessary? What protection and guarantees should be provided by the state? How much choice should individual workers have in a compulsory system?

Most countries with mandatory funded pillars impose compulsory participation on workers in dependent employment. Self-employed workers usually are not covered, because it is difficult to ascertain their incomes and monitor compliance—and perhaps also because self-employed workers are considered to be sophisticated enough to look after their own long-term interests. Chile, Switzerland, and Australia, among countries with mandatory fully funded pillars, follow this approach. In contrast, Argentina has imposed compulsory participation on all workers, including those in self-employment. Compliance by self-employed workers nonetheless is very weak; in Chile, for example, where participation by self-employed workers is voluntary, only one in 10 choose to contribute in an active and systematic way.[5]

There are other aspects to this question. For example, a strong case can be made for exempting some groups of workers, such as younger workers or those who continue to work beyond the normal retirement age. The Netherlands and Switzerland, for instance, exempt workers under the age of 25 from contributing to funded pillars, and several countries, including Singapore, allow older workers either to not contribute or to contribute at reduced rates. Young workers should, however, be covered by term life and disability insurance, especially if there is no separate unfunded public pillar in operation.

Workers with very low incomes also could be exempt. Switzerland uses a concept of "coordinated earnings," requiring compulsory contributions on earnings falling within a band that is set annually and which corresponds to between 40 and 120 percent of average economy-wide earnings. In this way, it has attained an admirable integration of its unfunded public and funded private pillars. As low-income workers receive a high replacement pension from the public pillar, the Swiss approach avoids forcing low-income workers to oversave when they are young and eliminates the anomaly of paying them unduly high replacement pensions when they are old.[6] Argentina, Hungary, and Poland do not use this approach in their new pension systems, and therefore are running the risk of discouraging active participation by low-income workers.[7]

Another group of workers that could be exempt is those that have strong philosophical objections to government-imposed compulsory participation (see below).

What Form of Compulsory Participation?

The form that compulsory participation should take generally is a concern for funded plans that generate long-term savings. Increasingly, these plans are of the defined-contribution variety and tend to be fully funded, fully vested, and fully portable.

Occupational defined-benefit plans provide some retirement income insurance (Bodie 1990), but it is now increasingly recognized that the value of this insurance is contingent on the integrity and solvency of employer plans, on continuing employment with the same employer, and on the treatment of pre- and postretirement inflation (Bodie and Merton 1992).

Historically, occupational pension plans have played an important role because of the underdevelopment and weakness of long-term insurance and financial markets, even in the industrial countries. Initially, they conferred no vesting or portability rights, and only retiring workers received benefits. Workers changing employment in mid-career could not transfer their accumulated pension rights to their new employers. Company pension plans effectively operated on the so-called "Tontine" principle of insurance, which pays all accumulated capital to the last survivor of a group. Coverage of company pension plans was small and their cost was low. Most plans were not funded. When funding started, it took the form of book reserves, and only over time did this shift to holding external assets: first government and other bonds, then equities, and more recently international securities.

As financial markets have become stronger and employment patterns less stable, and as regulation of pension funds and protection of the rights of employees has increased, there has been a slow but steady trend away from defined-benefit to defined-contribution plans. This trend is most evident in Australia, New Zealand, and South Africa, but it is also pronounced in Switzerland and the United States and is spreading to other countries with large occupational pension plans, such as Canada, Ireland, the Netherlands, and the United Kingdom.

Defined-contribution plans deal more effectively than defined-benefit plans with vesting and portability rights, which are increasing in importance as employment patterns become less stable. They can be fully funded, almost by definition, provided they are based on actual individual capitalization accounts. While they transfer the performance risk of pension funds to workers, this risk can be reduced by the use of properly diversified portfolios and sophisticated annuity products (Bodie and Crane 1998; Burtless 1998; Alier and Vittas 2001).

Some countries combine defined-contribution plans with targeted pension levels. The best example is Switzerland, which specifies the obligatory part of its funded pillar as a defined-credit system,[8] with the ultimate objective being achievement of a targeted pension level at retirement (Smalhout 1996; Queisser and Vittas 2000). Optional variable contribution rates also may contribute to the attainment of targeted pension levels (Vittas 1993). Most countries that operate defined-contribution plans effectively permit such variable contribution rates, although their role could be made more explicit in the relevant pension laws.

What Rate of Saving (Contribution)?

The appropriate rate of saving depends on the targeted pension level and on whether or not there exists a separate redistributive public pillar. Experience from Latin America suggests that a contribution rate of less than 5 percent is inadequate for long-term capital accumulation. An additional 2 to 3 percent is necessary to cover operating fees and premiums for term life and disability insurance.

In Chile, the total contribution rate used to be around 13 percent: 10 percent for long-term capital accumulation, plus around 3 percent for operating fees and insurance premiums. In recent years, the latter rate has fallen, reaching 2.1 percent in 2000. In Argentina, the contribution rate for the second pillar is 11 percent (7.5 percent for long-term capital accumulation plus 3.5 percent for operating fees and insurance premiums). In Mexico, the minimum contribution rate is 6.5 percent to the individual retirement account plus another 5 percent that is credited to an account operated by a housing finance institution. The government adds a flat contribution that corresponds to around 2.5 percent of the average wage. Operating fees are deducted from these contributions, but disability and term life insurance, which covers survivor benefits, is operated by the traditional social security institution, IMSS, and involves a premium of 2.5 percent.

In Hungary, the contribution rate to the compulsory funded pillar was initially set at 6 percent, with provision for its increase in two annual steps to 8 percent. However, the government that took office in 1999 has indefinitely postponed implementation of this provision, and has frozen the contribution rate at 6 percent. In Switzerland, there is no minimum required contribution rate: Swiss law requires only that employer contributions are at least equal to those of employees. In practice, employers cover two-thirds of annual contributions. The minimum legal requirement is for credits to be made to notional individual accounts, based on the worker's age combined with a minimum notional return of 4 percent per year. Plans that achieve high investment returns may operate with zero contribution rates.

In general, a rate of 10 percent for long-term capital accumulation would be adequate for a reasonable replacement rate of between 40 and 50 percent. This assumes that investment returns exceed wage growth rates by 2 to 3 percentage points, and that active working life is at least twice as long as passive retirement life-the latter calculated to include the life expectancy and benefits of dependent survivors (Vittas 1993). A lower replacement rate would be achieved if the gap between investment returns and wage growth is smaller or if careers are interrupted. Under these conditions, a 10 percent contribution rate would still be adequate if the targeted replacement rate from the funded pillar amounts to 35 percent and if this is supplemented by a pension of similar magnitude from the unfunded public pillar.

What Benefits?

Benefits can take several different forms: lump sums on retirement, lifetime pensions, pensions for surviving dependents, pensions for disability, and withdrawals for housing, education, and healthcare. Historically, there was a clear distinction between provident funds that paid benefits in lump-sum form and pension funds that offered life annuities. Over time, however, the distinction has become blurred. Most pension funds now allow commutation into a tax-free lump-sum payment of up to one-third of the present value of accumulated balances, while provident funds require the purchase of a minimum-sum annuity. Singapore introduced a minimum-sum annuity requirement in 1988.

Pension systems that are based on personal pension plans require either the purchase of life annuities or the use of scheduled withdrawals (also known as income drawdowns in the United Kingdom, and allocated annuities in Australia). Scheduled withdrawals, which were an innovation of the Chilean pension reform of 1981, are recalculated annually, taking into account investment returns and the remaining life expectancy of pensioners and their dependents; they do not, however, provide longevity insurance. In Chile and in other countries following its lead, lump-sum withdrawals are allowed if the annuity payment exceeds a certain replacement rate (usually 70 percent of reference salary).

A differentiation between compulsory accumulation and compulsory annuitization is advisable when designing pension schemes. This is because private annuity markets suffer from structural problems and are not well-developed, even in the industrial countries.[9] To a large extent, the underdevelopment of annuity markets is due to the crowding-out effect of social security and occupational pensions that predominates in industrial countries. Pending the development of more efficient annuity markets, it would be preferable to limit compulsory annuitization to a level of around 35 percent of average earnings and to subject any excess balances to scheduled withdrawals, with flexible arrangements made for major health and other emergencies (James and Vittas 2000; McDonald et al. 2000). Development of variable annuities with floors and caps as well as the use of more transparent participating annuities could address some of the problems facing annuity markets. The 35 percent target should apply to the combined pension from the unfunded public pillar and the private funded one; workers thus should be encouraged to accumulate enough retirement savings to support a replacement rate of around 70 percent of preretirement income, but only one-half of this should be required to be annuitized.

In addition to benefits for retired workers, pension systems need also to provide disability insurance, to cover active workers and their dependents from the effects of serious accident, and term life insurance, to protect the dependents of active workers in case of death. In Latin American countries, these insurance policies are organized on a group basis, a feature that lowers costs and which also could be used in annuity business.

Other benefits for active workers could include provisions allowing preretirement withdrawals for housing, education, healthcare, and to cover various lumpy costs whose timing is unforeseen, such as funeral or wedding expenses. Many countries allow the use of pension or provident fund balances for such purposes, but this does introduce the risk of depleting accumulated balances and leaving too little capital for retirement—or alternatively may require that the mandated contribution rate be set too high, as is notably the case in Singapore. The blanket prohibition of early withdrawals for housing, education, or healthcare would unfairly penalize low- and middle-income workers, however, and would weaken support for participation in retirement saving plans. An appropriate compromise would be to permit withdrawals up to a sensible aggregate limit, and possibly to require the repayment of early withdrawals or the replenishment of account balances. A sensible aggregate limit might be to allow withdrawals equal to 100 percent of accumulated balances or to 30 percent of projected balances at normal retirement age, whichever is lower.[10] Young workers would be bound by the first limit, and older workers by the second.[11]

What Institutional Structure?

The institutional structure of funded private pillars, which affects the administration of accounts, collection of contributions, payment of benefits, and management of accumulated assets, is one of the most important aspects of the functioning of compulsory pension systems. There are two basic choices: between centralized public and decentralized private management, and, in the case of private management, between company-based closed funds and open funds managed by specialized financial institutions.

With regard to the first choice, experience in both industrial and developing countries shows that private decentralized management has achieved higher efficiency, a better quality of service, and higher real returns than public centralized management. The rare exceptions to this pattern, exemplified by the high operating efficiency of the Central Provident Fund of Singapore and the Employees' Provident Fund of Malaysia, serve to confirm this rule. However, even in these countries, and especially in Singapore, the real rate of return credited to workers' accounts has been very low, despite the pursuit of sound macroeconomic policies and the attainment of high economic growth with low inflation (Valdés-Prieto 1998). In many countries, especially in Africa and Latin America, the investment performance of central public sector agencies has been disastrous (World Bank 1994) and the quality of service has been very poor. In OECD countries, private pension funds generally have achieved higher investment returns than public pension funds (Davis 1995); the quality of service of private funds also has been superior.

Supporters of centralized public management point to the lower marketing and operating costs of public agencies and argue that the lower investment returns of past experience were due to failure to ensure the insulation of fund management from political interference. Several countries, including Belgium, Canada, France, Ireland, Norway, and Sweden, have created in recent years public pension funds with better incentives to attain higher investment returns and strong safeguards for insulation from political interference. However, in all cases the public pension funds represent a fraction—in some cases a very small fraction—of total pension fund assets under management. Moreover, it remains to be seen if the new investment rules for such public funds will survive political interference; in this they have yet to be tested. Proponents of the nationalization of pension fund management, such as Orszag and Stiglitz (2001) and Heller (1998), underestimate the implications of the vast public agency that would be necessary to handle this task, not only in terms of the risk of political interference in corporate governance and performance but also in terms of the functioning and innovation record of financial markets.

The choice between closed and open funds is a more delicate one. A weakness of open funds, such as those found in Chile, Argentina, and other Latin American countries, is their high operating costs. This is mainly due to high selling commissions and other marketing costs, and is related to the right given to workers to switch their accounts among competing pension fund management companies.

Employer-based pension funds have much lower operating costs, mainly because they avoid these marketing costs (Rocha, Gutierrez, and Hinz 2001).

It should be stressed, however, that the level of operating fees of Latin American open funds tends to be exaggerated. Operating fees are levied in the form of collection fees, and these translate into high asset fees during the first years of operation of open funds.[12] Calculated over the active career of workers, the fees of open funds in Chile and several other Latin American countries are much lower, corresponding to between 70 and 150 basis points of assets under management (James and others 1999 and 2001). These fees compare favorably with those charged by most mutual funds in the United States and other countries, but are higher than the operating costs of employer-based closed funds (Rocha, Gutierrez, and Hinz 2001).

The operating fees charged by open funds in Latin American countries may decline as the systems mature and as regulatory measures, such as limiting account switching and permitting multiple accounts and multiple funds, are taken to reduce their marketing intensity.[13] Such a trend is already evident in Chile, where operating fees have declined substantially. These amounted in 2000 to a collection fee of 13.9 percent of contributions-equivalent to an average asset fee of less than 70 basis points for a 40-year active contribution period.[14] But what is most important is the net investment return after operating fees are deducted. The Chilean and other Latin American pension funds have achieved and continue to achieve high net real rates of return.

Employer-based closed funds typically have low operating costs and high investment returns, especially in Anglo-American countries, which have tended to invest heavily in corporate equities and bonds (Rocha, Gutierrez, and Hinz 2001). The problem with employer funds is that such good performance typically is found among the pension funds of larger employers that operate traditional defined-benefit plans. In the United States, smaller company funds tend to incur higher operating costs, especially when they are organized as 401(k) plans. Operating fees of as much as 200 basis points are not uncommon among such plans. In addition, 401(k) plans, of both small and large employers, tend to encourage investment in the equity of the sponsoring employer, a practice that generally is considered to be highly imprudent.[15] The basic problem with employer-based closed funds is that workers are captive and depend on the integrity and professionalism of their employers and the board of trustees in pursuing good performance.

One compromise solution would be to allow hybrid funds. For instance, employer-based plans offering fully vested, fully funded, and fully portable benefits could give workers the right to opt out and join independent funds. Alternatively, group contracts could be allowed for independent fund management companies, especially if such contracts could be negotiated by employers and offered to their employees on an optional basis. In this way, pension funds would benefit from economies of scale and group discounts, while the pressure would persist to achieve high investment returns with low operating fees.

The operation of private pension funds with individual accounts benefits from considerable economies of scale, and there is a persistent trend toward greater concentration in pension fund management. In Chile, the number of pension funds declined from 21 in the early 1990s to eight by the year 2000; in Argentina, in the same period it fell from 25 to 13. In Bolivia, at the start of the new system only two managers with proven international experience were authorized. In view of this trend, and to avoid workers being forced to save with noncompetitive private sector institutions, one option would be to permit the participation of a fund managed by a public sector agency. Argentina, Mexico, Kazakhstan, and Uruguay have taken this approach.

The participation of a publicly managed fund requires a level playing field, however, such that neither the private nor the public funds are placed at a competitive disadvantage; the publicly managed fund also needs to be effectively protected from political interference. A better option would be to centralize the administrative functions of pension funds, such as the keeping of records, collection of contributions, payment of benefits, and sending of statements, and assign the management of assets to a small number of managers on the basis of competitive bidding and with clearly defined asset allocation policies (Glaessner and Valdés-Prieto 1998; James et al. 1999). Such an approach has been successfully applied in the case of the Thrift Savings Plan for the Federal Employees Retirement System in the United States. Sweden also has adopted the centralized approach to the administration of pension funds, but allows individual workers to select from a large group of asset managers through a system of "blind accounts," whereby the asset managers do not know which workers have selected them (Palmer 2000).

A lesson of recent experience is that reformers need to be careful when they try to lower operating costs. Centralized collection of contributions has been pursued in a number of countries, but results have been less than satisfactory because of the inefficiency of the public agencies used for this purpose. Notably, in Kazakhstan and Poland, contributions were collected but individual records were deficient, with the result that a substantial proportion of collected funds remained unallocated two years or more after the introduction of the new system. When trying to improve on the performance of reform programs in other countries, policymakers clearly need to ensure that the proposed cures are not worse than the disease.

What Regulation and Supervision?

A government that imposes a mandatory retirement saving system has an obligation to ensure that it is safe, works well, is simple and easy to understand, and will deliver the promised benefits. This obligation clearly is strongest in developing countries, where millions of affected workers may lack familiarity with the workings of modern financial markets.

The main focus of regulation should be on prudential and protective norms and on fiduciary standards. First and foremost are licensing rules that should ensure that only persons satisfying a stringent "fit and proper" test are allowed to act as sponsors, founders, directors, trustees, or senior executives of pension funds. Other rules should require a specified minimum capital, asset diversification and market valuation, external financial audits and actuarial reviews, and extensive information disclosure and transparency. Of particular importance are rules on fund governance, internal control systems, legal separation of the assets of the pension fund from those of the management company, and custodial arrangements. All of these prudential and protective rules are necessary to ensure the financial soundness of pension funds; to prevent fraud, self-dealing, and other potential conflict-of-interest situations; and to safeguard the interests of workers.

Although noncontroversial, such regulation is difficult to achieve. Ensuring an efficient and adequate supply of auditors, actuaries, and custodians, not to mention experienced examiners and supervisors, is a tall order for most developing countries. In Chile, effective external custody of pension fund assets was secured by requiring that, for the first 10 years of the new system, all assets be held with the central bank. Private custodianship was allowed only in the 1990s. The development of automated central securities depositories in many countries has since simplified the requirement for safe external custody.

Other rules that have been practiced in Latin American countries are more controversial. One account per worker, one fund per company, and uniform pricing rules have aimed at ensuring simplicity and transparency and thus at providing protection for workers, but their usefulness is open to question. Such rules can be justified in systems that offer constrained choice—although they probably should be supplemented with regulations and limits on operating fees, agent commissions, and account switching—but they would be out of place in systems that emphasize personal choice. In the latter, they would in the longer run need to be relaxed, to offer more effective choice to workers.

To enforce compliance with the panoply of prudential and protective regulations requires the creation of an effective, well-funded, properly staffed, and proactive supervision agency (Vittas 1998a). Latin American countries, and to a lesser extent the reforming countries of Eastern Europe, have been more successful than most OECD countries in developing effective supervision of private pension funds. Following modern practice, supervisors should enlist the support and cooperation of auditors, actuaries, and custodians.

In several high-income countries, pension fund supervision lacks adequate, timely information and is slow to take corrective action. Given the long-term nature of pension contracts, it is imperative that a system of supervision be developed that is proactive and effective, that stimulates transparency, and that ensures compliance with basic prudential and protective rules.[16]

What Investment Rules?

Investment rules are highly controversial. In the early years of pension reform, when accumulated fund assets are small,[17] they may be of limited relevance, but as assets start to expand proper investment rules are essential. Many developing countries have imposed detailed investment rules for diversification purposes, setting upper limits on different assets by type as well as by issuer. These can be justified by the low level of development of local capital markets, the lack of any tradition of private pension provision, and the lack of familiarity of most workers with complicated financial assets. However, investment rules should always emphasize safety and

profitability, and should never aim to direct funds into socially
desirable projects.

Among the reforming developing countries, Chile has avoided
imposing minimum investment requirements and has expanded the
choice of available asset classes as pension funds have increased in
size and maturity. Other countries, including Argentina, Bolivia,
Mexico, and Uruguay, have imposed minimum investment rules,
although in most countries a pattern of gradual liberalization is also
evident or intended. Critics of investment limits have emphasized
the losses in forgone income that could have been avoided if a more
liberal system had been in place (Shah 1997; Srinivas and Yermo
1999), but they typically have not taken into account the specific
prevailing conditions. In reality, the performance of mutual funds in
developing countries, which are heavily invested in bonds and
money market instruments, and the apparent lack of investor confidence in the integrity and transparency of local equity markets,
strongly suggest that in a more liberal system pension funds would
have tended to follow more conservative investment policies—probably achieving lower returns than under the regulated regime.

In industrial countries, detailed investment rules may not be necessary. Reliance on the "prudent expert" rule and the concept of
benchmark portfolios (see below) may be adequate. Data show that
pension funds in countries that rely on the prudent expert approach
have been able to achieve higher investment returns than pension
funds in countries that have imposed quantitative limits on different classes of assets (Davis 1998; European Commission 1999).

Most developing countries and several industrial ones either
prohibit pension funds from investing in foreign assets or apply
tight limits on such investments. To some extent, the motivation for
these controls is prudential, since local pension funds may not have
the expertise to select foreign assets. But to a much larger extent,
limits on foreign assets are motivated by balance-of-payment considerations and by the desire to promote the development of local
capital markets. Pension funds and other institutional investors
have the potential to stimulate the development of local capital
markets (Vittas 1998b and 2000). While they are neither necessary
nor sufficient for capital market development (Vittas 2000), there
is considerable empirical evidence showing a close correlation
between pension funds and other institutional investors and capital
market development.[18]

In developing countries, rules that prohibit or severely constrain
investment in foreign assets may be counterproductive if the rest
of the economy and financial system are integrated with foreign

markets. For instance, in countries where large utilities, industrial firms, and financial institutions are strategically owned by foreign entities, a blanket prohibition on foreign investments would force pension funds to invest in local companies that either are unattractive to foreign strategic owners or are otherwise too small to elicit foreign interest. Investment rules on pension funds should be consistent with the degree of international economic integration. This argument is particularly important for the countries of Eastern Europe that are aiming for closer integration with the European Union, but it is also increasingly relevant for countries in East Asia, Latin America, and the Middle East.

Perhaps the leading concern about investment in overseas assets and derivative products relates to the facilitation of what could be called the institutional flight of capital from developing countries with poorly functioning capital markets to high-income countries with strongly developed and efficient markets. One solution to this problem, advocated by Bodie and Merton (2001), would be to use international asset swaps with pension funds based in other countries. This would permit the international diversification of pension fund assets without a large outflow of capital. The only movement of capital across the exchanges would be to cover the net gains or losses suffered by national pension funds in these asset swaps.[19] As regards the use of derivative products, authorization could be extended on an individual basis to those pension funds that demonstrate effective asset management and internal control. This approach was formally introduced in Switzerland in 2000, having been previously practiced on an informal basis.

What Guarantees?

Pension guarantees play an important part in compulsory pension systems. Aimed at providing effective protection to workers, they need to be designed to avoid the problems of moral hazard that afflict all systems of financial guarantees. Pension guarantees can take four different forms: a minimum pension, a minimum investment return, a minimum annuity conversion factor, or protection from insolvency.

Minimum Pension

A minimum pension guarantee is essential where there is no separate public pillar and the social assistance pension is low. Chile offers a minimum pension guarantee of about 25 percent of the average wage to workers who have contributed for at least 20 years. Prior to its recent reform, Argentina's separate public pillar offered a basic universal pension of around 30 percent of the average covered wage after a minimum contribution period of 30 years.

Minimum pension guarantees can give rise to moral hazard problems. If they are not formulated properly, they can encourage strategic manipulation by workers who seek to contribute for the minimum period and for the minimum amounts that would entitle them to draw the minimum pension. Conversely, as in the case of Argentina, the requirement of contribution to the public pillar for at least 30 years may act as a strong disincentive for participation by self-employed and other workers who may be uncertain about their ability to contribute for such a long period. One solution may be to apply a proportionality rule, broadly similar to that used for the public pillars in Switzerland and the Netherlands. Under such a rule, the state would offer (or guarantee) an accrual factor of, say, 0.75 percent of the average wage for each year of contribution, with a minimum that would be no lower than the social assistance pension. Thus, for a 40-year contribution period, the minimum pension guarantee would amount to 30 percent of the average wage.

Minimum Return on Investment

Providing a minimum investment return guarantee expressed in absolute nominal or real terms is not advisable. Such a guarantee could distort incentives and exert undue influence on investment policies. Switzerland requires as a minimum the annual crediting of a 4 percent nominal return to the notional retirement accounts that are held for each covered worker. The minimum return is credited alongside the required age-related contributions. Accumulated balances on these notional accounts become relevant when people change jobs and join the pension funds of their new employers or on retirement. There are no penalties for failure to achieve the minimum return on an annual basis, although fund managers appear to have adopted conservative investment policies to ensure that their annual returns do not fall below this level (Queisser and Vittas 2000).

In Singapore, a minimum nominal return of 2.5 percent is guaranteed, but as this is a state-run plan the guarantee has little impact. Since it is expressed in nominal terms, it also has little meaning.

It would make more sense to guarantee the minimum nominal or real profitability relative to the average achieved by all pension funds. This would protect workers from large deviations in returns. Chile requires a minimum real return that is no less than 50 percent of the average real return achieved by all pension funds on a 36-month moving average basis (recently extended from a 12-month basis). Argentina imposes a similar requirement, expressed as no less than 70 percent of the nominal return of all pension funds.

Guaranteeing relative minimum profitability is linked with minimum solvency requirements and investment reserves. It results in more uniform, and perhaps also more conservative, investment policies. However, it can be justified by the imposition of the one account per worker and one fund per company rules, which create a large exposure of individual workers to the performance of individual managers. A minimum relative rate of return would protect workers from aberrant behavior by individual fund managers.[20] In both Chile and Argentina, fund managers are required to make up any shortfall in returns from their own funds. This provision is not explicitly provided in the case of Switzerland.

For the industrial countries, other solutions for protecting workers from excessive fluctuations and deviations in returns may be more appropriate. The prudent expert rule has worked well for defined-benefit plans, where the investment risk is borne by sponsoring employers, but it remains to be seen whether it will work equally well for defined-contribution plans. One possible approach would be to require management companies to spell out clearly the investment policies of funds that they promote, and to make those management companies liable for any shortfalls that result from deviation from their stated policies.[21] In countries where the only constraints on fund management are fear of loss of business and of damage to their reputation, the use of benchmark portfolios and detailed investment guidelines may be a better approach.

There are some practical problems in defining benchmark portfolios, but these difficulties should not be exaggerated since benchmarks are widely used by pension funds to monitor the performance of asset managers. Formal statement of investment policy objectives (SIPOs) are required by the new mandatory provident fund system of Hong Kong, and are required, on a less formal basis, in the United Kingdom. However, no country requires fund managers to make up any shortfalls in returns that may result from unauthorized deviations from the published SIPO.

Minimum Annuity Conversion

Switzerland is the only country that stipulates a minimum annuity conversion factor, set at 7.2 percent since the introduction of the compulsory system in 1985. Proposals are under discussion for a significant decrease in this factor, to reflect the fall in interest rates and the increase in longevity.

The annuity conversion factor is used when workers retire and convert their accumulated balances into a life annuity. Although a minimum conversion factor stipulated in absolute terms may not be advisable, as it may either expose annuity providers to a high reinvestment risk or may fix the conversion factor at too low a level, some regulation of annuity prices (as well as products) may be warranted. At the very least, there should be extensive publicity and analysis of the products and prices offered by different insurance companies.

Protection from Insolvency

Finally, protecting workers from the failure of insurance companies that provide term life and disability cover, as well as annuities, seems essential, especially in a mandatory retirement saving scheme. To prevent moral hazard problems and excessive risk taking, regulators need to ensure that financial institutions have adequate capital for the risks they assume, are properly diversified, and are not exposed to a major mismatch of their assets and liabilities (Merton and Bodie 1992).

How Much Individual Choice?

Although this may sound like a contradiction in terms, individual choice can be an essential element of a compulsory saving scheme. In Singapore and Malaysia, individual workers can decide how to invest their own balances, above a stipulated minimum level, with the proviso that they choose among approved instruments. These instruments used to be limited to owner-occupied housing, but they now cover approved mutual funds investing in domestic and foreign securities.

In Chile, Argentina, and other Latin American countries, individual workers can choose their fund management company and can switch their account from company to company. In Chile and Argentina, account switching in fact took place on such a large scale that it became a major problem. At the peak of the problem in Chile, nearly one in two active accounts was switched annually; the corresponding ratio in Argentina was one in three active accounts. Account switching seemed to be motivated by the interests of selling agents rather than those of workers. To contain the problem, both countries have introduced rules that restrict the frequency of switching to one per year, and have introduced more cumbersome procedures for account switching.

In Chile, Argentina, and other reforming countries, the one account per worker, one fund per company, and uniform pricing rules seem to constrain individual choice. There are various ways of improving these systems to increase individual choice and enhance efficiency, while retaining the compulsory element of saving for retirement. Some of these improvements would be appropriate also to the industrial countries, where they could make compulsory retirement savings plans more palatable.

First, workers could be allowed to hold multiple accounts and management companies could be allowed to operate multiple funds. These could be limited to a small number, say, three, to facilitate verification of compliance.

Second, group contracts could be allowed. These could offer discounts to group members and could be arranged according to employer or other group sharing a common bond. Individual workers also could be allowed to opt out of company-based group plans (although they might be discouraged from so doing by the higher operating fees they would incur). The right to opt out would exert pressure on group plans to earn net investment returns as good as those earned by nongroup plans.

Third, individual workers could be given the right to invest in pension funds that are subject to less regulation (especially to fewer and less restrictive investment rules), under the understanding that in exercising this right they would lose government protection and guarantees. Workers who value the minimum pension and minimum relative profitability guarantees above having a wider range of investment options could stay with the more heavily regulated funds; workers who value choice above protection could opt for the less regulated ones. Similarly, where the system is based on benchmark portfolios, workers who do not wish to be covered by state regulations and protections could opt for funds that are subject to fewer regulations.

Finally, and perhaps most controversially, workers who have philosophical objections against compulsory saving for retirement purposes could be exempted from such plans, provided they sign a declaration to that effect. Opting out of a compulsory system would at the least require a conscious decision. While that decision, particularly among young workers, might still merely represent myopic behavior, requiring them to sign a declaration every three or five years could impress upon them the need for saving for their retirement at an earlier stage than might otherwise be the case.

It would probably be inadvisable to offer most of these additional elements of individual choice when pension reform is first implemented. From a practical point of view, it would probably be better to introduce them once the private funded pillar is well established.

Conclusion

To recapitulate, policies to promote saving for retirement and old age ideally should use both tax incentives and compulsion.

The case for compulsory provision is based on the needs to overcome the myopic behavior of a large minority of workers and to protect society from those who make inadequate provision for their old age.

Tax inducements may facilitate compliance. The socially superior way of providing tax inducements would be through a credit transfer that is added to individual capitalization accounts, provided a minimum rate of saving is observed. This would encourage participation by low-income groups. Allowing exemption of contributions within specified lower- and upper-income limits could also encourage adequate saving for retirement by middle-income and high-income workers.

Compulsory provision imposes an obligation on the state to ensure that the system is safe, works well, is simple and easy to understand, and will deliver the targeted benefits. Important policy issues include the extent of compulsory coverage; the form and size of compulsory saving; the management, regulation, and guarantees of the compulsory system; and the extent of individual choice.

This paper argues for imposing compulsory participation on workers in dependent employment, exempting the very young (younger than 25 years of age), the very old (more than the normal retirement age), the very poor (those earning less than 40 percent of the average wage), and the self-employed. It suggests that compulsory participation should take the form of individual accounts, but with constrained choice, and that a contribution rate of 10 percent for long-term capital accumulation would be reasonable and adequate. Allowing use of variable contribution rates to attain targeted pension levels also would be advisable.

A minimum level of compulsory annuitization should be required, and this should be less than the targeted level of compulsory accumulation. Balances in excess of the minimum level of annuitization could be used in a more flexible way, both before and after retirement. Withdrawals for housing, education, and health-care could be allowed, but should not exceed the lower of 100 percent of accumulated balances or 30 percent of projected balances at retirement.

Management of accumulated assets should be decentralized, but one of the fund managers could be a public sector agency, provided a level playing field is in place and the public sector agency is protected from political interference. Independent open funds, employer closed funds, and group contracts could be allowed, with workers having the right to select their fund type. Vesting and portability rights should be ensured. Limits on operating fees and selling commissions, as well as on the frequency of account switching, could be imposed to lower operating costs and fees.

The regulatory framework needs to be robust and effective. A panoply of prudential and protective rules would be necessary to cover "fit and proper" tests for the founders, sponsors, directors, trustees, and senior executives of pension funds; asset diversification and market valuation rules; legal segregation of assets and safe external custody; independent financial audits and actuarial reviews; and adequate disclosure and transparency. An effective, proactive, well-funded, and properly staffed supervision agency also would be necessary.

Tight investment rules could initially be justified for countries with weak capital markets and limited tradition of private pension provision. However, in the long run, adoption of the prudent expert approach with publication of statements of investment policy objectives would be preferable and more efficient. Various guarantees covering aspects such as minimum pension levels and relative investment returns need to be provided to protect workers from aberrant asset managers, but care must be taken to address effectively the risk of moral hazard.

The paper also argues for greater individual choice, including the creation of a dual regulatory structure. One part of this structure would be characterized by heavy regulation and a constrained choice of investment funds, limits on operating fees and on account switching, and strong government safeguards and guarantees. This would cater for those workers with low risk tolerance. The other part of the structure would be more liberal but based on strong conduct rules. It would offer greater choice of investment funds, allowing multiple accounts and liberal account switching, with no limits on operating fees but with no or fewer state guarantees. This would cater for workers seeking a higher return and willing to tolerate a higher level of risk.

There are many options from which to choose. Decisions on which options to take will reflect their political acceptability. Clearly, it will be easier for countries to build on what they already have, unless their existing arrangements are totally deficient and unsustainable.

Notes

1. Occupational pensions used to be compulsory for most eligible employees of companies that operated defined-benefit plans. Compulsory participation is not a feature of defined-contribution plans, such as the proliferating 401(k) plans of the past two decades or so, although employers offer matching contributions and undertake educational and promotional campaigns to stimulate voluntary participation.

2. In the United States, IBM and AT&T changed their employer-based pension system in recent years, moving from a generous defined-benefit system to a less attractive cash-balance system. In both cases, the companies acted without adequate consultation with covered employees, causing the latter to campaign publicly against the proposals made. Both IBM and AT&T have faced difficult conditions in competitive markets. Their change of approach underscores the importance of employer solvency and integrity, neither of which should be accepted without question.

3. Switzerland also is notable in that it imposes no ceilings on the contributions to either compulsory pillar. There is, however, a proposal under discussion to place a limit on the tax-exempt contributions to the pillar of occupational pensions (Queisser and Vittas 2000).

4. A tax exemption at the basic rate of income tax is equivalent to offering a tax credit against a person's tax liability rather than taxable income.

5. Self-employed workers may for various reasons opt to register with a private pension fund, but may fail to maintain an active contribution record. This is the prevalent experience in Argentina.

6. Such an approach would exclude self-employed workers with very low earnings, and could provide an additional justification for exempting all self-employed workers from compulsory participation to the funded pillar.

7. The treatment of unemployment spells, maternity leave, military service, and university education creates complications that may have a serious effect on defined-benefit final salary plans, though their impact on defined-contribution systems would be less important. Some countries (e.g., Switzerland) require compulsory contributions on all types of income,

including unemployment and disability benefits, to their unfunded public pillars but not to the funded private pillars. This policy would be consistent with a high level of integration of the two pillars.

8. This is broadly similar to the cash-balance plans introduced by many company plans in the United States over the past 15 years or so. However, in the Swiss system, the minimum legal requirements are spelled out much more clearly and also include the decumulation phase (a fixed minimum annuity conversion factor is specified).

9. These structural problems include the impact of adverse selection due to asymmetric information and socioeconomic factors (Friedman and Warshawsky 1990; Blake 1999; Brown 1999; James and Vittas 2000). Because annuity contracts are irrevocable, inflexible, and nonportable, they require considerable trust in the long-term solvency and integrity of annuity providers. This trust is weakened by the considerable uncertainty regarding long-term improvements in longevity and the reinvestment risk emanating from the duration mismatching of assets and liabilities of annuity providers.

10. Allowing early withdrawals could mitigate any opposition to investment rules that prohibit the extension of loans to members. In many developing countries, employer-sponsored provident funds play a multifaceted role as short-term saving clubs, loan-granting credit unions, and retirement saving plans.

11. Reverse mortgages could be used to provide liquidity to old people who have invested heavily in their own houses and end up being "asset rich" but "income poor." Reverse mortgages are an interesting concept, but have yet to be successfully implemented in any country. They raise some important policy issues, such as how to protect very old people from aggressive selling agents and how to ensure that insurance companies would be able to meet their financial obligations.

12. Operating fees may take several different forms: collection fees are based on contributions and are similar to the front-load fees charged by most mutual funds; asset fees are levied on account balances; performance fees are calculated on investment returns in excess of a stipulated level; exit fees are charged when workers switch out of a fund; and benefit fees are levied on pension payments. In Chile and most Latin American countries, only collection and benefit fees are allowed. Mexico has permitted all types of fees, but collection fees predominate.

13. None of the reforming countries in Latin America has imposed limits on operating fees or on agent commissions. However, a strong case can be made for such limits in mandatory pension systems, especially those offering constrained choice.

14. For a 40-year contribution period, a collection fee of 1 percent of contributions is equivalent to an asset fee of about 5 basis points. This is a useful simplified key, although it should be borne in mind that the

relationship between collection and asset fees is nonlinear. For a contribution period that covers the last 30 years before retirement, the simplified key is 7 basis points; for a contribution period covering the last 20 years before retirement, it is 10 basis points.

15. In 401(k) plans, investments are worker directed. On average, around 30 percent of assets are invested in the equity of sponsoring employers, but there are individual plans where company stock represents as much as 60 to 80 percent of assets. To some extent, this pattern is explained by the matching contribution made by employers, which is often made in company stock rather than cash. The recent collapse of U.S. energy corporation Enron has underscored the high risk of investing in a non-diversified portfolio.

16. The worst offenders in this respect have been the U.K. regulatory agencies. Not only in the area of pensions but also in banking and insurance, U.K. regulators have failed to adopt a proactive approach in ensuring effective supervision. As a result, the U.K. financial system has suffered from many scandals, including the BCCI collapse, the Maxwell case, the Lloyds insurance market abuses, the mis-selling of personal pension plans, and the fiasco of Equitable Life.

17. Tight investment limits on equities and foreign assets should be tolerated in the early years of pension reform, if adoption of conservative policies would overcome opposition to the implementation of pension reform and authorization of private pension funds. However, as a practical rule, investment in domestic equities should be allowed once pension fund assets reach 5 percent of GDP. International diversification would be essential when pension fund assets exceed 20 percent of GDP.

18. The empirical evidence has been compiled by Gregorio Impavido and Alberto Musalem in a series of papers (Catalan, Impavido, and Musalem 2001; Impavido and Musalem 2000). It is important to note that in many countries, including Malaysia, Singapore, and Switzerland, foreign pension funds and other international investors may have been as important in stimulating local market development as the domestic pension funds (Vittas 2000).

19. The fear of institutional capital flight is one of the main reasons why policymakers in developing countries have not shown much interest in Kotlikoff's proposal to select an international asset management company and invest all assets in a properly constructed world index (Kotlikoff 1994). This approach aims to minimize operating costs, maximize asset diversification, achieve an optimal combination of risk and return, and insulate pension fund assets from political risk. It would also ensure that all workers of the same cohort receive the same returns. However, the fact that no industrial country—nor even any individual pension fund in any industrial country—has adopted Kotlikoff's proposal has weakened its appeal for policymakers of developing countries.

20. The minimum relative return guarantees used in Chile and Argentina and the uniformity of asset portfolios that they induce have come under considerable criticism (Shah 1997; Srinivas and Yermo 1999). The criticism overlooks, however, the need to protect individual workers from very bad outcomes. Moreover, the result would not be much different from pension funds offering constrained choice of indexed funds.

21. For instance, a pension fund may publicize an investment policy that allocates 60 percent of assets in a broad equity index and 40 percent in a broad bond index. If it were to deviate from this policy and allocate 80 percent in equities, and if this were to result in a lower return than the publicized allocation, the fund manager could be required to make up the shortfall in returns.

References

Alier, Max, and Dimitri Vittas. 2001. "Personal Pension Plans and Stock Market Volatility." In Robert Holzmann and Joseph E. Stiglitz, eds., *New Ideas about Old Age Security: Toward Sustainable Pension Systems in the 21st Century.* World Bank, Washington, D.C.

Blake, David. 1999. "Annuity Markets: Problems and Solutions." *The Geneva Papers on Risk and Insurance* 24(3):358-75.

Bodie, Zvi. 1990. "Pensions as Retirement Income Insurance." *Journal of Economic Literature* (March).

Bodie, Zvi, and Dwight B. Crane. 1998. "The Design and Production of New Retirement Savings Products." Harvard Business School Working Paper 98070. Harvard Business School, Cambridge, Massachusetts.

Bodie, Zvi, and Robert C. Merton. 1992. "Pension Benefit Guarantees in the United States: A Functional Analysis." In R. Schmitt, ed., *The Future of Pensions in the United States.* Philadelphia: University of Pennsylvania Press.

————. 2001. "International Pension Swaps." Boston University, Boston, Mass. Processed.

Brown, Jeffrey. 1999. "Private Pensions, Mortality Risk, and the Decision to Annuitize." National Bureau of Economic Research (NBER) Working Paper Series 7191. NBER, Cambridge, Mass.

Burtless, Gary. 1998. "Financial Market Risks of Individual Retirement Accounts: The Twentieth Century Record." The Brookings Institution, Washington, D.C..

Catalan, Marcelo, Gregorio Impavido, and Alberto R. Musalem. 2001. "Contractual Savings or Stock Market Development: Which Leads?" *Journal of Applied Social Science Studies* 120(3):445-87.

Davis, E. Philip. 1995. *Pension Funds: Retirement-Income Security and Capital Markets: An International Perspective.* Oxford: Clarendon Press.

———. 1998. "Regulation of Pension Fund Assets." In H. J. Blommenstein and N. Funke, eds., *Institutional Investors in the New Financial Landscape.* Paris: Organisation for Economic Co-operation and Development (OECD).

European Commission. 1999. *Rebuilding Pensions: Security, Efficiency, Affordability.* Brussels: European Commission.

Friedman, Benjamin, and Mark J. Warshawsky. 1990. "The Cost of Annuities: Implications for Saving Behavior and Bequests." *The Quarterly Journal of Economics* (February): pp. 135–54.

Glaessner, Thomas, and Salvador Valdés-Prieto. 1998. "Pension Reform in Small Developing Countries." World Bank Policy Research Working Paper 1983. World Bank, Washington, D.C.

Helbling, Carl. 1991. *Les institutions de prévoyance et la LPP.* Bern: Haupt.

Heller, Peter. 1998. "Rethinking Public Pension Initiatives." International Monetary Fund (IMF) Working Paper 98/61. IMF, Washington, D.C.

Holzmann, Robert. 2000. "The World Bank Approach to Pension Reform." *International Social Security Review* 53(1):11–34.

Holzmann, Robert, and Joseph E. Stiglitz eds. 2001. *New Ideas about Old Age Security: Toward Sustainable Pension Systems in the 21st Century.* World Bank, Washington, D.C.

Impavido, Gregorio, and Alberto R. Musalem. 2000. "Contractual Savings, Stock and Asset Markets." World Bank Policy Research Working Paper 2490. World Bank, Washington, D.C.

James, Estelle. 1998. "Pension Reform: An Efficiency-Equity Tradeoff?" In Nancy Birdsall, Carol Graham, and Richard Sabot, eds., *Beyond Tradeoffs.* Washington, D.C.: Brookings Institution Press.

James, Estelle, Gary Ferrier, James Smalhout, and Dimitri Vittas. 1999. "Mutual Funds and Institutional Investments: What Is the Most Efficient Way to Set Up Individual Accounts in a Social Security System?" World Bank Policy Research Working Paper 2099. World Bank, Washington, D.C.

James, Estelle, James Smalhout, and Dimitri Vittas. 2001. "Administrative Costs and the Organization of Individual Account Systems: A Comparative Perspective." In Robert Holzmann and Joseph E. Stiglitz, eds., *New Ideas about Old Age Security: Toward Sustainable Pension Systems in the 21st Century.* World Bank, Washington, D.C.

James, Estelle, and Dimitri Vittas. 2000. "The Decumulation (Payout) Phase of Defined Contribution Pillars." World Bank Policy Research Working Paper 2464. World Bank, Washington, D.C.

Kotlikoff, Laurence J. 1994. "A Critical Review of the World Bank's Social Insurance Analysis." World Bank Educational and Social Policy Department. World Bank, Washington, D.C.

McDonald, Oonagh, David Blake, et al. 2000. *Improving Security and Flexibility in Retirement: Summary Report. Retirement Income Working Party.* London: The Pensions Institute.

Merton, Robert C., and Zvi Bodie. 1992. "On the Management of Financial Guarantees." *Financial Management* (Winter), 87–109.

Orszag, R. Peter, and Joseph E. Stiglitz. 2001. "A Taxonomy of Pension Reform Issues: Ten Myths about Social Security Systems." In Robert Holzmann and Joseph E. Stiglitz, eds., *New Ideas about Old Age Security: Toward Sustainable Pension Systems in the 21st Century.* World Bank, Washington, D.C.

Palmer, Edward. 2000. "The Swedish Pension Reform Model: Framework and Issues." Social Protection Discussion Paper 0012. World Bank, Washington, D.C.

Queisser, Monika, and Dimitri Vittas. 2000. "The Swiss Multipillar Pension System: Triumph of Common Sense?" World Bank Policy Research Working Paper 2416. World Bank, Washington, D.C.

Rocha, Roberto, Joaquin Gutierrez, and Richard Hinz. 2001. "Improving the Regulation and Supervision of Pension Funds: Are there Lessons from the Banking Sector?" In Robert Holzmann and Joseph E. Stiglitz, eds., *New Ideas about Old Age Security: Toward Sustainable Pension Systems in the 21st Century.* World Bank, Washington, D.C.

Shah, Hemant. 1997. "Toward Better Regulation of Private Pension Funds." World Bank Policy Research Working Paper 1791. World Bank, Washington, D.C.

Smalhout, James H. 1996. *The Uncertain Retirement.* Chicago: Irwin Professional Publishing.

Srinivas, P. S., and Juan Yermo. 1999. "Do Investment Regulations Compromise Pension Fund Performance?" World Bank, Washington, D.C.

Valdés-Prieto, Salvador. 1998. "The Private Sector in Social Security: Latin American Lessons for APEC." In Asian Development Bank, *Promoting Pension Reform: A Critical Assessment of the Policy Agenda.* Manila: Asia Development Bank.

Vittas, Dimitri. 1993. "The Simpler Algebra of Personal Pension Plans." World Bank Policy Research Working Paper 1145. World Bank, Washington, D.C.

———. 1998a. "Regulatory Controversies of Private Pension Funds." World Bank Policy Research Working Paper 1893. World Bank, Washington, D.C.

————. 1998b. "Institutional Investors and Securities Markets: Which Come First?" World Bank Policy Research Working Paper 2032. World Bank, Washington, D.C.

————. 2000. "Pension Reform and Capital Market Development: 'Feasibility' and 'Impact' Preconditions." World Bank Policy Research Working Paper 2414. World Bank, Washington, D.C.

World Bank. 1994. *Averting the Old Age Crisis: Policies to Protect the Old and Promote Growth*. New York: Oxford University Press.

————. 1999. *Czech Republic: Capital Market Review*. World Bank, Washington, D.C.

Financial Networks
and Banking Policy

Patrick Honohan and Dimitri Vittas

Introduction

THE INTERDEPENDENCE OF BANKS AND governments, the inexorable
sequence of banking booms and busts, and the prevalence of regulatory controls all have a centuries-long history. Developing and
transition economies are confronted with the need for liberalization
at a time when deregulation in the market economies has presaged
costly bank failures. At the same time, although there is little reason to believe that the unregulated financial system is always for
the best, the growing complexity of the world financial system
begins to militate against successful policy activism.

Banking cannot function without a basic regulatory and ownership framework satisfying certain minimal criteria. But an overreg-
ulated banking system can also underperform. The move to dereg-
ulate banking systems has been followed by a wave of bank failures. Although bad policies, bad banking, and bad luck each had a
part to play in these failures, suggesting the existence of a learning
curve that may imply fewer banking failures in the future, the
analysis also highlights the strong pressures to assume excessive

The authors are grateful to Millard Long and to participants at the IEA
World Congress for helpful comments. This paper appeared in Holger
Wolf, ed., *Contemporary Economic Issues; Vol. 5: Macroeconomic Policy
and Financial Systems* (Proceedings of the International Economic
Association World Congress), published in 1997 in London by Macmillan.
It is reprinted by kind permission of Palgrave/Macmillan.

risks, notably in waves of euphoria associated with property booms (especially in industrial countries) or in concentrated or self-lending (especially in the developing world).

In seeking policy solutions we suggest that it is important to recognize that the structured interconnectedness or network characteristics of banking and finance have certain policy implications: they are prone to externalities; they are robust to partial failure, and offer multiple alternative paths if one is blocked; and their complexity is such that intervening in one area will typically produce far-reaching and hard-to-predict effects. The three considerations pull policy design in opposite directions: although networks are not fragile, the pervasive externalities call for intervention; but the complexity makes successful intervention hard to design.

Deregulation and Liberalization: What Went Wrong?

The Indispensable Institutional Framework

Defining the exact degree and nature of the optimal constraints on bank ownership rights and the best design for regulatory structures is not a simple matter for a sophisticated financial system. But for economies that have difficulty in reaching even a basic level of adequate financial sector performance it seems possible (at the risk of some reductionism) to define the major prerequisites of the minimally adequate or indispensable institutional framework (IIF). Underlying the idea of such a framework is the attempt to avoid the most glaring misalignments of private incentives with the public good.

The IIF has three elements, relating respectively to central banking, banks, and the contractual framework. Central banks should have the political and operational autonomy to influence interest rate and credit conditions, with a view to protecting the value of the currency and the viability of banking, and in particular should not be constrained to fund open-ended fiscal deficits. Such autonomy can be sought through legislation, but will have little real effect unless buttressed by political tradition and the force of public opinion or by external pressures such as those often conveyed through the conditionality associated with International Monetary Fund (IMF) balance of payments support. Banks should have ownership and control structures that ensure that they are primarily autonomous profit centers, rather than responding passively to the demands of their borrowers or of the government. Regulatory intervention in their activities should be chiefly directed to ensuring solvent and safe and fair operation, and regulations should certainly not undermine solvency. Finally, governments must try to avoid legislative or administrative action that stands in the way of the basic functioning and enforceability of financial contracts.

Different types of banking malaise are characteristically associated with the absence of each of these elements. Experience in Latin America shows, for example, that a lack of central banking autonomy typically results in chronic inflation, which shrinks the domestic financial market. Even if commercial banks operate as autonomous profit centers under such circumstances (as some have done in Argentina and Brazil), the financial system as a whole suffers because savers place their money in real assets or in foreign financial markets. Alternatively, there are many instances in which the absence of autonomous commercial banks in an otherwise stable financial system with low inflation has resulted in endemic insolvency, as commercial banks are forced to lend to unprofitable firms and carry nonperforming loans on their books.

In this view, most of the issues that preoccupy the analysts of sophisticated banking systems are inherently of secondary importance. Issues such as the desirability of risk-weighting for capital requirements, bank privatization, the pros and cons of deposit insurance, and the relative merits of bank-by-bank credit ceilings and open market operations are irrelevant if an IIF is not in place. Other aspects, such as governance within banks-the agency problems of managers in relation to shareholders—are also important but derive their logic essentially from the overall incentive framework.

Although the list of requirements of an IIF is a brief one, it is nuanced. Slogans are inadequate here. Privatization and central bank independence in particular are two slogans whose inadequacy has been exposed by instances in which the forms have been adopted without the intended substance.

Deregulation and Banking Crises

An ownership and regulatory framework satisfying these criteria and going beyond them coevolved with early banking systems in industrial countries. But by the middle of this century the paraphernalia of regulation, both prudential and substantive, had gone far beyond this minimum. Excessive regulation, not only through-out the developing and planned economies but also in the industri-al world, had transferred too many powers to regulators and gov-ernments, restricted the pool of potential bank owners, distorted and muddied incentives, and degraded banking skills. Besides, even before the wave of promarket ideology of the 1980s, technological developments were making it easier for the financial system to bypass much of the regulation.

The resulting move to liberalization has been followed by a widespread increase in the incidence of bank failures, however. The proximate causes of these crises have been categorized as bad luck, bad policies, and bad banking (Solheim 1992). The three can inter-act, with bad policy undermining good banking and vice versa.

Bad luck refers to factors outside the control of policymakers and bankers, such as a prolonged international economic reces-sion, the collapse of a major country or region (such as the disin-tegration of the Soviet Union, which had such an adverse econom-ic impact on Finland as well as on several countries of Eastern Europe), the collapse of an important market for a commodity-producing country (such as the large fall of the oil price in the mid-1980s), or a major natural disaster. Attributing bank failures to bad luck smacks of blame shifting, as prudent policymakers and bankers could make an allowance for unfavorable external devel-opments and could accordingly adopt more conservative policies. But it may be uneconomic to provide against the simultaneous occurrence of two or more external shocks. An overcautious poli-cy would probably have bigger costs in terms of forgone output and economic growth.

Bad policies on the macro side include expansionary monetary and fiscal policies leading to unsustainable economic booms. Chile in the late 1970s and Mexico and Argentina in both the 1970s and 1980s are only the best-known examples of overvalued exchange rates combined with excessive expansion of both business and household lending. Even when not accompanied by macroeconom-ic booms, the maintenance and subsequent collapse of unrealistic exchange rates has been at the root of many bank failures. Unsustainable fiscal policies have contributed to aberrant lending surges by encouraging indebtedness by businesses and households. For example, high marginal rates of income taxation combined with tax exemption of mortgage interest stimulate household bor-rowing (especially where, as in Sweden and the United Kingdom, changes in the tax treatment of mortgage interest are announced long before they become effective).

Bad policies at the micro level include the failure to strengthen supervisory agencies and create mechanisms for dealing with problem loans and imminent bank failures. In the United States, the thrift debacle was precipitated by cuts in supervisory staff and failure to perceive the growing problems of related lending and abuse of the new business powers that were granted to savings and loan associations in the early 1980s. In developing countries, many failures resulted from reliance on politically or socially motivated directed credit from development banks to state enterprises or priority sectors, where grants would have been more appropriate. Poor financial discipline also contributed, including undue forbearance where timely intervention in troubled banks was needed.

Bad banking may be subdivided into three categories: imprudent lending, abusive self-lending, and fraudulent behavior. Imprudent lending seems to have afflicted all countries with banking problems. It is often associated with a "herd instinct" and negative externalities. If, as the textbooks say, banks have a comparative informational advantage in analyzing and screening potential borrowers and in assessing the prospects of the projects they finance, this advantage can evaporate under competitive pressures. Individual banks fail to take into account the effect on total market prospects of their own lending decisions. Banks almost everywhere succumbed to the lure of real estate finance and the presumed safety of collateralized lending. They also failed to take full account of the effects of asset price inflation on the economic feasibility of the financed projects. Bankers involved in making lending decisions seem to have explicitly or implicitly assumed that increases in land or house prices would continue unabated, even though they may have been rising at an abnormally high pace.

Such collective incompetence and limited institutional memory is difficult to explain outside a dynamic model that exerts systemic pressures on bank loan officers to adopt optimistic assessments during the expansion phase of an economic cycle and thus charge low risk premiums, to be followed by very pessimistic reactions during the economic downturn, when risk premiums may be raised to unjustifiably high levels. Thus, bankers succumbing to systemic market pressures may be exaggerating the business cycle. Some banks resist the temptation and avoid suffering large losses, but they are clearly unable to stem the wave of euphoria.

Abusive self-lending to related companies, either at preferential terms and conditions or when the prospects of those companies are very poor, is another manifestation of bad banking. Thus, banks in Chile, República Bolivariana de Venezuela, Colombia, Mexico,

Spain, Turkey, and Greece abused on several occasions the trust of their customers and provided excessive loans to related companies. Controlling self-lending and ensuring that it does not exceed levels that are compatible with prudential norms and is not extended at below-market terms and conditions is a major challenge for regulators and supervisors in all countries. It is, however, interesting that related lending is less of a problem among large banks in developed countries. In these countries, self-lending seems to occur either in marginal institutions or through finance companies that raise their funds from commercial banks but that are not properly monitored and scrutinized in how they utilize these funds. Lending through uncontrolled finance companies was a big problem in Sweden and, especially, in Japan during the 1980s. Related lending also gives rise to a moral hazard problem, as banks with substantial amounts of self-lending tend to throw good money after bad when the performance and prospects of related companies suffer sudden and substantial deterioration. Spain in the late 1970s and Chile in the early 1980s are the best-known examples of this phenomenon.

Outright fraudulent behavior is probably less important as a source of failure than other forms of bad banking. Nevertheless, it often causes failure among small banks; in large banks, isolated frauds may generate big losses without resulting in the collapse of the whole bank. Fraud rarely brings down a large segment of the banking system, but it may contribute to bank failures in an environment of bad policies and other types of bad banking.

The surge in banking crises may also be attributed to an inadequate understanding of the implications of liberalization and of the much higher risks inherent in a liberalized environment. Excessive regulations had weakened incentives to build up the required credit skills and to accumulate the necessary information capital for appraising credit applications. They also delayed the development of systems for monitoring and managing credit and price (market) risks. To that extent, a learning process may be under way that implies that the incidence of bank failures should decline in the future. Certainly bankers are now more aware of the risks involved and are likely to adapt their behavior accordingly. Furthermore, several countries have created more robust regulatory frameworks and have empowered their supervisory agencies to intervene at an earlier stage in the unravelling of a bank failure.

The fact that basic mistakes have been repeated, not only in such countries as Argentina and República Bolivariana de Venezuela but also in the United Kingdom, the United States, and Spain, suggests that the learning process at the level of individual institutions may be weak, or that institutional memories fade. As for the lessons learned by policymakers and bank supervisors, recently introduced and more robust approaches have not yet been tested. Indeed, many argue that new regulations are designed for "fighting the last war" and that future problems are more likely to arise in new areas.

Networks and Banking

The Network Metaphor

Disillusionment with the performance of interventionist policies and a degree of alarm at the consequences of deregulation leave the debate on optimal banking regulation wide open. Moving beyond the IIF introduced earlier brings us into disputed territory. The search for guiding principles has led to an explosion of theoretical work on various aspects of the microfoundations of banking and finance. Though it is too early for a synthesis of this work, a feature that has proved important in several disparate areas and which may have some broad policy implications is that models of banking and finance have begun to stress network characteristics.

A network can be thought of as a set of interconnected paths; it is the structured interconnectedness of economic relationships that we wish to convey by the term. In the economic context the paths typically link agents and offer a more effective or less costly way of communicating than simple bilateral trade. A different type of network, the neural network, is also relevant to information and learning problems. A body of mathematical and statistical theory is devoted to various issues in different types of network. Some of the networks studied by applied mathematicians have economic relevance, as with electrical, telecommunications, and transport networks. There also are many economic analyses of particular types of network, and a growing number of applications of results from the related theory of complex systems.[1] But, given the diversity of these applications, there does not appear to be an organized economic theory of networks as such.

Even in the absence of such a theory, it appears that most economic policy issues surrounding networks relate to three recurrent characteristics of many networks: externalities, structural redundancy, and complexity. First, because of externalities to which they are prone, unregulated networks are likely not to achieve Pareto optimality. Second, network structures can be robust to the failure of one node or segment because alternative (redundant) paths through the network are available. Third, the complexity of the interconnections is such that intervening in one area will typically

produce far-reaching and hard-to-predict effects elsewhere, as the
network adapts to a new equilibrium configuration. The three considerations pull in opposite directions: although networks are not
fragile, the pervasive externalities call for intervention; but the
complexity makes successful intervention hard to design.

The potential applicability to banking should be evident. For
example, on the one hand, the system is prone to contagion
through depositor runs, suggesting the need for prudential regulation. On the other hand, large and famous banks can and do fail
without disastrous economic collapse. Furthermore, the externalities involved make it well-nigh impossible to design policies that
will align the incentives of bank management and ownership with
social welfare.

It is not our intention to develop a network theory of banking as
such, but rather to employ it as a metaphor, concentrating on policy implications of network externalities, redundancy, and complex
adaptive behavior. This policy discussion is resumed in the next
section, but to justify and motivate the approach the remainder of
this section looks more closely at the various ways in which the
recent theoretical literature has identified network characteristics in
banking and finance. The examples come from each of the classic
aspects of banking: payments, liquidity, and credit.

Network Externalities in the Payments System

That network externalities are prevalent at the heart of the payment mechanism has often been noted in the literature. The conventional explanation for why money dominates barter is based on
such externalities (Ostroy 1973; Williamson and Wright 1994), and
the same idea recurs in policy-oriented contexts, such as the analysis of optimal currency areas.[2] Externalities also arise in modern
payment systems networks linking banks in clearing and settling
different types of payment instruments. These externalities can provide market power to those banks that have access to the wholesale
payments network or to check clearing systems, and regulators are
often called upon to ensure access for others that might be excluded. As with the telecommunications network, if the externalities
entailed in payment networks cannot be adequately internalized by
private institutions, they could generate the need for price or access
regulation, though this is arguably of greater significance in respect
of the wholesale, or interinstitutional, payments system than for
retail transactions (Saloner and Shepard 1992).

The competitive and regulatory implications of ATM networks
provide an interesting illustration. A recent study by Matutes and

Padilla (1994) presents a model that describes the dilemma of banks considering whether to join their ATM network with that of competitors. Having a compatible network enhances the product the bank can offer to potential depositors, who will benefit from enhanced network externalities; but for the same reason this compatibility risks eroding the bank's market power. Both the decision to join and the related pricing decisions need to take account of the network aspects. There are clearly potential public policy issues here in computing optimal access prices for ATMs. Similar issues arise with credit cards, seen as a means of payment.

Network Externalities in Liquidity

Network effects in liquidity are most evident in the stock exchange and other organized exchanges such as those for commodities, futures, and options. So far as bank liquidity is concerned, network effects are at play at both the micro and macro levels. A subtle micro argument implying negative network externalities in liquidity has been suggested in recent theoretical work by Matutes and Vives (1992) and Yanelle (1989). They point out that, since the attraction to a depositor of a particular bank depends on the number of its other depositors (after all, size implies stability and liquidity), large but otherwise inefficient banks may prevail in the market.

At the macro or system level an extensive literature (following the original work of Diamond and Dybvig 1983) explains that a network externality is at the heart of that regulator's nightmare, the bank run. According to the literature, early deposit withdrawals by some customers from a bank that has tied up its resources in illiquid loans may lead to collapse. The externality derives from the fact that my deposit would be safe if most other depositors left their money in, but all deposits would be at risk if some withdrew. The bank run externality forms the center of one argument for deposit insurance.[3]

The Credit Network

Credit too involves a network: the web of interrelated credit arrangements between different agents has substantial potential for externalities of the network type. Credit information exchanges, consumer credit bureaus, and the like[4] work well only if most suppliers participate. Other externalities arise in the credit network, though not all of them are strictly "network externalities" in the usual sense of depending on the number of participants.

Gale (1993) points out the "lemons"-type feature in lending decisions, where each bank is faced with a pool of applicants, some of whom have been turned down by other banks in the network. Faced with such adverse selection, the individual bank will be fearing the "winner's curse." The bank's confidence that it is making a profitable lending decision can thereby be undermined.[5] Unless each banker's own screening ability is good enough to outweigh the risk of suffering from the winner's curse, the impact on the volume of credit could theoretically be very severe.[6] Where information is scarce and mostly private, as in developing economies, the adverse selection argument is likely to assume relatively greater importance, thus inhibiting the growth of intermediation.

Traditional populist concerns about concentration of economic power in banks can be reinterpreted in terms of their role in another network: that of corporate control. A recent theoretical literature emphasizes the manner in which debt contracts increasingly govern the transfer of control over poorly performing corporations.[7,8] Bank credit plays a central role here, both in regard to transfer of control over existing productive resources and because access by entrepreneurs to control of additional resources is dependent on their ability to obtain credit. In terms of the network metaphor, banks act as hubs that are on the preferred routes for much of the pattern of control over productive resources in the economy.[9]

Neural Networks in Credit

Neural networks are rather different in character from the networks we have been considering up to now, but they also have clear relevance. Finance, and especially banking, demonstrates neural network characteristics in that repeated interactions between participants, or repeated use of nodes, help build information capital (cf. Shubik 1990). Repeated interactions can also, through the development of reputation effects, reduce the importance of market imperfections relating to opportunistic behavior.

We should not assume that neural network–type learning clearly leads to an optimal allocation of loanable funds. The banker typically uses fairly crude decision rules in deciding whether or not to grant a credit. These rules can be revised, but the criterion for revision is their success in inducing a favorable result for the bank. As the banker's objective function will not usually correspond closely to that of the economy as a whole,[10] the decision rules that are being reinforced will not necessarily be those that maximize economic welfare over time. In simple situations this may not matter much, but where such features as externalities and increasing returns are quantitatively important, initial conditions can strongly influence the evolution of the economy (Arthur 1989). These initial conditions can include the stock of creditworthiness and how it is distributed among potential borrowers. By relying on tried and trusted credit paths the banking system may be locking the economy into an inferior growth path.

No one has yet carried out much formal analysis of how the evolution of economies might depend sensitively on initial conditions as a result of the credit network,[11] but such dependence is likely to become a widely discussed link between the new theories of endogenous growth and policy analysis of institutions. It could, for instance, enrich the theoretical basis for the empirical links between financial institutions and growth discussed by King and Levine (1993a and 1993b) and perhaps help to explain their results.

Redundancy

Examples from finance can also be provided for the other two characteristics that we have highlighted for networks; namely, redundancy and complex adaptation. For redundancy, the arbitrage possibilities underlying covered interest parity would be an example in the payments area. The availability of liability management as an alternative to asset sales for generating liquidity also illustrates redundancy. Redundancy is so familiar in the credit market that we have a neologism for its most common manifestation: "disintermediation."

Complex Adaptation

The payments systems of Ghana and Liberia around 1990 provide an interesting example of sharply divergent evolutions: Ghana had no coins, and Liberia had no banknotes. This curious contrast was the outcome of fiscal pressures impacting subtly different regulatory and institutional structures in the two countries (Honohan 1993).

The scale of the U.S. stock market collapse of October 1987 reflects a leverage induced by the unravelling of a network of linkages put in place by market participants to provide liquidity. In this case, a rather modest initial disturbance was greatly magnified as an overburdened liquidity network attempted to readjust.

Credit markets also have the potential for multiple equilibriums and the potential to respond to changed circumstances in unpredicted ways. Surely the best-studied example of complex adaptation to policy change under conditions of structured interconnectedness is the U.S. savings and loan collapse, where the metamorphosis of a large segment of the system, following a number of shocks, was clearly contingent on a set of interlocking mechanisms and contractual links (including deposit insurance).

Optimal Feasible Regulation

The Conventional Wisdom and Some Proposed Refinements

There is an accepted core of wisdom concerning the essential design features of the "financial constitution"[12] underlying prudential regulation for the modern financial system. The aim is to apply a stable, liberal regulatory environment; create a contestable market with free qualified entry and exit; and ensure appropriate incentives for efficiency and innovation. Such a constitution does not place arbitrary entry, branching, and merger restrictions, but it does require risk diversification (including limits on lending to related parties and on large exposures) and the accumulation of capital reserves to absorb losses. Appropriate prudential norms to ensure adequate risk-based capital backing and effective internal systems of risk management and control are mandated. Can one do better than this by going further in regulation?

We have seen that a kind of contagious euphoria has frequently preceded banking crises. This looks like another network externality, this time negative, and the corrective policy known as "speed limits" that has been proposed to prevent overlending during the euphoric phase of the economic cycle makes sense in these terms. These speed limits would be limits on the growth rate of asset accumulation by financial institutions. They could be linked to each institution's capital position, allowing more rapid growth for those whose capital allowed them to assume the greater risk that is inevitably associated with rapid growth. As the limits would only bite during occasional spurts of rapid expansion, their static distortions would be moderate, and it would not be as easy for the financial network to bypass them as it is for it to bypass permanent restrictions.

Increasingly elaborate regulatory rules on capital adequacy have been proposed (beyond those already adopted), both in terms of the calculation of risk-weightings, including new attempts to cope with the various risks associated with derivatives, and in terms of varying the capitalization requirements over time, depending, for example, on the state of the macroeconomy.[13] Although overcomplicated regulatory rules may demonstrably improve incentives in a worked-out model of a single bank's behavior, they may fall foul of the complex adaptive pattern of the financial network as a whole. In the present state of knowledge, network considerations would argue for caution against overcomplicating the rules. After all, it is much easier to identify and unwind the unintended system consequences of simple regulatory rules.

As an alternative to increasing the complexity of regulation and the burden of supervision, some have suggested making failure more costly for the management and shareholders of the banks themselves. For example, recognizing that those who control profitable banks holding a valuable franchise will tend to be prudent in order to avoid loss of the franchise, some authors have considered models that call for preferential tax treatment or subsidies for banks. Other models generate the conclusion that restrictions on entry or branching, for example, though resulting in monopoly profits, can pay for themselves in terms of improved credit allocation and a reduced risk of failure (cf. Gorton 1994).

Since widespread bank crises are often associated with the negative externalities created through overlending and optimistic assumptions during the euphoric expansion phase of a cycle, and through the underlending and pessimistic outlook during the dysphoric contraction phase, we may have some doubt that franchise value will do the trick. Limiting the number of banks does not appear to have sheltered countries with highly concentrated banking markets from the excesses of the bank lending cycle. For one thing, if banks remain aloof, finance companies and other types of financial institutions may become involved and may propel the expansion phase with both imprudent and abusive self-lending. And if finance companies are not allowed to emerge, then the nonfinancial companies themselves may expand their trade credit and other forms of lending directly to other businesses or households. Commercial paper and other securitized markets may also emerge to provide the finance that is demanded by an expansion-minded economy but which is not provided by the financial sector.

Limiting entry into banking in an attempt to increase its franchise value will also militate against innovation and technological progress, as new banks are more likely to adopt new practices, new products, and new technologies than old banks. By freezing the network, entry limitations stultify it.[14]

Translating theoretical predictions into practical recommendations furthermore requires an awareness of the political economy dimensions of the issue. However subtle the rationale for their introduction, tax breaks, subsidies, or other advantages for banks may well open the door to crude distortions achieved by special interest lobbyists. This is usually observed when attempts are made to protect a sector from competitive pressures. As a result, the general presumption against such privileges seems hard to overturn.

Limits to Supervision

It is one thing to introduce regulations, another to supervise the performance and solvency of the regulated institutions. One must be realistic about the information and expertise available to regulators.[15] Network considerations greatly complicate their lives. The blurring of boundaries between banking and other financial institutions is a key factor here, and not only because the associated decline in bank profitability[16] increases their vulnerability, as evidenced by a general tendency to decline in their credit ratings.[17] The erosion of boundaries goes hand-in-hand with an increase in network interdependencies affecting banks.

One aspect of this is the growing importance for banks of the management of portfolios for which market price risk (interest rate, stock price, or exchange rate changes) is more important than credit risk.[18] Bandwagon effects in these speculative markets probably increase the instability of interest rates and asset prices, and thereby of other macroeconomic conditions. This in turn feeds back to the vulnerability of banks.

More generally, because of the much wider variety of contingencies that can have a material effect on the solvency of banks, it is harder to assess the capacity of each bank to face future risks. When banks were conducting a traditional bills, loans, and deposits business, the application of simple ratios gave a pretty good assessment of the health of the bank, at least when combined with a qualitative assessment of the probity and general administrative and managerial competence of the principals. Nowadays, with highly leveraged and frequently traded contingent assets and liabilities in the picture (including open-ended insurance commitments, securities underwritten, and a range of mathematical derivatives), not to speak of the uncertainties entailed by counterparty risk (including that generated by reinsurance contracts that may be repudiated in bad times), maintaining an up-to-date evaluation of solvency seems well-nigh impossible.[19] This is true for the bank's own management and doubly so for the supervisor, especially when, as in many cases (most recently in the case of Daiwa Bank), the bank's management sets out to deceive the supervisor.

Furthermore, the complex ownership structures characteristic of a reemerging breed of financial conglomerates may serve to conceal not only potential conflicts of interest, but also the true leverage involved, as, for example, where intergroup loans or guarantees are present. The apparent exposure (as in the Barings case) of owners of mutual fund units to the collapse of a banking affiliate of the fund manager is just one example of the inadequacy of "firewalls" apparently built into conglomerate structures. These are instances of the complexity characteristics we have already noted for networks. It is hard for the supervisor to predict how a particular disturbance might impact the equilibrium structure and ultimately the solvency of an elaborate network, whether that network be a single financial conglomerate or several interacting conglomerates.

Network redundancy is also clearly relevant here. Regulatory arbitrage becomes virtually uncontrollable when the dividing line between regulated banks and unregulated nonbanks no longer clearly delineates financial products that are close substitutes. Attempts to regulate or reregulate a particular instrument or activity often result merely in the emergence of a close substitute provided by a nonbank, perhaps with explicit or implicit ownership links with the bank.

Acceptable Risk of Failure

If financial crises and collapses cannot be entirely avoided, it is also true that most bank failures are absorbed reasonably smoothly, largely because of the network redundancy of which we have spoken.

Of course bank failures have distributional effects, but how substantial are the systemic costs that they impose on society? There are historical episodes that involved bank failures and in which there was massive economic disruption characterized by a slump in output, soaring unemployment, exchange rate depreciation, inflation, and so on. But many of these occurred against a background of macroeconomic policy failure or of adverse external nonfinancial shocks, and should be seen as consequences rather than independent causes of widespread distress. Besides, the bulk of instances of bank failure are not of that character. In particular, while the deposit contract is theoretically prone to runs by uninformed depositors at times of heightened uncertainty caused by a bank failure, the frequency of such contagion effects is not high. They also usually affect only a part of the banking system and for a short time, and they usually are offset by the interbank market or by the central bank.

Even where a large part of the banking system has become insolvent, the position has usually been met by government subsidy with only limited deadweight losses.

It seems that the finance network contains sufficient redundancy to continue to function despite isolated failures. Ensuring this capacity, rather than attempting to forestall all possible bank failures, may be the key to feasible bank regulation. The implications for competition policy here clearly conflict with the idea of ensuring a franchise value for banks. While the latter is seen, among other things, as being required to prevent excessive risk taking, it could be counterproductive if pursued to the point where it leads to just a few institutions handling the whole of a relatively closed and fragile system.

Where the consequences of bank failure are spread widely through taxation, and where they do not result in catastrophic disruption to the operation of the financial system or of the economy, it is possible to take a more relaxed view of bank failure than is customary. From this perspective, one may think of the regulatory system as a mechanism for limiting the exposure of the taxpayer to risk. At some price, bank failure becomes an acceptable risk.

Conclusion

Despite the growing complexity of banking and financial systems, there are some unambiguous messages. For one thing, we have seen that application of a few simple structural rules goes a long way to avoiding the worst kinds of financial sector failure. That many recent instances of such failure can be documented shows that this finding is not a vacuous one. Indeed, its implementation is still the major policy priority in probably most transition economies, and is also required elsewhere.

But banking policy has always been more ambitious than this, both at the macro and micro level. Dissatisfaction with the diminishing effectiveness of the controlled banking regimes in the decades after the Second World War led to substantial deregulation. In its wake came several waves of bank failure and bank crisis, only some of which could be rationalized as the manifestation of previously hidden insolvency. Certainly bankers went through a learning process before adjusting to the deregulated regime, and they seemed particularly vulnerable to a form of contagious euphoria, often manifested in overlending to property developers. Given the recurrence in history of carbon-copy banking failures, however, it is clear that private learning will not go so far as to eliminate all bank failure.

The design of optimal policy, not only for achieving safety but also for ensuring the effectiveness of the banking system, and an equitable share in its services for all sections of the community, is still a major policy concern. But the disappointing performance of both the regulated regime and the deregulated leaves a vacuum that theoreticians have been trying to fill. A feature of many theoretical studies of banking is the recurrence of the concept of a network to describe either the system as a whole, or aspects of it. Among the characteristics of many networks are their proneness to externalities, their redundancy (ensuring that flows cannot be obstructed by blocking just one path), and their tendency to adapt in a complex manner to disturbances. Taken together, such characteristics can on the one hand justify regulation, but on the other hand point also to the likely ineffectiveness of much regulatory effort and to the unpredictability of the system's response to regulatory measures.

Applying this perspective to current policy issues leads us to suggest a degree of modesty in banking policy. A basic regulatory framework is certainly needed to reduce the incidence of bank failure; we are not advocating *laissez faire*. We emphasize measures to ensure risk diversification and adequate capital reserves. We even allow for growth and portfolio limits, linked to capital resources, on the grounds that such controls are institution-neutral and will not be as readily undermined by network effects as other types of regulation. But we argue that both overelaborate regulation and the alternative of increasing franchise value, through limited entry or otherwise, fall foul of network-based critiques. We are against restrictions on branching, mergers, and business powers, against elaborate capital requirements (too difficult to calculate and verify), against entry restrictions to increase franchise value, and against proscription of universal banking (because no conclusive case has been made against it).

Supervision has a role in verifying the presence of effective internal information and management systems and in early intervention to avoid the heavy costs of forbearance. However, the blurring of boundaries between banking and the remainder of the financial network has placed an upper limit on the effectiveness of supervision. We will have to put up with bank failures, mitigated by deposit insurance to protect small savers, and indeed we argue that—partly because of network redundancy—the social costs of bank failure are not as high as is sometimes thought.

Many of the other commonly discussed policy objectives, mostly relating to the dynamic effectiveness of the banking system and to issues of fairness, can be rationalized in terms of correcting for network externalities. For example, the universal bank can be seen as a way of internalizing a whole segment of the financial network in a single institution. The appropriate role of policy here depends crucially on correct specification of the model; when the relevant networks have complex adaptive characteristics, the wrong model can give very misleading results.

While the forces of redundancy, as exemplified by regulatory arbitrage, militate against subsidy or directed credit solutions to problems of fairness, network ideas suggest that the marginal impact of small interventions here can be so large as to justify the distortions involved.

Notes

1. Liebowitz and Margolis (1994) show how the concept of a network externality—i.e., one that depends on the number of other participants—can be misused.

2. Cf. Dowd and Greenaway (1994), who argue that membership in a currency union will be more attractive the more participants it has.

3. Dewatripont and Tirole (1994) do not, as is usual, rely on the bank run as the main justification for prudential regulation: instead, they see the authorities as representing the interests of small depositors, thereby avoiding costly duplication of monitoring activities that would otherwise have to be carried out by the depositors.

4. For instance, similar organizations operated for non-life insurance. The same applies to the multiple listing services used in the United States to buy and sell houses.

5. In game-theoretic terms, this is an instance of coordination failure in the presence of strategic complementarity.

6. This network effect is independent of other arguments, based on informational asymmetries in the credit market that prevent the banking system from lending enough (or occasionally induce it to lend too much) to achieve a social optimum (cf., for example, de Meza and Webb 1990).

7. Because of the agency problems entailed by the extension of credit, credit contracts specify the circumstances under which control will pass from the entrepreneur. These contracts are designed to help align the interests of the borrower with those of the lender. For instance, a feature of the

standard bond contract is that it removes any incentive for the entrepreneur to conceal the true value of the firm. Only if the value of the pledged firm truly falls below the cost of repaying the bond will the entrepreneur default (Diamond 1984). Other, more subtle mismatches between the objective functions of entrepreneur and investor lead to more complex financial contracts, in which the circumstances under which transfer of control will occur is a key element (Aghion and Bolton 1992; Hart and Moore 1994).

8. Bolton and von Thadden (1998) present a model in which the positive network externalities in liquidity associated with dispersed firm ownership have to be traded off against the reduced effectiveness of corporate control when ownership is dispersed.

9. The variety of debt contracts used by financial intermediaries in these control relationships—i.e., the financial instruments—may be seen as analogous to alternative modes in a transportation network. Many specialized financial intermediaries are involved in only a limited range of modes, but the trend to deregulation has meant that it is increasingly banks that are closest to offering a full range of modes, thereby acting as full hubs in the network.

10. Especially if the bank is relying on debt contracts whose payoff to the bank is a strictly convex function of the economic benefits of the activity being financed.

11. This can be seen as an instance of complex adaptive behavior of the system.

12. Cf. Vittas (1992a). In essence, this can be seen as a fleshing out of aspects of the IIF (indispensable institutional framework) introduced earlier.

13. Dewatripont and Tirole (1994) provide a sophisticated analysis of such a framework.

14. As well as increasing systemic fragility.

15. Recall also that reliance on prudential regulation assumes the availability of a skilled, impartial, and authoritative official supervision agency, something that is not always easy to provide. It is not hard to be convinced of the practical relevance (where regulators lack experience or authority) of such problems as theoretically illustrated by Boot and Thakor (1993). Their model describes an imperfect regulator reacting to new information that suggests that an earlier regulatory judgment was too lax and that bank management is assuming too much risk. Because corrective action now will expose the regulator's earlier error of judgment, the regulator too becomes caught up in the risk taking, and gambles, along with the management, on the success of the risky strategy in being able to alone conceal the regulatory error.

Heavy reliance on regulation furthermore has the effect of retaining in the system the scope for corruption to drastically worsen economic performance. Adapting Shleifer's and Vishny's (1993) model to bank regulation, we can picture a corrupt regulator turning a blind eye to optimistic loan classification, or tolerating excessive lending to related parties, in return for a side payment (e.g., a low-interest loan). The lowering of prudential standards will spread throughout the system, encouraging a socially excessive level of risk taking, with adverse budgetary consequences when implicit or explicit deposit insurance kicks in.

16. With traditional core banking activities opened to new competitors.

17. Which in turn reduces their capacity to intermediate at the top end of the market. Market segmentation and the high credit rating of banks in the industrial countries derived from the old regulatory regime that is now being progressively dismantled. Note, however, that despite all the changes, line-of-business and ownership restrictions remain important in most industrial countries (Borio and Filosa 1994).

18. Securitization of bank loans has contributed to this process, and has been part of the wider process of unbundling and repackaging assets into derivative securities.

19. In fairness, and while supervision will never be able to provide early warning of all failures, it is arguable that the major technological leaps in the area of derivative instruments are already behind us and that prudential technology now has a chance to catch up. In particular, the mathematical complexity of compound derivatives should not be beyond the mastery of government regulators.

References

Aghion, P., and P. Bolton. 1992. "An Incomplete Contracts Approach to Financial Contracting." *Review of Economic Studies* 59:473–94.

Arthur, B. 1989. "Competing Technologies, Increasing Returns, and Lock-in by Historical Events." *Economic Journal* 99:116–31.

Baumol, W. J., and J. G. Sidak. 1994. "The Pricing of Inputs Sold to Competitors." *Yale Journal on Regulation* 11:171–02.

Berglöf, E., and E.-L. von Thadden. 1994. "Short-Term versus Long-Term Interests: Capital Structure with Multiple Investors." *Quarterly Journal of Economics* 109:1055–84.

Bolton, P., and E.-L. von Thadden. 1998. "The Ownership Structure of Firms: The Liquidity-Control Tradeoff in the Privately Held Firm." *Journal of Finance* 53:1–25.

Boot, A. W., S. I. Greenbaum, and A. V. Thakor. 1993. "Reputation and Discretion in Financial Contracting." *American Economic Review* 83:1165–83.

Boot, A. W., and A. V. Thakor. 1993. "Self-Interested Bank Regulation." *American Economic Review Papers and Proceedings* 83:206–12.

Borio, C. E. V., and R. Filosa. 1994. "The Changing Borders of Banking: Trends and Implications." *BIS Economic Papers* 43. Bank for International Settlements, Basle.

Caminal, R., J. Gual, and X. Vives. 1990. "Competition in Spanish Banking." In J. Dermine, ed., *European Banking in the 1990s*. Oxford: Basil Blackwell.

Caprio, J. G., Jr. 1996. "Bank Regulation: The Case of the Missing Model." World Bank Policy Research Working Paper 1574. World Bank, Washington, D.C.

de Meza, D., and D. Webb. 1990. "Risk, Adverse Selection and Capital Market Failure." *Economic Journal* 100:206–14.

Dewatripont, M., and J. Tirole. 1994. *The Prudential Regulation of Banks*. Cambridge, Mass. MIT Press.

Diamond, D. W. 1984. "Financial Intermediation and Delegated Monitoring." *Review of Economic Studies* 51:393–414.

Diamond, D. W., and P. H. Dybvig. 1983. "Bank Runs, Deposit Insurance and Liquidity." *Journal of Political Economy* 91:401–19.

Dowd, K., and D. Greenaway. 1994. "Network Externalities and Switching Costs: Towards an Alternative View of Optimum Currency Areas." *Economic Journal* 103:1180–89.

Gale, D. 1993. "Information Capacity and Financial Collapse." In Mayer and Vives (1993).

Gorton, G. 1994. "Bank Regulation when 'Banks' and 'Banking' Are Not the Same." *Oxford Review of Economic Policy* 10(4):106–19.

Hart, O., and J. Moore. 1994. "A Theory of Debt Based on the Inalienability of Human Capital." *Quarterly Journal of Economics* 109:841–80.

Honohan, P. 1993. "Financial Sector Failures in Western Africa." *Journal of Modern African Studies* 31:49–65.

King, R. G., and R. Levine. 1993a. "Financial Intermediation and Economic Development." In Mayer and Vives (1993).

———. 1993b. "Finance and Growth: Schumpeter Might Be Right." *Quarterly Journal of Economics* 108:717–38.

Liebowitz, S. J., and S.E. Margolis. 1994. "Network Externalities: An Uncommon Tragedy." *Journal of Economic Perspectives* 8:133–50.

Litan, R. E. 1992. "Banks and Real Estate: Regulating the Unholy Alliance." In L. E. Brown and E. Rosenberg, eds., *Real Estate and the Credit Crunch*, Conference Series No. 36. Boston: Federal Reserve Bank of Boston.

Matutes, C., and A. J. Padilla. 1994. "Shared ATM Networks and Banking Competition." *European Economic Review* 38:1113–38.

Matutes, C., and X. Vives. 1992. "Competition for Deposits, Risk of Failure and Regulation in Banking." Financial Markets Paper 18. Centre for Economic Policy Research, London.

Mayer, C. P., and X. Vives, eds. 1993. *Capital Markets and Financial Integration.* Cambridge, Cambridge University Press.

Ostroy, J. M. 1973. "The Informational Efficiency of Monetary Exchange." *American Economic Review* 63:597–610.

Saloner, G., and A. Shepard. 1992. "The Adoption of Technologies with Network Effects: An Empirical Examination of the Adoption of Automated Teller Machines." National Bureau of Economic Research (NBER) Working Paper 4048. NBER, Cambridge, Mass.

Shleifer, A., and R. W. Vishny. 1993. "Corruption." *Quarterly Journal of Economics* 108:681–716.

Shubik, M. 1990. "A Game Theoretic Approach to the Theory of Money and Financial Institutions." In B. J. Friedman and F. H. Hahn, eds., *Handbook of Monetary Economics I.* Amsterdam: North Holland.

Solheim, J. A. 1992. "The Norwegian Experience with Financial Liberalization and Banking Problems." In Vittas (1992a).

Vittas, D., ed. 1992a. *Financial Regulation: Changing the Rules of the Game.* EDI Development Studies. World Bank, Washington, D.C.

———. 1992b. "Introduction and Overview." In Vittas (1992a)

Williamson, S., and R. Wright. 1994. "Barter and Monetary Exchange under Private Information." *American Economic Review* 84:104–23.

World Bank. 1989. *World Development Report 1989: Financial Systems and Development.* World Bank, Washington, D.C.

Yanelle, M. O. 1989. "The Strategic Analysis of Intermediation." *European Economic Review.* 33:294–304.

Part III

Taking the Longer View

Retirement Reading for Sophisticated Bankers

Charles P. Kindleberger

AT A RECENT CONFERENCE I MET an old acquaintance, a banker of European antecedents, who asked me for a list of 100 books on economic and financial history to read in his forthcoming retirement. What a beguiling task! It proved, however, that 100 was the wrong number. I easily picked 35 to 40 favorites, but the circle widened after that to such an extent that choices became too close. It was with difficulty that I stretched the list to the round total of 50 books.

One can make one's own rules in a task of this sort. I felt justified in including a very small number of French and German works. Novels also are permitted, since 19th century novelists are long on realism: Defoe was a forerunner. There are one or two books prominent in the history of thought on money and finance that cannot be excluded, and for good measure I have thrown in some general and social history and analysis with a financial flavor. Unless it is particularly well written, I have, however, omitted most of the profound work on banking and finance. I am not trying to educate retired bankers—it is too late for that—but to interest and possibly to amuse them.

The list is long on Europe, short on the United States, blank elsewhere—the consequence of professional deformation. I gave no regard to whether a book is in print or out of print, since interlibrary loans, especially in the United States, are more and more possible. Annotations are of varying length, dependent less on the merit of the work than on how lively is my memory and how full are my notes. Braudel, Dickens, and de Roover make the list with two books; elsewhere, where the call is too close, like a book-of-the-month club I offer an alternative selection.

The list is divided into general history, including social history; banking and financial history, including a handful of classics in the history of financial thought; novels; and biographies, including correspondence and autobiographies. Within each grouping, the order is alphabetical by author. No one is expected to begin with number 1 and read through to number 50. Many people state and even believe that they like history, or biography, or fiction: the lists under the several groups are so short that it should be simple to find a good place to start.

General History

1. Luigi Barzini (1954), *The Italians* (New York: Atheneum)

By virtue of his place in the alphabet, Barzini is first on the list. This is a little disconcerting, for *The Italians* is a work of sociological history, not economics and finance. Nonetheless, one can learn much from Barzini, a brilliant journalist. He writes about general Italian characteristics such as *clientismo*, the wish of everyone to have a protector and of the powerful to be surrounded by clients, and stresses the differences between north and south in a barrage of pungent aphorisms: southerners make money in order to rule, northerners rule in order to make money. The southerner is looking for power, prestige, authority, and fame; the northerner is almost a pure *homo economicus*, wanting a better job, land, capital, degrees, credit, industrial shares, a rich wife, and rich daughters and sons-in-law to ensure the defense and prosperity of the family.

2. E. W. Bovill (1958), *The Golden Trade of the Moors* (New York: Oxford University Press)

For centuries, the Moors plied back and forth across the Sahara desert, carrying salt to the alluvial gold deposits of the Ashanti above the Gold Coast. In the beginning the exchanges were silent, the Moors leaving salt on the river bank and backing away, the Ashanti bringing forward what they deemed the appropriate amount of gold. Salt and gold were added or taken back until an implicit price was settled. The Ashanti needed salt to preserve meat, and at one time the price paid was a pound of salt for a pound of gold. Some caravans of as many as 1,800 camels were lost. Guides were blinded by exposure to the blazing sun but knew where they were by tasting the sand. When the Ashanti converted to Islam, one trip to Mecca, bearing gold for expenses, crossed the Sahara west to east. Stopping for a few weeks in Alexandria, it left behind an inflation that lasted years.

3. Fernand Braudel (1966 and 1973), *The Mediterranean and the Mediterranean World in the Age of Philip II,* Volumes 1 and 2 (New York: Harper and Row)

Braudel was the leading historian and founder of the *annales* school in France. The *annales* school sought to change the teaching of history from the study of dynasties, wars, and high politics to study of the daily life of an epoch as it was shaped by geography and climate, and the study of how people lived and communicated with one another. The first volume in particular, which treats the inland sea as a highway that unites its shores, is marvellous, even exciting, reading. Volume 2 unaccountably reverts to the traditional history of kings and diplomacy.

4. Fernand Braudel (1983), *Civilization and Capitalism, 15th–18th Century,* Volume 2: *The Wheels of Commerce* (New York: Harper and Row)

All three books of *Civilization and Capitalism* are brilliant, erudite, even dazzling. In them, Braudel, the *pointilliste*, describes life in the gap between the medieval period and the factory age, with detailed lists of practices, artifacts, connections, and episodes. They do, however, require the stamina of a long-distance runner. The first volume, *The Structure of Everyday Life*, deals with traditional peasant society; the third volume, *The Perspectives of the World*, deals with the way that "distant trade" binds up the world (and the national) economy. The sprinter might be best directed first to Volume 2, *The Wheels of Commerce*, which treats of local markets—fairs, shops, and market towns—and the beginnings of capitalistic production in cottage industry, as organized by merchants.

5. Gordon A. Craig (1982), *The Germans* (New York: New American Library)

Craig is the leading American historian of contemporary Germany. In this book, he distills from years of research some general conclusions about the Germans, their history, and their prevailing attitudes, and hazards a few guesses about the future. I was originally drawn to the book by the chapter "Money," which, while almost devoid of monetary history in the institutional sense, is penetrating on German attitudes toward money as revealed by history and quotations from leading figures such as Faust, Wagner, and Marx. Other chapter topics include Jews, women, literature, and the military; there also is an appendix, taking off from Mark Twain, on "The Awful German Language."

6. P. G. M. Dickson (1967), *The Financial Revolution in England: A Study in the Development of Public Credit* (New York: St. Martin's Press)

This may strike some retired bankers as a heavy monograph, as it traces the development of British government finance after the Glorious Revolution that in 1688 replaced the Stuarts with the House of Orange. Tax farming gave way to bureaucratic handling of tax revenue and government expenditure; chaotic debt instruments, many at the level of the spending units such as the army and navy, were scrapped in favor of regularized public debt. The period covered embraces the establishment of the Bank of England, the South Sea bubble, and Dutch investment in England. Solid, but not bedtime reading.

7. Stanley Hoffmann et al. (1963), *In Search of France* (Cambridge, Mass.: Harvard University Press)

This volume fills the need for a companion piece on France to Barzini on Italy and Craig on the Germans. Too much of it, perhaps, for our purpose, deals with politics and domestic and foreign policy, but it does include two penetrating sociological analyses by Wylie and Pitts, the former on the French peasant and village, the latter on aristocratic and bourgeois values. The dominance of aristocratic values that emphasize virtuosity, whether on the field of battle, in conversation in the salon, driving an automobile, eating splendiferously, or in the boudoir, is shown to inhibit economic growth, except where such growth depends on scientific achievement.

8. Stephen A. Schuker (1976), *The End of French Predominance in Europe: The Financial Crisis of 1924 and the Adoption of the Dawes Plan* (Chapel Hill, N. C.: University of North Carolina Press)

This book is badly titled, with the subject matter conveyed rather in the subtitle. Schuker, a modern historian, shows in detail how French financial weaknesses, which had their origin in tears in the French social fabric, frustrated France's political aims in the post–

First World War settlement. The book is meticulously researched in the archives of four countries, and makes compelling reading.

9. Warren C. Scoville (1960), *The Persecution of Huguenots and French Economic Development, 1680–1720* (Los Angeles: University of California Press)

My recent interest in the Huguenots was aroused by the question of whether the emigration of the tenth of their number that refused to abjure Calvinist Protestantism after the Revocation of the Edict of Nantes in 1685 hurt the economic development of France. Scoville is somewhat indecisive on the point: the emigrants took with them wealth and skills, especially in glass and papermaking and in silk, but while French economic growth slowed after their departure, the wars of Louis XIV and bad harvests also were major contributing factors. Chapter 9, on finance and agriculture, is particularly absorbing. Readers who wish to pursue an interest in the Sun King-who said on his deathbed: "too many palaces, too many wars"—have a wide choice of guides, from Nancy Mitford to Charles W. Cole.

10. Lawrence Stone (1967), *The Crisis of the Aristocracy, 1558–1641*, abridged edition (London: Oxford University Press)

Stone pins down the watershed between medieval and modern England to the period 1580–1620, when capitalist institutions and ethics began to replace the aristocratic love of gambling, conspicuous consumption, and honor. Chapter 9, on credit, reminds one of today's credit-card addicts and their need for financial restructuring-except that these debtors were many of them aristocrats—with unpaid bills and debts to moneylenders. The world today may be a junk-bond casino, as Felix Rohaytyn has characterized it, but the Elizabethan age saw individual indebtedness of dukes and earls as high as £60,000; and this at a time when the pound sterling was a heavy currency.

11. Barry Supple (1959), *Commercial Crisis and Change in England, 1600–1642: A Study in the Instability of a Mercantile Economy* (Cambridge: Cambridge University Press)

A solid study in the disturbed monetary conditions of England at the opening of the modern period, with an account of the debates over bullionism, the foreign exchanges and foreign exchange control, mercantilism, and the money supply. The debates often have an echo of present-day controversy.

12. Pierre Vilar (1969), *A History of Gold and Money, 1450–1920* (London: New Left Books)

Of the several books on the history of money, this is by far the best. There is a strong emphasis on the impact of the New World on European finances, starting with Columbus, who over the three months and five days that his voyage took mentioned in his diary 65 times his interest in finding gold. Vilar also provides a brilliant chapter on the silver mountain of Potosi (in modern Peru): a city of 160,000 people at its peak, including 700–800 criminals and 120 white prostitutes; at 4,000 meters' elevation, 500 kilometers from the nearest port; a city that spent 8 million pesos to celebrate the accession of Philip II; a city that was possibly jewel of the Empire, more likely "accursed mountain." The book, as it covers the European price revolution brought on by the influx of specie and the economic discussion thereby initiated, is scholarly; it is nonetheless a page-turner.

13. Charles Wilson (1941), *Anglo-Dutch Commerce and Finance in the Eighteenth Century* (Cambridge: Cambridge University Press)

This is a scholarly account of two transitions: in Holland, from trade to highly sophisticated finance; and of commercial and financial supremacy from Amsterdam to London. Dutch investors lent heavily to Britain, and invested in British shares, through a series of financial ups and downs, ending with the switch of Dutch lending from London to Paris after 1784 and especially after the French occupation of Amsterdam in 1793.

Financial History and Classics in the History of Financial Thought

14. Walter Bagehot (1873), *The Collected Works of Walter Bagehot,* Volume 9: *Lombard Street,* Norman St. John-Stevas, ed. (London: The Economist Books).

Bagehot (pronounced Badge-ette) was for years the editor of *The Economist,* started in 1848 by James Wilson, his father-in-law, and wrote prolifically on economic and political subjects. *Lombard*

Street is his most famous work, describing the operations of the London money and capital market at the end of the third quarter of the 19th century. It articulates and rationalizes, with some misgivings, the role in financial crisis of the Bank of England as "lender of last resort" (see also my selection number 32, below). The debate is inconclusive as to whether Bagehot was a better writer than economist, or vice versa. There is no doubt, however, that he was a superb writer.

15. Jean Bouvier (1960), *Le Krach de l'Union Générale, 1878–1885* (Paris: Presses Universitaires de France)

This is an absorbing description of the bankers' quarrels that are so prevalent in French financial history. An outsider, Eugène Bontoux, a Catholic with connections with the French nobility, left the *grandes écoles* to start a bank in Lyons at the time when France was recovering from the doldrums of the 1870s (after the Franco-Prussian indemnity). Bontoux challenged the Protestant-Jewish banking establishment of Paris, started off a boom in foreign and domestic investment, and fell flat. The establishment chose not to pick him up. The details, in French, are delicious. An equally absorbing but more extended book by Bouvier is his 1961 *Le Crédit Lyonnais de 1863 à 1881: Les années de formation d'une banque de depôts* (Paris: S.E.V.P.E.N.).

16. Murray Teigh Bloom (1966), *The Man Who Stole Portugal,* second edition (New York: Scribners)

This book was written following the death in 1965 of one Albas Reis, a Portuguese, who in the 1920s forged orders to the London printer Waterslow instructing them to deliver to him the plates for printing the Portuguese 500-escudo note. He printed and spent some 200,000 notes (worth about US$5 million), roughly one-fifth of which he used to purchase foreign deposits and securities. The rest produced a Keynesian economic expansion in Portugal, until Reis was caught. An earlier book on the subject is C. Kisch's 1932 *The Portuguese Bank Note Case: The Story and Solution of a Financial Perplexity* (London: Macmillan).

17. Martin G. Buist (1974), *At Spes non Fracta: Hope and Co., 1700–1815* (The Hague: Martinus Nijhoff)

This is an account of the Dutch merchant bank established by a Scot, John Hope, and especially the work of Peter C. Labouchère, the leading partner during the Napoleonic wars and son-in-law of Sir Francis Baring of Baring Brothers, London. The Hope and Co. bank clung to commodity trade and speculation throughout the 18th century, instead of specializing. When Labouchère was cut off in St. Petersburg during the Napoleonic continental blockade, he bought up commodities that were in short supply, on speculation. The bank also was involved in lending the United States money for the Louisiana Purchase in 1803, transmitting funds owed by Spain to France by way of Mexico, Baltimore, London, and Amsterdam; it also notably surviving the Amsterdam financial crises of 1763 and 1772 that toppled rival banking houses. The Latin motto of the title, incidentally, translates as "But Hope Is Not Lost."

18. John Carswell (1960), *The South Sea Bubble* (London: Cresset Press)

There is a plethora of books about the South Sea bubble in London and the Mississippi bubble of the Scotsman John Law in Paris. This book, while focusing primarily on John Blunt's activities in London, covers both. The two bubbles were pricked in 1720, Mississippi first and then the South Sea, whereupon the speculators departed for Amsterdam and Hamburg to conflate insurance bubbles in those centers. The financial machinations at times become intricate, and the connections among trade, the national debt, and frenzied stock exchange speculation can be hard to follow. The Carswell book is a solid one, however, and is the one I know best. On the Mississippi bubble there is a relatively new 800–pager by Edgar Faure (*La Banqueroûte de Law,* Paris: Gallimard, 1977), written, it has been cynically said, to get him into the French Academy. The first 20 or so pages are devoted to how the French pronounced Law's name. Notable among the accounts in English is Charles MacKay's *Extraordinary Popular Delusions and the Madness of Crowds*, originally published in 1841, reissued in 1980 by Harmony Books in New York. *Extraordinary Popular Delusions* also contains shorter pieces on the South Sea bubble and the tulip mania of 1636.

19. Youssef Cassis (1984), *Les Banquiers de la City à l'Époque Eduardienne* (Geneva-Paris: Librairie Droz)

This is a study of 460 London bankers, from a variety of disciplines, in the Edwardian period prior to the First World War. The bankers are examined in sociological terms; their origins, education, wealth, social standing, marriage customs (in terms of whom they marry), and relations with the British aristocracy and the political elite observed. Unlike much sociology, this is interesting reading. The leading cast of merchant bankers is divided into Quakers, Anglicans, and old-foreign and new-foreign groups, with a number of Jews among the last two categories. Cassis, who wrote this from Geneva but on the basis of English material, including some previously unexamined diaries, observes that the bankers were powerful and rich, were largely descended from other bankers, and included only a few self-made men. He exonerates them from the charges of exercising dominant political power and of starting the First World War. Their ranks, moreover, were far from solid on even such issues as free trade and the gold standard. The book will probably be translated into English; for those who do not want to wait, this original version is highly recommended.

20. Center for Medieval and Renaissance Studies, University of California, Los Angeles (1979), *The Dawn of Modern Banking* (New Haven: Yale University Press)

This is a collection of studies by leading medieval scholars in the United States and Europe that covers the rise of banking in Italy and Spain, the shift of focus to Southern Germany, the rise of the bill of exchange and of credit in England, and banking without banks in the Middle East under the Islamic ban on interest. It includes a particularly useful discussion of usury laws and their limited impact on the development of bank lending. For newcomers to the subject, it provides a running start to an understanding of the development of modern banking in the 17th century.

21. Paul Emden (1938), *The Money Powers of Europe in the Nineteenth and Twentieth Centuries* (New York: Appleton-Century)

This is a most agreeable book of sketches, pastiches, and anecdotes about banks and bankers of Britain and continental Europe. Some of the stories are funny, such as the account of Labouchère, who, on being turned down for a partnership in Hope and Co., asked if things would be different were he married to Sir Francis Baring's daughter, and then on being turned down for the hand of the daughter asked if things would be different were he a partner in Hope. (He got both the job and the girl.) Emden, who should not be confused with Paul Erdman, whose *The Crash of 1979* almost made the novel section, is a bright and breezy journalist of the sort whose books not only pass the time in retirement but fill it up.

22. Richard Ehrenberg (1928), *Capitalism and Finance
    in the Age of the Renaissance: A Study of the Fuggers*
    (New York: Harcourt Brace)

This classic study of the Fugger bank in Augsburg in the 16th century focuses on war and money: Money is needed to buy soldiers;
but with soldiers, one can acquire money. The Fuggers were
involved with Venice, Austria, the Holy Roman Empire, and the
financial markets of Lyons, Bruges, and Antwerp (and through
them with the Spanish crown, which proved their ultimate undo-
ing).The period was one of struggling capital markets. The financial center of Europe was moving northward from Lucca, Florence,
and Venice; Genoa, a rival of the Fuggers for the Spanish treasure
that was overdue in payment for loans when it reached Seville,
hung on longer. The mistake that brought down the Fuggers, and
many a bank before and since, was lending too much to kings on
inadequate security.

23. James S. Gibbons (1859), *The Banks of New-York,
    Their Dealers, the Clearing House and the Panic
    of 1857* (New York: D. Appleton)

If you liked Martin Mayer's 1976 work *The Bankers* (New York:
Ballantine), you will like *The Banks of New-York.* Published more
than a century earlier, Gibbons's study explains how banks worked,
setting forth the duties of the president, cashier, teller, note teller,
runner, porter, and so on, and including at the end a description of
the brand-new clearing house and the recent excitement in the international panic of 1857. There is much talk of embezzlement and
monitoring: "There is perhaps no record of a bank fraud extant of
which the perpetrator was not honest *yesterday*" (his italics). The
clearing house in an average market exchanges US$25 million daily:
A good game for the modern retired banker would be to decide how
much of Gibbons's lessons and advice is relevant today.

24. Bray Hammond (1957), *Banks and Politics in
    America: From the Revolution to the Civil War*
    (Princeton, N. J.: Princeton University Press)

I knew Bray Hammond, for many years the secretary of the Board
of Governors of the Federal Reserve System, but did not read his
books. I list *Banks and Politics in America* here because I want to
include some material on U.S. finance that is of general, rather
than scholarly, interest. It is also worth picking up Hammond's

1970 *Sovereignty and the Empty Purse: Banks and Politics in the Civil War* (Princeton, N. J.: Princeton University Press). For those inclined toward the scholarly, the following blockbusters should be considered: Milton Friedman and Anna Schwartz (1963), *Monetary History of the United States* (Princeton, N.J.: Princeton University Press); Margaret Meyers, Benjamin Beckhart, and James G. Smith (1931), *The New York Money Market,* (New York: Columbia University Press); W. Randolph Burgess (1927), *The Reserve Banks and the Money Market* (New York: Harper and Brothers); and Marcia Stigum (third edition, 1989), *The Money Market* (Homewood, Ill.: Dow-Jones, Irwin). Choose your tipple.

25. John Maynard Keynes (1919), *Collected Writings, Volume 2: Economic Consequences of the Peace* (New York: Harcourt Brace)

This is a curious item, difficult to classify. It perhaps even belongs under "fiction." It is a brilliant polemic that changed the course of history; by saying that the Germans could not pay the reparations sketched out at Versailles, it practically ensured that they would not. Loaded with purple passages, including descriptions of the "big four" (Clemenceau, Orlando, Lloyd George, and Wilson, with whom the British adviser Keynes seldom met), it is explained by its detractors as an attempt to justify to the Bloomsbury set Keynes's failure to join them as a conscientious objector during the First World War, or as a reaction to his intimacy with a German negotiator, Dr. Melchior of the Warburg Bank in Hamburg. The overall conclusion, that Germany might be able to pay US$10 billion in reparations but not an amount many times that, is undoubtedly just. A biting French answer to Keynes's line of argument, however, is given in Etienne Mantoux's 1946 *The Carthaginian Peace or the Economic Consequences of Mr. Keynes* (New York: Scribner's). Mantoux, who was killed in the Second World War, asserted that the rise of Hitler was a consequence of the political, not the economic, clauses of Versailles.

26. John Berry McFerrin (1939), *Caldwell and Company: A Southern Financial Empire* (Nashville, Tenn.: Vanderbilt University Press)

This is a sleeper. Written during the 1930s as a doctoral dissertation, it was published in 1939 by the University of North Carolina Press, went out of print, and was reissued 30 years later in

Tennessee, where the original investment house that failed with a bang in November 1930 had flourished. Caldwell and Co. was an aggressive issuer of municipal bonds that leveraged up by requiring the issuing city to maintain the money in its banks until used, and employed the funds to buy more banks and insurance companies. When municipal bonds fell after the stock market crash, Caldwell scrambled for cash for a year before his empire collapsed around him. This, like the *Union Générale* of Bouvier (see number 15), is a cautionary tale, albeit one not on the spectacular scale of the South Sea and Mississippi bubbles.

27. David S. Landes (1958), *Bankers and Pashas: International Finance and Economic Imperialism in Egypt* (Cambridge, Mass.: Harvard University Press)

This book, somewhat like that of Iris Origo (see number 28), originated in the discovery of a mass of 1860s correspondence, between Edouard Devieu in Paris and Alfred André in Alexandria, of a private Paris bank that later was absorbed into De Neuflize, Schumberger et Cie. The 1860s were a time of boom and bust in cotton, as the U.S. Civil War first took cotton off the market and then let loose a large accumulation. The completion of the Suez Canal in 1868 added complications, with the cupidity of the Egyptians and the canal's exploitation by French, British, and to some extent, German bankers calling to mind the 1970s boom and bust in oil. Another book on the same subject from a wider but shallower range of sources is the 1974 *Spoiling the Egyptians*, by John Marlowe (a pseudonym) (London: Andre Deutsch). The title comes from the thought that anything other than extremely harsh financial conditions would have been "spoiling the Egyptians."

28. Iris Origo (1957), *The Merchant of Prato: Francesco di Marco Datini* (New York: Knopf)

Prato is a town outside Florence. During the Black Death, which started about 1348, Datini stayed in Florence and corresponded with his wife in Prato. He kept this correspondence and kept also his business letters to correspondents in Avignon, Barcelona, and elsewhere—a total of more than 150,000 documents. Origo, an American woman married to an Italian, drew on this archive and advice from economic historians Raymond de Roover and Federigo Melis to write this fascinating account. Datini was more trader than banker, perhaps, but was a prudent, infinitely patient man who refused to lend to kings or prelates, who financed no wars, and who stayed clear of political quarrels. The late Alexander Gerschenkron, to whom I recommended the book, was astounded that Datini would undertake such complex and risky multilateral transactions that over three years would net him only 10 percent overall.

29. Ellis T. Powell (1915), *The Evolution of the Money Market, 1385–1915: An Historical and Analytical Study of the Rise and Development of Finance as a Central Coordinated Force* (New York: A. M. Kelley)

This monograph has two points of interest, one substantial. The point of substance is that it is a history of the London financial market expressed in terms of natural selection and evolution—the survival of the fittest, with the gradual disappearance of organisms incapable of adaptation. The lesser point is that the copy in the Kress Rare Book Library at the Graduate School of Business Administration of Harvard University has had written in the inside cover:

> This book was compiled by Powell from his notes on my historical lectures at the School of Economics, including even some of the little jokes with which I tried to keep the class awake (the lectures were delivered from 7 to 9 p.m.). Not a word of acknowledgement of course.

Kenneth Carpenter told me that the handwriting of the note was that of H. S. Foxwell, an avid book collector as well as an economist, who sold one accumulation of books to the Goldsmith's Library of the University of London and a second to the Kress Library at the Business School.

30. Raymond de Roover (1949), *Gresham on Foreign Exchange: An Essay on Early English Mercantilism* (Cambridge, Mass.: Harvard University Press)

This is an account of the operations of Queen Elizabeth's "exchanger," who borrowed funds in Bruges and Antwerp and transmitted them to London. Gresham's Law, that good money drives out bad, did not in fact originate with Gresham, but was ascribed to him by McCleod in the 19th century entirely in error. There nonetheless is much of interest in this account of ways of remitting funds. A later exchanger under Queen Elizabeth was Horatio Palavicino, of Italian origin and with large French interests in alum, an unpleasant and unbeloved man whose life is written up in Lawrence Stone's 1956 *An Elizabethan, Sir Horatio Palavicino* (Oxford: Clarendon Press).

31. Raymond de Roover (1966), *The Rise and Fall of the Medici Bank, 1397–1494* (New York: W. W. Norton)

This is a fascinating account of banking and trade in the medieval period by the leading financial historian of the post–Second World War era. Like earlier Italian bankers—the Ricciardi, the Bardi, the Peruzzi, and the Aiaccuoli of northern Italy (so-called Lombards although they came especially from Tuscany)—the Medici had Italian and international networks of branches to serve domestic and international trade and the papacy. Like the earlier bankers, the Medici after their heyday under Cosimo from 1429 to 1464 were brought down at the end of the century by unauthorized loans to sovereign borrowers, notably the Duke of Burgundy. Additional troubles sprang from an unexplained depression. The spread of the bank was wide, with headquarters in Florence and branches in Rome, Venice, Naples, Milan, and Pisa and abroad in Avignon, Geneva, Lyons, Bruges, and, of lesser significance, in the provincial town of London.

32. Henry Thornton (1802), *An Enquiry into the Nature and the Effect of the Paper Credit of Great Britain, together with the Evidence,* edited with an introduction by F. A. Hayek (London: Frank Cassel)

Henry Thornton was a Quaker, banker, Member of Parliament, friend of William Wilberforce, and fighter against slavery. He also wrote one of the pioneering books in monetary theory. He was a member of the committee that wrote the *Bullion Report* of 1810, ascribing the depreciation of the pound sterling during the Napoleonic Wars to overissue by the Bank of England rather than to a series of particular circumstances such as bad harvests, the Continental blockade, and subsidies to British allies on the Continent. But *Paper Credit* is his classic statement, far ahead of the understanding of money and banking of his day, judicious in its unwillingness to side entirely with the Keynesian view that money should expand with business or with the Currency School that recommended a fixed supply. The book contains a well-developed theory of the lender of last resort, rationalized 70 years later by

Bagehot. The book may be somewhat austere for reading after dinner, particularly if that dinner is preceded by cocktails and followed by brandy. It is perhaps a better candidate for reading near the last in this list of 50, rather than at the beginning.

33. J. G. Van Dillen, ed. (1934), *History of the Principal Public Banks* (The Hague: Martinus Nijhoff)

This volume deals with the large public deposit banks, starting with the bank of St. George in Genoa (1272), and includes essays by leading economic historians of the time: Heckscher on the Bank of Sweden (in its dealings with the Bank of Amsterdam); Luzzato on the Bank of Venice; and van Dillen, the editor, on the Bank of Amsterdam that flourished from 1609 to the French occupation of the city in 1791. These banks operated on the whole with 100 percent reserves, issuing deposits against all kinds of coin and bullion, which they first assayed. Their contribution was to furnish a standard money and to spare merchants the trouble—called transactions costs in modern economics—of testing monies received. A distinction thus arose between bank money (liabilities of the deposit banks) and variegated coin, with different exchange rates. A monograph that deals with the centuries mainly before the 16th and 17th, and that goes as far back as 1240 and Catalonia, is A. P. Usher's 1943 *The Early History of Deposit Banking in Mediterranean Europe* (Cambridge, Mass.: Harvard University Press).

Novels

34. Honoré de Balzac (1837), *César Birroteau* (Paris: Le Livre de Poche)

This is one of a series of cautionary tales of the 19th century about the dangers of speculation, written after the boom of 1828 in Paris building sites. The hero, César Birroteau, is a perfumer who strays from the path of the business he knows to buy building lots around the Madeline, despite the strong warnings of his shrewd but shrewish wife. Readers with a propensity, however mild, to gamble may find the story uncomfortable. Other Balzac novels on banking include *La Maison Nucingen*, about a banker who had 5 million francs but wanted 10 million, and *Melmoth Reconcilié*, about a cashier who sold his soul to the devil and forged the Nucingen signature on a letter of credit for 500,000 francs.

35. Daniel Defoe (1724), *Roxana, the Fortunate Mistress* (London: Oxford University Press)

Defoe's best-known work of economics is Robinson Crusoe. It is economics because it illustrates the choices Crusoe had to make when he was alone, and the distribution of income and specialization in production that was necessary when he was joined by Friday. In financial history, however, it is the novels about rascals—Roxana, Captain Jack, and Moll Flanders—rather than those about heros that are most edifying. Defoe was a journalist, a merchant, and a traveler. He was continuously in debt, and had strong ideas on the stock market, commerce, and morality. A favorite theme was the moral danger of poverty, encapsulated in the prayer "Give me not poverty, oh Lord, lest I steal." Roxana is no better than she should have been, but the details of her financial adventures convey a rich picture of trade and finance in Britain in the 17th and 18th centuries.

36. Charles Dickens (first serialized 1846), *Dombey and Son* (London: Oxford University Press)

Dombey, age 48, was mainly a banker; his son is eight when the book opens. The son dies before fulfilling the father's ambition to become a partner. The novel is sentimental in the extreme, but has many isolated passages mocking banks and bankers.

37. Charles Dickens (first serialized 1856), *Little Dorrit* (Boston: Houghton Mifflin)

Little Dorrit deals with debtor prison, bureaucracy, and swindling—the last inspired by the railway mania of 1847 that collapsed in 1848, rather than by the boom of the early 1850s that imploded in 1857. Merdle, the swindler (Dickens' distaste for him will be understood by those who know gutter French), is said to be enormously rich, to make killings here and there, to be in the City, a Member of Parliament, trustee of that, president of the other. But Dickens is irritatingly vague on exactly what his technique of swindling is. Bureaucracy is caricatured by the Circumlocution Office, where work described as "form-filling, corresponding, minuting, memorandum making, signing, countersigning backwards and forwards, and referring sideways, crosswise and zigzag" goes on.

38. Friederich Spielhagen (1877), *Storm Flood (Stürmflut)* (New York: German Classics)

Storm Flood is a novel that compares a rare 1874 storm that broke down the coastal defenses in the Baltic Sea with the financial storm in Germany of 1873. It is said to be based on the career of Geheimer Oberregierungsrat H. Wagner, politician and speculator, and on a private railroad project launched by unscrupulous promoters.

39. Christina Stead (1938), *House of All Nations* (New York: Simon and Schuster)

Stead spent five years in the 1930s working in a bank in Paris, and has written a brilliant novel describing life in what is essentially a bucket shop. The title comes from the medieval period when merchants often congregated in a national house, as in the German house in Venice and Antwerp's "House of All Nations." The Banque Mercur of the protagonist Jules Bertillon conveys an echo of John Law, the failed banker of the Mississippi bubble of 1720 in Paris, who published letters in the *Mercure de France*. The dialogue is highly aphoristic; for example: "Money is king, especially in a republic."

40. Anthony Trollope (1874), *The Way We Live Now* (New York: Bobbs-Merrill)

A taste for Trollope is usually cultivated as one approaches retirement, and normally is focused on the Barchester or the Palliser series. For a retiring banker, however, *The Way We Live Now* or *The Three Clerks* (New York: Harper and Brothers) may be a little more in point. *The Way We Live Now* deals with a swindler, Augustus Melmotte, and was inspired by the investment boom of 1872–73 that produced a series of novels based on profligacy, or what in Adam Smith's rhetoric was "profusion." The central investment that attracts the suckers is a railroad from Salt Lake City to Mexico City. In the end, Melmotte is undone.

The Three Clerks also deals with swindling, as well as with the civil service that the clerks served. In this and in some of the Palliser novels, Trollope adverts consistently to the battle in England over whether or not to go along with the rest of the world in adopting the decimal system. The clerk that succumbs to temptation to speculate is enticed to do so by Undecimus Scott. In Trollope's *The*

Eustace Diamonds (Harmondsworth: Penguin), the issue of decimalization turns on a five-farthing penny, of which 100 make 10 shillings. See also *The Correspondence of Lord Overstone*, number 48 on this list.

41. Emile Zola, (1891) *L'Argent* (Paris: Le Livre de Poche)

This is a *roman à clef* about a speculator named Saccard, patterned after the real-life Jules Mirès, a sleazy character who had a spectacular career in the 1850s and 1860s in Paris but who in the end came a cropper. Gundermann, the Germanic banker, is drawn from James de Rothschild, the French member of the Frankfurt family who never lost his strong German accent. Saccard forms a *banque universelle* that has a meteoric rise and fall. Greed abounds.

Biography and Correspondence

42. Andrew Boyle (1967), *Montagu Norman* (London: Cassell)

The official biography of Lord Montagu Norman by Sir Henry Clay (*Lord Norman*, London: Macmillan), for years the economist of the Bank of England, is pallid compared with this journalistic biography. Norman, governor of the Bank of England from 1920 to 1944, was an enigmatic character in many ways: scion of an ancient banking family, he liked to visit the United States incognito as Professor Skinner, and had strong views he was not always able to articulate with clarity. In July 1931, as sterling was under attack, he had a nervous breakdown and was absent when sterling went off gold in September that year. He would rescue troubled banks in secret, so as not to alarm financial markets, and his greatest—but a retrospectively dubious—achievement was to restore the pound to gold at the parity of 1925 (D. E. Moggridge, in the subtitle to his 1972 *British Monetary Policy, 1924–1931* (Cambridge: Cambridge University Press), recalled this as *The Norman Conquest of $4.86*). Keynes's cross-examination of Norman in the testimony before the Macmillan Commission of 1931 was a battle of titans. Norman was partial to Hjalmar Horace Greeley Schacht, intermittently president of the German Reichsbank and antipathetic to the French in general and to Emile Moreau, governor of the Bank of France from 1926 to 1930, in particular.